T0231933

Medical Information Systems Ethics

"Whatever, in the course of my practice, I may see or hear (even when not invited), whatever I may happen to obtain knowledge of, if it be not proper to repeat it, I will keep sacred and secret within my own breast."

Hippocratic Oath

"I hope the principles here laid down will afford some light either to this or some truer method of philosophy."

Isaac Newton

Series Editor
Bruno Salgues

Medical Information Systems Ethics

Jérôme Béranger

WILEY

First published 2015 in Great Britain and the United States by ISTE Ltd and John Wiley & Sons, Inc.

Apart from any fair dealing for the purposes of research or private study, or criticism or review, as permitted under the Copyright, Designs and Patents Act 1988, this publication may only be reproduced, stored or transmitted, in any form or by any means, with the prior permission in writing of the publishers, or in the case of reprographic reproduction in accordance with the terms and licenses issued by the CLA. Enquiries concerning reproduction outside these terms should be sent to the publishers at the undermentioned address:

ISTE Ltd
27-37 St George's Road
London SW19 4EU
UK

www.iste.co.uk

John Wiley & Sons, Inc.
111 River Street
Hoboken, NJ 07030
USA

www.wiley.com

© ISTE Ltd 2015

The rights of Jérôme Béranger to be identified as the author of this work have been asserted by him in accordance with the Copyright, Designs and Patents Act 1988.

Library of Congress Control Number: 2015942609

British Library Cataloguing-in-Publication Data
A CIP record for this book is available from the British Library
ISBN 978-1-84821-859-8

Contents

Introduction

The past several years have been a turbulent time for the French healthcare system. With an institutional environment in the midst of dramatic change, patient care is in a perpetual state of transformation under the effects of factors such as evolving healthcare needs and emergence of new technologies playing an increasingly large role in cost-saving policy.

Collectively, hospital establishments represent assets that are important as much for our healthcare system as for the social role they play. However, they are currently facing significant concerns such as demographic challenges; evolving management tasks, which notably include the hyper-specialization of certain techniques; changing financial regulations with the introduction of fee-for-service practices; quality of services and reception; continuity of the care process; human and organizational management; and obligation to inform, all against a background of budgetary restriction.

This period has been conducive to value conflicts, divergences of opinion and opposing points of view, and even clashes, notably mainly concerning the development of healthcare expenditure control policies, with care opposing cost, providers opposing economists or managers, and the right to individual healthcare opposing the obligation of solidarity and efficiency. In the resulting ethical debates, tensions have appeared between the morals of conviction and the morals of individual and collective responsibility, and between clinical medicine and public healthcare, contributing to strategic and organizational dysfunction in the healthcare sector.

To all this, we can add revolutionary developments in information technology, with new communication devices such as the Internet, e-health, m-health, medical big data, and the complexity of internal and external transmission, notably in hospitals, due to the existence of medical information carrier systems (hospital information system (HIS), radiology information system, personal medical file (PMF), confidential physician cancer reporting, telemedicine, intranet networks, etc.). Currently, "data intelligence" appears to be the strategic response for the management of the use and deviance of the latter. Consequently, exploitation of big data is a sensitive subject, as it directly touches the private life of everyone. The number of situations in which difficult problems of strategic choice are faced in matters of personal data management grows larger every day. The increasing digitalization of digital data, the ever-growing capacity to store digital data and the resulting accumulation of information of every type have given rise to certain fears and uncertainties due to their multiple (and complex) usages, their impacts on highly diverse populations, which are difficult to measure, and the fact that information is sometimes impossible to control.

In this context, ethics cannot constitute an absolute response; it is not an exact science that, using theorems and axioms, leads to a universal truth; it can only hope to tend towards that direction. Its aim is to contribute orientations that do not seek a consensus but which reveal existing antagonisms. Thus, divergences of opinion effectively illustrate the difficulties to be faced by healthcare professionals with regard to medical information in disciplines, such as cancer treatment, in which sensitivity due to the idea of sickness and death in the near future is very high.

I.1. Questions on which our study is based

In the face of these accelerating changes and expanding ruptures, a feeling of chaos has arisen where there was previously a semblance of order, values, principles and well-established rules. The manipulation and use of medical information are perpetually seeking a balance between medical confidentiality (a fundamental principle of classical medicine) and transparency (a fundamental principle of the modern public sphere).

Our healthcare system, and our society more generally, has now entered an era of perpetual questioning where no certainty can ever be definitively reached. Has the evolution of technology and of mentalities abandoned certain human values, rules and principles in the face of increasing consequences of medical information? Are the rights to access and truthfulness of this information being called into question? Generally speaking, has the concept of medical confidentiality retained its validity and meaning in this modern techno-democracy? Can procedures to control and manage the diffusion of information formulated on an ethical basis contribute to bringing risks of misuse under control to a certain extent?

In short, are the computerization and digitalization of medical data endangering certain fundamental social and moral principles of classic Hippocratic medicine, such as the confidentiality and security of medical information?

So many questions indicative of a certain degree of anxiety and a loss of trust in healthcare actors and even in the very values of our healthcare system have given rise to a sense of profound destabilization in global terms. This feeling of chaos naturally makes it a complex matter to project possible developments to come, and thus to plan anticipatory responses. Can ethical reflection on the subject make it possible in the medium term to preserve a predominant place for confidentiality in the eyes of healthcare professionals?

We may note that the development of ethics-centered reflection in the field of healthcare is not limited solely to considerations pertaining to bioethics, clinical or biomedical research, or therapeutic innovation. For several years now, ethics has also focused on the emergence of new technologies, particularly those to be used for medical information and communication within healthcare structures.

More generally speaking, it results from multitudes of decision-making situations involving values. These new technologies pose the problem of knowing how to inform and who to inform. Is inequality of access to medical information morally and socially acceptable? How do these technologies contribute to relational, behavioral and organizational changes between healthcare professionals and their patients? Have technological advances banalized the "sacralization" of medical information by making it more and more accessible to all? In a more serious scenario, is it possible that this modernization of information and communication tools, illustrated notably by telemedicine, poses the risk of relegating the clinical and therapeutic practice of medicine to second place?

This leads us to question ourselves regarding the societal values and ethical principles involved in the design and use of healthcare information systems (IS) for the exchange and sharing of medical information with healthcare actors, as well as better access to medical data for users of our healthcare system.

One of the major questions posed by this book is how the technological modernization of the use of digitized medical information and medical big data can work hand in hand with increased ethical sensitivity to create an IS with a human face. What are the repercussions of an IS on the mentalities and social values of healthcare actors from a structural, technological, strategic, methodological, organizational, relational or cultural perspective?

We can therefore contextualize this ethical reflection within the perspective of the evolution of IS, in a time of both recent technological developments and new medical communication tools, as well as of new healthcare structures that are in the process of being introduced.

It is on the following questions that our book will rely in order to develop an intellectual approach to questioning focused on IS ethics. The objective of these reflections is not only to contribute to the appearance of facts but also to go deeper and perceive their real meaning.

In the case with which we are concerned, this is indeed an ethical reflection on which we must ground ourselves to know how society as a whole[1] must address and treat the questioning of existing IS. Ethics hark back to a corpus of human values and principles that goes beyond the principles of medical ethics alone. This in a nutshell is the entire concern of our book: which ethical principles and essential social values must guide the design and implementation of healthcare IS? This ethical questioning around IS represents a significant part of what can be called the symbolic accompaniment of New Information Communication Technologies (NICTs). It attests to a "growing awareness of the challenges of operative transcendence at odds with symbolic transcendence handed down by tradition" [HOT 04]. This awareness is what justifies the presence of philosophers within these conceptual debates.

I.2. Objectives and contributions of this book

Most of the problems and even legal disputes that develop between healthcare professionals and patients stem from a lack of communication due to insufficient awareness of the importance of the patient's information, lack

---

1 Healthcare professionals, software developers, public authorities and citizens.

of time and almost non-existent training of the healthcare professionals in communication. In these conditions, communication becomes a veritable tool that should be used to reorient the doctor–patient relationship [MAN 06], wherein information represents both the product of this communication and the bond of the relationship.

Of course, we do not claim to analyze all the mechanisms of the development and use of an IS for the whole patient care process in depth, but only the phases during which medical information takes on its full importance. Thus, we will focus on addressing, from an ethical point of view, sharing, transmission, and storage of medical information for the management of care and diagnosis, leaving aside the resulting therapeutic and clinical part. One of the major challenges of our research is to establish a context of analysis based on a universal, abstract and rational ethical requirement[2] culminating in a practical and concrete set of ethics based on daily work in the field.

Our objective is not to publish directives for the creation and use of medical information via NICTs but to highlight issues and make some recommendations related to ethical principles. This emphasizing of the ethical dimension of an IS makes it necessary for us to work from two perspectives simultaneously – that of the individual and that of the system as such – with the goal of ensuring the required minimum of consistency. For this reason, transforming an IS into an ethical system will depend on the nature of the ethical standards surrounding the aforementioned system [JOH 07, WRE 07, ZHE 07, COE 10]. This ethical framework will help us to avoid positioning dictated by short-sighted pragmatism, the desire for power, economic interest, and so on.

The goal is to know whether the objectives and the means used fulfill the same ethical requirements on the subject. Which circuits for the diffusion of medical information are given priority? Is it necessary for the regulation of medical data to be subjected to ethical concerns?

The development of recommendations for the creation, use, methodology and means to be implemented in order to ensure the efficient operation of an IS, as well as the intellectual projection of a theoretical "ideal" computer tool, may, in the near future, be of use to the computer publishers, healthcare

---

2 Always considered as an end and never as a means.

establishments or care institutions as an "ethical charter" for the design and implementation of IS whose end goal is care support.

In summary, there are multiple expectations with regard to this book:

– shedding precise illumination on the various IS and circuits used by healthcare actors and structures;

– understanding ethical and technical expectations of IS managers in the healthcare industry, as well as those of users (healthcare professionals and patients/users of the healthcare system) and industrialists;

– achieving better readability of the various uses and implementation of an IS within the different structures of care support;

– creating a model and ethical analytical evaluation of IS to set up a scoring system for expectations, achievements and means implemented;

– developing an "ethical charter" involving recommendations, actions and developments to be carried out in the creation, implementation and use of an IS;

– creating a tool for the setting up and ongoing improvement of the ethical performance of hospital IS.

Our ultimate goal, thus, is simply to help readers to have a clearer understanding of the ethical issues provoked by a subject such as this. This, in our opinion, is the primary condition necessary in order to have a social dialogue going beyond the current financial and material considerations. By bringing to light a framework based on new ethical–technological reflection, we hope that this book will supply the first elements of a development plan that will contribute to noticeable changes in mentalities and ways of working, as well as a strategic and organizational transformation with a "human face" for an IS and its use in doctor–patient communication. The objective here is to establish a certain consistency and meaning in this landscape of perpetually evolving technology in order to provide the best care possible for the patient.

With this in mind, we will introduce the basic ethical principles surrounding the use of medical information in the field of healthcare. This will give us the opportunity to approach subjects addressing the emergence of this information in the face of human ethical concerns in society, and its importance in the field of cancer treatment. To do this, we will rely on bibliographic research on literature, conferences and books on the subject.

Next, we will describe the various systems and circuits of information acquisition, transmission and storage used by different actors and structures in the sector, and will present the field studies on which our research is based.

We will identify and understand the purposes and emerging reflections around the ethics of IS design on the one hand, and its production, characteristics and methods used on the other hand, based on the description of the computer-based process via the intermediary of semi-directive interviews conducted with actors who are particularly deeply concerned with this subject, as well as via the development of a field study in the form of a questionnaire. These analyses will be made possible due to the development of an ethical model that will supply quantitative weighting of all these results.

In section 3.3. of Chapter 3, we will enter into a personal reflection on the recommendations, actions and perspectives to be imagined from a behavioral, strategic and structural point of view, leading to production and effective use of IS. All this will help us to make an analysis of the construction of an "ideal" computerized tool that best fulfills the ethical expectations of the cancer treatment sector. This will be combined with an ethical charter for IS intended for patient care, as well as a tool for the introduction and ongoing improvement of hospital ethical performance in the IS. Note that this ethical charter will be the subject of an opinion survey among healthcare professions and users[3] on these recommendations of actions to take, as well as on the perspectives contributed by our theory, with the goal of ensuring that these conclusions will be in sync with the expectations and concerns of actors on this subject.

I.3. Toward medical ethics

This section will involve the construction and detailed examination of the conceptual and theoretical framework in which our reflections have been formulated. A context like this must necessarily include descriptions of the various ethical concepts and principles involved in the production and use of an IS in cancer treatment. This will also contribute to the establishment of a definition of our research subject within a field itself, which must be defined in both theoretical and practical terms. For this reason, we will measure the

3 The same as those involved during field surveys.

challenges of an IS and attempt to surmount both the various ethical questions it raises and the inevitable methodological obstacles and concerns inherent in the conducting of any field study. To do this, we will rely on bibliographical, documentary and literary research as well as semi-directive interviews with researchers, institutional bodies and companies with expert knowledge of the subject.

By definition, information is organized and constitutes a globally cohesive whole designated as an immaterial system. The issues and questions surrounding medical information are legitimate, and raising them already represents the first step and a certain increase in awareness of the value of the IS. This whole, then, brings together a quantity of ethical principles that help to give it meaning, coherence and humanity. For this, we do not need to invent new ethical principles or codes to frame an IS, as noted by Dominique Wolton [WOL 02][4], director of the Institute of Communication Sciences at the CNRS (Centre national de la recherche scientifique, or National Center for Scientific Research). According to him, "technology does not invalidate earlier principles; it is sufficient to apply existing ones to new technologies. We are not required to adapt our principles to new technologies; rather, these new technologies must be compatible with our principles".

Like all new technologies, Information Communication Technologies (ICTs) constitute both a promise and a risk; as such, they can provoke both interest and anxiety. However, they can also lead us to formulate some ethical questions in a new manner, considering the specific characteristics of their provisions and usages. This reinforces the need for social and psychological involvement in order to orient and guide the concrete details according to which an IS can be organized and structured. For this reason, healthcare norms and principles are actualized in good practice recommendations and are closely associated with values.

An IS generates information and norms that become part of a strategy, which is then made available to the healthcare professional. Indeed, all practical and political decisions that determine actions of human beings are themselves determined from a normative point of view and exert a normative effect in their turn. Thus, whatever is the strategy adapted by the healthcare professional during the use of medical information about his or her patient, it

---

4 Dominique Wolton is a former member of the *Comité Consultatif National d'Ethique* (National Advisory Council for Ethics on Bio and Health Sciences, or CCNE) and a member of the ethics committee of the CNRS.

is used as part of an institution that requires him or her to link his or her medical decision to an established rule or norm. In every case, he or she is constrained by the texts established for the well-being of healthcare users. Activities that take inspiration from values in fact seek to follow certain rules and norms to approach the value deliberately pursued, and it is easy to note that any research intending to survey the world of humankind and its activities is obligated to take values, rules and norms into consideration. Desiring to put these aside would mean treating the world of humankind like a world of pure Nature.

This is why the major challenge is to bring out possibilities of producing agreements founded on reason, based on values or principles recognized or recognizable by the largest number of people, and thus remain committed to universality [COR 09].

I.3.1. *Sources that feed our ethical reflections*

Our schema of reflectance draws part of its source and inspiration from the classical ethical theories we are used to consider, specifically, the Greek model of virtue[5], in which ethics concern first the individual (agent) who executes an action, and the so-called relational theories such as utilitarianism[6], contractualism[7] and deontologism[8], whose major concern is the moral nature and value of the actions executed by the agent. Our reasoning is based more broadly on a set of ethics oriented toward those who create or receive action involving an IS and are then subjected to its effects: patients, healthcare professionals and IS designers. This necessarily includes the application of universal principles that are both consensual and regulatory and tend toward social cohesion. A relational and communicational ethical code built on the basis of the diffusion of words thus makes it possible to bring meaning to therapeutic acts with the patient. It orients practices toward the relational dimension and creates continuity in space and time. In these conditions, we develop the idea of an ethical code used in a dialogue. What results is a deliberative approach in which the most appropriate ethical vision stems from a discussion between all the actors involved in the design, setup and usage of an IS intended for care support.

---

5 Moral principle of trying to be virtuous and of universal casuistic questioning.

6 Universal moral principle of maximizing consequences.

7 Universal moral principle affirming that every society is based on a social contract.

8 Universal moral principle of the categorical imperative (Kant). This ethical theory affirms that every human action must be judged according to its compliance (or non-compliance) with certain duties and is based on the respect of rights and duties.

Our ethical code drives a vision of medical decision-making that is both standardized and algorithmic, and is dissociated from a personalized and synthetic approach developed around patient needs.

In correlation, because in this society in which information is predominant and entities are made up of information, our ethical code is also oriented toward the telematic school of ethical thought introduced by Luciano Floridi, professor at Oxford University, on what ethics will be in an information society, and the characteristics of which are compatible with our subject of analysis [FLO 98]. Unlike classical models, which are intrinsically anthropocentric, individualist and social in nature, telematic ethics concern above all the environment in which information is generated and propagated (also called the "infosphere"), as well as the protagonists involved in the IS (which can be designated as being the "principal"). This infosphere represents a digital space composed of a lasting and volatile heritage present in an often undefined geographical space. It is an inherently intangible and immaterial environment, which makes it no less real or essential. This digital territory (intellectual, industrial, personal, cultural, etc.) belongs to an individual or a corporation, or falls under the responsibility of a person or an organization. All the software and other technological tools managed by this responsible entity are connected to this infosphere [CAR 00], as are all their legitimate users. This infosphere is composed of a set of subjects and objects that gravitate around computer devices. It also includes all the data belonging to an individual (or a corporation) and all the data concerning him or her, but which are outside his or her center of gravity (security, policy, etc.). In summary, the infosphere of a healthcare establishment brings together all the communicating objects of the structure, data and connections associated with the IS.

This approach is therefore considered to be allocentric, meaning that it tends to make other people the center of the universe, its concerns, its interests, and so on, and to center its own activities on what others do. For this reason, Luciano Floridi (the Italian philosopher) bases his ideas on the theory of information, and more particularly on the concept of entropy of information introduced by Shannon[9] in the mid-20th Century. For the author,

---

9 Claude Shannon, an engineer for the Bell Telephone Company, defined information as an observable and measurable value (1948); this became the main pillar of the theory of communication he developed with Weaver. This concept of information became the subject of a theory known as "information theory". This was a mathematical theory applied to techniques of telecommunication. This mathematical theory, stemming from the technical

entropy of information measures, in a way analogous to thermodynamic entropy, the degree of disorder of a system, or more exactly the knowledge that we have of it. If we understand something perfectly, we know how to locate all its details and can enumerate the series of them in order; thus the thing seems ordered. This means that there is a direct relationship between the organization of a system and the knowledge we have of it. Likewise, the weaker the entropy (i.e., the more ordered a system is), the more it is understood, and vice versa.

On the basis of this theory, Floridi developed his reflectance around the ethics of information using global entropy of information as a criterion applied to his concept of the infosphere, the environment in which information develops. According to him, "ethical behavior will diminish entropy because it renders information more meaningful, while an increase in entropy would be harmful to everyone". Thus, an action considered "just" or considered as ethical will lead to a reduction in overall entropy, and to an increase in the understanding we have of it.

Conversely, incorrect information or already understood data will increase entropy by disorganizing the infosphere. In this context, the ethical issues[10] raised by this digital universe are better grasped and understood if we associate them with events or concrete facts in the real environment [FLO 02]. For example, the concept of confidentiality can be connected to the presence or lack of parameters in an IS, enabling the blocking of the identification of the patient to whom the medical information is linked. Accessibility to medical information can be associated with the existence of a so-called sharing platform within the IS in which the patient can have access to his or her own medical information.

In complement to this, according to Fessler and Grémy [FES 01], the concept and the term "info-ethics" can be examined on two levels:

– the human relationships existing in all IS of a structure as soon as individuals are connected to one another via the tools of the IS;

---

concerns of telecommunication, remains the basis of the concept of information science to this day.

10 Ethical issues such as confidentiality, medical secrecy, medical data protection, respect for private life, accessibility of medical information, sharing of responsibilities and the respect and maintenance of patient autonomy.

– healthcare structures have an additional dimension *vis-à-vis* humankind; they concern changes in human beings.

As we have just seen, information becomes the principal subject of moral action. The principal objective of telematic ethics is to determine what is good for an item of information, and more generally for its near environment: the infosphere. It distinguishes right from wrong, what must be done and the duties of the moral agent, based on four fundamental laws: entropy must not be caused in the infosphere; production of entropy must be prevented in the infosphere; entropy must be excluded from the infosphere; and good condition of information must be favored by the expansion of information (quantity), its perfection (quality) and its diversification (variety) in the infosphere [FLO 98].

Finally, our framework of reflection belongs most naturally to the concepts of medical ethics, bioethics and environmentalist ethics, which have a more patient-oriented approach and thus reposition the receiver of action at the heart of the ethical discussion and move the emitter toward its periphery. According to Floridi [FLO 98]:

> Good and bad no longer describe actions in themselves, but relate to what is good or bad for the infosphere. [...] Telematic ethics elevates information to the position of a life form. It elevates information to the position of universal receiver of any action. Now there is something more elementary and fundamental than life and suffering: being, understood as information, and entropy.

I.3.2. *The Hippocratic Oath at the root of medical ethics*

The word "ethics" suggests both antiquity and modernity, harking back to both distant origins of moral discourse and extreme topicality. To speak of medical ethics is to evoke the genealogy of thought, to go back toward a forgotten dimension and almost "to lay bare the structures of the West" originating from ancient Greece with the Hippocratic Oath, as stated by the jurist and psychoanalyst Pierre Legendre [LEG 85].

It is indisputable that philosophy has fed on centuries of reflection on medical ethics ever since the Hippocratic Oath, and on critical study of medical knowledge and its modes of acquisition. These classical medical ethics texts have ensured the continuity of ethics from Hippocrates until today. But the term "ethics" also means something that has become omnipresent and almost triumphant. Badiou notes that "this word 'ethics', which smacks so strongly of Greek or philosophy class, which evokes the famous bestseller *Nicomachean Ethics*, is in the limelight" and that ethics, come straight from Antiquity, has been "belatedly" voted in. What establishes the roots of medical ethical authority is the fact that ethics springs from philosophy and that Greek medicine is itself a philosophical activity. In late Antiquity, the famous Galenian phrase "the best physician is also a philosopher" meant nothing else.

A reading of the various writings in the Hippocratic corpus shows that Greek medicine did indeed include a great deal of practical wisdom, with the capacity for ethical deliberation on one hand and moral respect applicable to every patient and every citizen on the other, implying even greater importance for the person responsible for the health and lives of other human beings.

It is in these observations, which appeared for the first time in a classical text, that we find the premises of four future major principles of modern bioethics:

– *Principle of non-malfeasance*[11]: *Primum non nocere*: "First do no harm;" that is, act only within the realm of one's knowledge and abilities, otherwise a physician must delegate the power of action to his or her colleagues. This maxim means that risk, inconvenience and burden to the patient are acceptable only proportionally to the good they yield for him or her. It, therefore, implies a duty of diligence and caution, which must not however slide into therapeutic nihilism.

– *Principle of autonomy*[12]: secrecy has a sacred status: "I will keep secrets and regard them as inviolable".

– *Principle of beneficence*[13]: "In every house I enter, it will be for the relief of the ill:" do everything possible to be useful to the patient, and above all do nothing that may harm him or her. The good of the patient has always been the guiding principle of medical action and of the doctor–patient relationship; the doctor is, in a sense, "there for that". This principle thus

11 Avoiding harm in order not to cause injury to anyone.
12 Making the individual to participate in a decision-making process, ensuring his or her enlightened consent via clear, precise, adapted and understandable information.
13 The action undertaken must be beneficial and contribute to well-being to the person.

represents the driving force, the moral energy that underlies every care action.

– *Principle of justice*[14]: "In every house I enter, it will be for the relief of the ill, keeping myself pure of any deliberate injustice, abstaining from every sort of immorality".

To these four principles is added the idea that the doctors must be exemplary, keeping themselves apart from any corruption or abuse of power that their position may confer on them, with the concept of unconditional respect for life as a constant backdrop.

Thus, the principles stated in the Hippocratic Oath guide the conduct not just of physicians but also of all professionals whose actions are dictated by the medical field. These principles are designed to be universal and were the subject of consensus in the International Code of Medical Ethics during the General Assembly of the World Medical Association in October 1983. In Europe, in January 1987, the European Council of Medical Orders formulated the most important principles intended to guide the professional conduct of physicians, irrespective of their mode of practice, in their relationships with patients, the medical community and one another.

I.3.3. *Ethical reflection centered on principles and adjusted by rules*

The objective of this chapter is to propose an alliance between ethics and anthropology by applying an analytical model of the principles and ethical rules underlying the development and setup of an IS in the healthcare sector.

The roots of the word "ethics" lie in the Greek term *ethos*, meaning "mores" (Cicero), or "habits" (Plato and Aristotle). Ethics involves the "habitat" and "character of a person". Thus, the way in which we inhabit the world represents the way in which we are someone. According to the philosopher Jean-François Mattei, the expression "to be inhabited" takes on its whole meaning and symbolic value here. Seen from this perspective, ethics is a reflection on the habits that must be formed to render a space habitable. Thus, ethics questions the values that underlie action, which can result in a conflict of values in a world of ideas. It "naturally finds its source of reflection in action" [HER 97]. Ethics is an individual tendency to act according to virtues in a given situation to seek out the right decision. It has

---

14 The action performed is based on equality and equity toward individuals.

meaning only in a proper situation in which it admits argumentation, discussion and paradoxes.

In the context of technology, ethics deals with acts and actions that have an incomparable causal reach toward the future and are accompanied by provisional knowledge that, despite its incomplete nature, also spills over into everything that has been previously known. To this we must add the value of actions in the long term, and very often their irreversibility as well. All of this places responsibility at the center of ethics, including the horizons of space and time, which correspond to those of ethical principles.

Ethics is situated upstream of deontology and the law, certain fundamental principles of which it has given rise to. From ethics to law and from law to ethics, there is a permanent dialectic movement that, it may be imagined, is causing society to progress toward a greater humanity.

Consequently, we can establish the following phrases:

– *Morals*[15] produce individual awareness of good and evil and the extension of this awareness to relationships with other people.

– *Ethics* regulates and adjusts morals by inserting them into common principles, taking context into account.

– *Deontology*[16] codifies ethical principles by constituting general rules applicable to a specific sector of human activity.

– *Law* generates concretized and binding rules for the population of a given group.

In ethics, the principle constitutes the base, represented "in the form of a commandment" [LEC 07]. It is immutable, universal and intangible, and its value is not influenced by the course of history. For this reason, all societies tend toward this universality, illustrating the unicity that surrounds us. The universal is present in the multiplicity of things, and thus of human beings.

---

15 All the rules of correct mores. Morals represent the "world of facts" in which the conflict of duty appears. These represent a set of obligations that are categorically imposed.
16 From the Greek *déon*: "what must be done", "a set of rules expressed formally and explicitly, the transgression of which is liable for sanction", according to the *Dictionary of ethics and moral philosophy*. It constitutes a system of moral obligations and imperatives applied to a given professional sector.

All theoretical discourse is rational discourse applied to the universal. By its very essence, the Italian term *Uomo Universale* designates the theoretical and abstract man of Leonardo da Vinci. This conquest of the universal necessarily includes a refusal of immediate particularity. The universal thus yields an ordered whole according to unitary laws illustrated by rules.

The purpose of ethical rules is to bring order to a social group by giving orders to citizens, thus preventing "anarchy"[17]. The rules can be revised and modified according to context, environment, space and time; thus, they are specific to each country and culture [LEC 07]. Because of its status as a means, the rule has less an ethical meaning than a pragmatic and utilitarian value. It has a strong instrumental connotation, providing ethical principles with a concrete expression that causes them to exist. According to the *Dictionary of ethics and moral philosophy*, these rules "tend more to impose a response in problematic situations that may be encountered by the professional in the exercise of his profession than to expose and arbitrate the moral dilemmas that these situations may cause". Thus, ethics rise up in the cracks of the deontological code to confront moral dilemmas by questioning. There are only rules for a given situation; they cannot be applied to every situation, and their use concretizes the rightness of an approach and a course of action to be taken in a defined context.

Against a background of disorientation of spirits and anxiety concerning the future of our healthcare system, we believe it is indispensable to go back to the fundamental tenets of medical ethics. What are our human values? How can we include and apply them in reality? In expressing our values, we discover that they are shared by others.

Modern research in healthcare ethics focuses on its importance for the personal values of individuals in order to understand the behaviors and relationships existing in the human–machine interface. The clarification of personal, professional and institutional values constitutes a precondition for any reflexive approach to healthcare ethics. Thus, it examines the consistency and compatibility between the different value systems involved in the medical information environment, that is, the infosphere.

---

17 Literally "the absence of principle", or *anarkhia* in Greek.

In the context of our theoretical analysis of ethics, we have drawn heavily on the book by Beauchamp and Childress [BEA 01], which proposes the application of principlism, "a principlism that is non-dogmatic and normative but not imperative". Their model is similar to the flexible version of principlism specifically applied to public healthcare and proposed by Massé [MAS 03], on which it draws heavily. For the authors, the model based on principles and values is composed of an analytical chart used to identify and consider moral problems; however, this model is relatively generalized and does not bring to light all the nuances of the various moral challenges of a specific issue. Thus, their model must be adapted for the principles to be concordant with the context and environment being studied. The authors speak of the concept of specifications, introducing the idea of balancing, which refers to a judgment and a deliberation imposed by the individuals on themselves in their analysis of the relative importance of each of the values or norms included in ethical reflectance.

According to Massé [MAS 03], ethics also refers to a set of so-called social values that are qualified as "personal, collective, or organizational, rather than absolute, as in the definition of morals". Ethical reflectance thus constitutes a place for debate and discussion of the values to be prioritized in the production and setup of a healthcare IS, with the objective being to reach a consensus in the analysis of our subject of study.

The Massé model proposes a framework to analyze the ethical challenges of public healthcare actions in order to adjust general and abstract principles to the realities and specific characteristics of the sector being studied. The norms proposed here greatly exceed the four principles usually discussed in bioethics, and the analysis chart includes ten values and two principles qualified as epistemological and political. The author states that the proposed model does not lay claim to exhaustivity, and that the key values that compose it do not tend toward universality, which can be dependent on the culture, beliefs and philosophy of a society.

The author maintains that the principles or values chosen have only a relative weight and should be considered as justifications, that is, as non-absolute norms that are never determinative in the final judgment. These values can therefore be of varying importance according to context, and each of them may be subject to open moral reasoning.

Table I.1 [MAS 03] indicates that each value falls within moral traditions and is based on ethical theories. These values, thus, can be used as a theoretical common thread at the time of judgment and analysis. They represent points of reference framing reflections on the action to be put in place.

Theories	Principles	Key values
Rights	Autonomy	Self-determination, private life, confidentiality
Deontology	Beneficence, non-malfeasance	Respect for healthy life, doing good, non-malfeasance
Justice	Justice	Justice, responsibility
Utilitarianism	Usefulness	Usefulness, common good
Virtue	Responsibility	Common good, solidarity, paternalistic responsibility, prudence

Table I.1. *Anchoring of key values in ethical theories*

Finally, in his study entitled *Ethical challenges in the Quebecois breast cancer treatment program*, Samuel Vézina [VÉZ 06] drew heavily on the Massé model in his analysis of the ethical framework of the breast cancer treatment program in Quebec. In it, he carried out an exercise of "particularization" of the values brought forth in the reflections made for the occasion.

On the basis of these various observations, we have constructed a system of ethical analysis based on four universal ethical principles, to which six ethical rules are associated.

I.3.3.1. *Four universal ethical principles*

In the face of this issue surrounding the management and use of medical information by an IS, the quality and harmony of the latter are dependent on the hierarchization of end purposes. For this reason, we must confront certain dilemmas, such as bringing a sense of meaning and purpose to the accessibility of medical data while guaranteeing the protection of personal data. An IS cannot define itself as a source of ethics because this is beyond its remit. However, it can tend toward it and recognize unethical actions. This questioning goes back to the most fundamental tenets of ethics. Are there universal values that are necessary for everyone? Can the uniqueness of individual consciousness be transposed to a transversal instrument with a collective and multidisciplinary purpose such as an IS? Our reflectance will be based on the questions that follow in order to develop an intellectual questioning approach oriented toward an ethics of ends and means, and the moral foundations of IS.

When we consult articles and books on ethics, we are quickly staggered by the abundance of references and underlying social values used by the authors: "well-being", "quality of life", "pleasure", "happiness", "concern for others", "compassion", "empathy", "solicitude", "altruism", "responsibility toward others", "communal solidarity", "sharing", "reciprocity", "interdisciplinarity", "prudence", "respect for others", and so on. This multiplicity of social values of every type has the unpleasant ability to create spiritual confusion. How can we sort through all these social values to find the principles that bring them together and can be used to achieve a clear discussion and analysis of the subject? What are the guiding principles and rules, the adjustment variables needed for ethical values to be accepted by the whole community? Finally, "how can a medical imaging company contribute added value and effectiveness to patient care?" [BON 07].

If we consult the international bioethics literature, we can see that four constants emerge again and again, depending on the country. References to the principles of "Autonomy", "Beneficence", "Non-malfeasance", and "Justice" appear unremittingly in every book, irrespective of its place of origin, culture, beliefs, philosophy or religion (see Table I.2).

Autonomy: This designates the fact that a person gives himself rules for his or her own conduct; the Greek terms *autos* and *nomos* mean "oneself" and "law/rule", respectively. The aim of this principle is to motivate the patient to participate in the decision-making process.
Beneficence: This contributes to the well-being of others. It must adhere to two very specific rules: the action undertaken must be beneficial and useful, that is, it must have a positive cost–benefit ratio.
Non-malfeasance: The purpose of this principle is to prevent harm being done to the person for whom one is responsible (the patient) and to spare him or her injuries or suffering that would be without meaning for him or her. Its end purpose thus implies doing good and abstaining from doing harm. This principle appears in the Hippocratic maxim *primum non nocere*[18], the motto of which is to do good for patients and to keep them away from harm and injustice.
Justice: The vocation of this principle is the sharing of available resources among all patients[19]. It is closely linked to the concepts of equality and equity, which are directly involved in the process of a court ruling. Ideally, every action should tend toward perfect equality, but depending on the circumstances and nature of the individuals, equity often imposes itself in order to establish priorities and a certain hierarchy in the acts to be performed. This principle reinforces a scope that can be designated as "macro-ethical" concerning all patients, while the three previous principles have a much more individual and relational scope and are considered as "micro-ethical".

Table I.2. *Vocation of the four ethical principles*

18 "First do no harm".
19 Resources of time, money and energy.

In the field of healthcare, a medical decision must be rational and constructed methodically using some simple, consistent, clear and previously defined ethical principles. The humanistic concept of support, which is a social dimension of care, enables the patient to reclaim part of his or her autonomy by taking him or her out of his or her state of passivity and mobilizing his or her resources. This puts us in a relationship in which the individual is at the center, in a position of respect for the person, and in which socio-educative or socio-curative approaches must be developed in the same way as socio-therapeutic action. It is in this sense that the social environment will recover its hospitalizable value.

As we saw in section I.3.3.1, the term "principle" is intended to give broad directions to action and to fix behaviors. It designates a fundamental orientation that inspires action. For many years, philosophers worked to "reduce all moral requirements to a single principle" [OGI 07], drawing inspiration from their glorious predecessors Aristotle[20], Kant[21], Bentham[22] and Mill[23]. Now, our modern society has the benefit of several major principles that are both stable and limited in number. Two books provide references on the subject of ethical principles in the healthcare field; these are *Public Health Communication Interventions* [GUT 96] and *Principles of Biomedical Ethics* [BEA 01]. Moreover, the latter was the first to establish and identify these four main ethical principles. According to Beauchamp and Childress, the place of ethics is that of conscience, questioning and dissidence, which must be framed by these four universal fundamental principles. This universality seeks to reveal itself to us through our concrete and practical achievements.

It was on the occasion of the drafting of the Belmont Report that these four major principles of biomedical ethics (respect for individual autonomy, beneficence, non-malfeasance and justice) were formalized in North America for the first time. Yet for all that, since their formalization and even before defining them, the authors of this report have emphasized that these principles represent a framework of reflection whose application is not self-evident: "These principles cannot always be applied incontestably to resolve specific ethical problems. Their objective is to supply an

---

20 The supreme good.
21 Good intentions.
22 The well-being of everyone.
23 Principle of non-harmfulness.

analytical structure intended to guide the resolution of ethical problems resulting from research enlisting the participation of human subjects"[24] [AMA 07].

For Lazare Benoroyo, "these ethical principles of bioethics – drawing their sources partly from outside the field of Hippocratic ethics – have tended to weaken the bonds uniting ethics and medicine and to call into question the legitimacy of the cardinal ethical aim that traditionally guided the production of care" [MON 11]. According to Beauchamp and Childress [BEA 01], consideration of a specific case makes it possible to confer a precise meaning on the principle, without which it is difficult to apply this principle correctly. According to the authors, "particularization (by case) is a way of reducing the overly general character of a norm and give it a greater capacity to guide action, while keeping it compatible with the moral meaning of the original principle".

Thus, whether we place ourselves in the recent history of North American medical ethics or in the older history of ethical philosophy, articulation of case and principle has always been thought necessary and productive for reflections of an ethical nature. These principles thus impose a moral obligation, but they leave room for the creativity of actors in the search for and development of solutions without imposing a canonical scale of values. Because they are not theoretically placed in a hierarchy, it is the responsibility of healthcare professionals to hierarchize them when seeking solutions in contentious situations. In this sense, this approach leaves room for freedom and for the creativity of those involved.

Moreover, according to Pierre Le Coz [LEC 09a], these four cardinal principles act simply as guides, helping to keep discussions from going off-track. In no case are they intended to resolve all ethical problems. A principle formalizes a value that is "intuitive, subjective and imprecise" in nature by giving it a verbal outline. The principle makes it possible for the value to impart a readable, easily shared meaning to a discussion or analysis. Ethics is not imperialist, rather it is a means of answering the question "how do we live together?" Establishing principles helps in bringing order and coherence to social values.

---

24 The Belmont Report.

However, it is important to add nuance to the universal aspect of these four ethical principles in terms of applicability. As specified by Le Coz [LEC 09b]:

> Each State is drawn back to its history, culture, and mores, and it would be wholly unrealistic to desire to wrench it away from this in the name of an abstract universal. This is why it does not seem possible to impose universal norms by requiring this or that State to comply with all requests. [...] States cannot be obligated to act as models for one another; they are always sent back to the solitude of their choice, forced to make decisions of which none can satisfy us fully and definitively, because there is always a value that is subordinated, if not sacrificed for another, as can be seen with the issue of donating eggs. Each State must make its own decision according to the values to which it is the most attached.

I.3.3.2. Six ethical rules

Ethical rules are intended to hone the framework of our ethical reflection on the subject. They are the adjustment variables used to respond as completely as possible to the issues that arise in the production and setup of an IS in the healthcare field.

Owing to its nature and impact on its environment, the IS will produce multiple repercussions affecting multiple sectors and actors. The consequences of a tool like this are multidisciplinary, and therefore cause numerous incidences of questioning the mentalities and social values of various fields from a structural, technological, strategic, methodological, organizational, relational and cultural point of view.

For this reason, we have used a large number of these ethical rules according to the sectors encountered during our analysis, for a total of six specific rules for the healthcare domain in France. These rules are associated with the fundamental ethical principles discussed earlier, as shown in Table I.3.

Fundamental ethical principles	Ethical rules
Autonomy	Respect for life
Beneficence	Usefulness
Non-malfessance	Proportionality
	Prudence
	Uncertainty
Justice	Solidarity

Table I.3. *Rules deriving from fundamental ethical principles*

Ultimately, an ethical deliberation tool based on four principles combined with six ethical rules is intended to contribute to the study of the end purposes of an action. This deliberative device has an evaluative and shifting reach.

This approach to ethical deliberation does not claim to resolve all the ethical issues created by the complexity of the problems surrounding NICTs in the field of healthcare. However, we believe that it constitutes a highly relevant model to guide reflections in medicine in an interdisciplinary context. This modeling is aimed at developing a meticulous reflexivity and an understanding of the decision-making impasses and challenges that takes into account the extremely complex character of human reality in medicine.

1

The Emergence of Medical Information in the Face of Personal and Societal Ethical Challenges

The considerable and ongoing progress made by medicine through applications of technologies and sciences suggests that we are moving toward a veritable "scientification" of the medical approach. These NTICs are becoming means of augmenting flows of information, exchanges, social interrelations and even access to programs, cases of cultural and social mediation notwithstanding. Services and tools are multiplying and being perfected but still are probably only in their early stages, causing real unease for both doctors and patients. Where will the human–machine fields of tomorrow fall, in relation to those of the doctor–machine? Certainly, within medical communication, a dialogue between a doctor, his or her patient, and the IS must now be taken into account.

In this chapter, we will establish why and how the sharing of medical information and its transparency has developed. This will also shed a more precise light on the distinction made between the terms "data", "information" and "knowledge". The inflation of medical knowledge and the brevity of its half-life make its control impossible for a single individual and demand a high-performance tool to access, acquire and manage it. This has resulted in the necessity of computerization for the sharing and exchange of data. This type of ethical debate applied to this information is an essential prerequisite for the comprehension, design and architecture of an HIS using it.

Of the information handled by healthcare structures, medical information – the objective of which is to describe the state of health of patients and the acts and procedures practiced on them – constitutes the most important information quantitatively and the most relevant qualitatively, as it is on this information that descriptions of care activities and production are based. It has become an integral part of the care process. All medical information poses the problem of its own legitimacy, of the duty to inform and of the right to disregard. It is a legal, technical, and ethical necessity, but there is a risk that medicine will shift from the dictatorship of the "unsaid" to that of the "everything said", that is, from paternalism to "information abandon"; these two extremes can have serious effects on the way in which the patient will experience his or her illness.

1.1. An information-consuming society

The society of consumption is a civilization born in the 20th Century, the economy of which is no longer based on the production of the necessary but rather on the production of the superfluous. It is considered to be an evolution. The upheaval of the 20th Century, which begun in the late 19th Century because of the industrial revolution, has reversed the proportions by assigning greater and greater importance to the superfluous and less and less to transcendence. This society has radically transformed mankind, from *Homo sapiens* to "homo consumens".

The world of consumption exists only in a representation that is perceived as reality. For this reason, objects consumed by individuals have no real meaning except as symbols. The term "society of consumption" is generally defined by inserting the idea of advertising as a tool bearing information on a product being sold. For a very long time, sales advertising has equaled the satisfaction of needs, with its objective being to satisfy the consumer's desires. Because desire exists only in mental form as the projection of a fantasy, objects are only images of a satisfaction that exceed their actual possession.

Consumption is no longer a means of fulfilling our primary needs but rather of differentiating ourselves from others. In Western societies, consumption constitutes a structuring element of social relations. It is omnipresent, creating new social relationships between people artificially by inventing symbols, acronyms and codes. It shows how our societies have become prisoners of consumption, which has taken the place of morals, and in which the body becomes an object, and capital subjected to consumption is recreated artificially in the form of symbols [ROD 08].

This is why personal medical information has become the subject of commercial issues. Subjected to pressure from commercial societies, of which they are sometimes promoters, healthcare professionals are likely to venture into the use of systems for the dissemination and use of information concerning their patients "without respecting the rights of the latter or taking into account legislation on the matter or medical ethics, the whole of which constitutes a complex corpus" [DUS 00].

In terms of the commercialization of medical information, it is most often personal medical information or information derived from the same that is at the forefront, that is, information concerning identified or identifiable individuals. An identifiable individual is defined as "a person who can be identified, directly or indirectly, notably by reference to an identification number or to one or more specific elements proper to his or her physical, physiological, physic, economic, cultural, or social identity"[1].

In the pharmaceutical industry, medical information is vital for the research and development of products and for the marketing those products. For their part, insurance companies and mutual funds wish to offer their affiliates the best services, and companies are willing to invest in prevention surveys, for example, to reduce the risks of accidents, illnesses and absenteeism.

Thus, to prevent any possible spiraling commercialization of medical information, Law 99-641 of July 27, 1999 introduced in Article 40-12 a new Chapter 5(3) of the law of January 6, 1978 pertaining to the communication of personal medical information and specified that data "issuing from the information systems targeted in article 710-6 [L.6113-7 new] of the code of public health; those issuing from medical files held as part of the liberal exercise of healthcare professions; and those issuing from information systems of health insurance companies, cannot be communicated for statistical purposes of evaluation or analysis of healthcare and prevention practices and activities except in the form of aggregated statistics or patient data put forth in such a way that the individuals concerned cannot be identified". There are no exemptions to this regulation except specific conditions assessed by the CNIL (*Commission Nationale de l'Informatique et*

---

1 Directive 95/46/CE of the European Parliament and the Council of October 24, 1995.

des Libertés, or National Commission for Data Protection), which specifically prohibits the interconnection of files likely to be harmful to efforts at anonymity.

In France and Europe, personal medical information is considered to be sensitive data, and the *groupe européen d'éthique* (European Group on Ethics) defines that this healthcare data "is an integral part of the personality of the individual and should not be considered exclusively as merchandise".

Today, the supply of goods and services available is greater than the demand. This abundance of products has led humans to surround themselves inexorably with objects. Eventually, humans will swear only by them, progressively abandoning themselves to becoming ever more functional. Consumption is becoming obligatory. As soon as a consumer takes possession of an object, he or she sends an external sign to the people around him or her, thus acquiring a certain power in society. This society has a need to produce objects and, thus, to be able to destroy them in order to exist. This renewal amplifies the idea of abundance and increases our dependence on the tangible.

Moreover, similar to commerce, which knew how to make the customer believe that he or she was king, medicine will be forced to bend to this consumerist principle. Medical relationships will have to fall in line with this model so that responsibilities will be clearly defined and indicated. Even though it is becoming consumerist, the caretaking relationship is not yet fully codified as such, except concerning the minimum necessary in the right to information. Thus, the increasing propagation of information in society imposes a certain degree of legitimacy on this information for the user of the healthcare system [FAI 06]; this legitimacy has been entirely established by the appearance of this significantly different way of interacting between healthcare consumers and healthcare service providers. There is still no model contract for what the doctor–patient relationship will involve in reality; there is more talk of the risks inherent in this medical relationship than there is talk of the objectives and means imposed by it. For this reason, our society is creating ever more possibilities and choices, which are often contradictory. Now the individual must examine, sort and rank each object or item of information on a rational value scale with the goal of being able to make choices and decisions regarding healthcare.

This evolution of consumerism in the field of healthcare marks a significant development in patient demand. These patients naturally wish the way in which they are treated to be accounted for and no longer have blind trust in practitioners. Healthcare professionals have therefore been obliged to adapt their services and the way in which they work to take this new order into account.

1.2. e-Health, m-health, the Quantified Self and Big Data

It is the combination of audiovisual and computer technology and telecommunications that accelerates the progression of these new technologies. The Internet stands as the legitimate heir to the triple alliance of the telephone, television and computer. The 1990s saw the Internet made available to the public at large; nowadays, this telecommunication tool has become an instrument of information, communication and exchange that is inescapable from a professional as well as a personal and familial perspective. The Internet has traveled across the surface of the globe like a water lily on a lake: the farther it goes, the faster it grows, and it is in the process of turning our vision of the world upside down. This is a new way of working, with primary materials consisting of dematerialized information. e-Health is also proving to be a remarkable system for sharing internal and external knowledge, providing enlightened users with a true culture of sharing. It seems to be an accelerator of empowerment, that is, of patients' management of their own healthcare status, with patients being more involved in medical decision-making.

According to Ewa Mariéthoz and Marika Bakonyi Moeschler [MAR 01], empowerment "enables patients to free themselves partially from the top-down decision-making of doctors in matters of treatment and to establish bilateral patient–doctor relationships based on communication, discussion, and negotiation". For this reason, this technology is often considered to be an emancipatory technology. It is enabling the patients to become better-informed. However, a usage study indicates that the diversity and complexity of these technologies only partially confirms this perspective. Thus, the notion of the expert patient harks back to elements other than online information alone and sharing with the practitioner remains a vital part of the relationship. The doctor thus retains his or her authority as an advisor while encouraging the patient's expertise with an eye to autonomization and therapeutic education.

Consequently, the emergence of the Internet in the field of healthcare has contributed to the existence of greater access to medical data for both doctors and patients. In these conditions, these NTICs have the power to act in-depth on social relationships, people's beliefs and the very nature of knowledge, which also contributes to certain fears and uncertainties because of their multiple (and often complex) uses; their hard-to-measure impacts affecting very different populations and their information, which is not always controlled. For this reason, it is becoming necessary to be more aware of and to better comprehend the use of NTICs in the medical sector.

This new technology has brought about behavioral changes between the actors, ethical reflections and, thus, consequences, such as:

– making it possible to access the whole body of medical information that is rich but inconsistent in terms of quality;

– increasing the number of exchanges via e-mail;

– creating "cyberpatients" through forums dedicated to health [EVE 02];

– developing projects to circulate medical data over a network;

– increasing awareness on the part of citizens and patients about the quality of healthcare offered and easier access for these individuals to healthcare-related education;

– creating a guidance tool in the system (putting the addresses and rates of healthcare professions, the platforms for urgent situations, the performance of healthcare, etc. online);

– contributing to epidemiological monitoring;

– causing healthcare and healthcare product providers to change and progress.

This also leads us to question ourselves about the reason (or reasons) driving citizens to search for information and advice on the Internet rather than asking for it directly from their usual physicians. The search for anonymity and greater freedom of expression are often mentioned. Does consultation no longer appear, as in the past, to be a time of adequate confidentiality and freedom for the patient? Is it possible that the very value of medical secrecy, designed above all to protect the patient, is being questioned? Freedom of expression implies that doctors know how to inspire trust in patients by developing a dialogue on all aspects of health, whatever the real reason for the consultation. Quality of healthcare information and confidentiality of medical data are the two ethical principles that come naturally to all of us. But we are entitled to ask ourselves questions about "freedom of access to medical sites, constraints related to documentary research, ownership of medical data, and traditional practitioner behavior" [EVE 02]. This motivates doctors to invest themselves in their mission of overall care of people. Here, we are part of a true reflection on the role of the physician in society and on the preparation of doctors to exercise their profession with regard to public expectations.

The Internet phenomenon also poses a number of security-related and technical problems, but above all, the issues it has brought about are cultural, as the hospital is obliged to consider itself as a satellite service and no longer as the center of the world. This NTIC raises societal questions, not so much on the part of the ever-increasing numbers of healthcare users who use it but on the part of classic producers of information pertaining to healthcare, including healthcare professionals. How can we best prepare healthcare professionals to use NTICs? How can we encourage the development of the concept of sharing or co-management of medical decision-making? Is the Internet a facilitative element or an obstacle to the duality of the doctor–patient relationship? In the medium term, will the Internet become the key to patient self-management, thus virtually eliminating the family doctor (see [SCH 09])?

However, the Internet can serve as a formidable instrument for accessing expert knowledge or skills remotely when the patient is unable to travel. Telemedicine and "cybermedicine" may in this case contribute to a positive evolution of the doctor–patient relationship as well as the sociocultural aspect of it. This naturally leads to new responsibilities on the part of the doctor – "tele-expert" and "guide" doctor for the patient (with the necessity of means) – as well as technical network providers (with requirements vis-à-vis security and medical secrecy).

This practice has the particular characteristic of separating the doctor from the patient. On the basis of this, we may ask ourselves if this doctor is risking the loss of his or her essence due to disruption of interpersonal relationships. What will be the patient's place in this system? Is it possible that the dematerialization of the doctor–patient relationship is contrary to a strengthening of human relationships?

Are we in the process of building new inequalities? What will be the guarantees concerning the confidentiality and security of personal data? What guarantees of skill will be established by remote consultation based on transmitted data?

On the basis of these questions, it seems advisable to study the resulting ethical requirements and risks. In this case, the use of this practice:

– must contribute a gain to patient care;

– must not replace, without a valid reason, a more human, more classical practice of medicine;

– must guarantee the fundamental rights of the patient, notably:

- to be informed of the actions taken and to use this information freely (free and informed consent of the individual),

- to choose his or her own doctor,

- to have access to quality healthcare,

- to have the benefit of medical secrecy, respect for private life and the confidentiality of personal data,

- to obtain an obligation of means but not result,

- to have access to compensation for wrongs caused by a possible malfunction of the system [PUE 06];

– must not interfere with the rights and responsibilities of the practitioners toward their patients and colleagues: risks of "virtualization" of the healthcare professional and the subsequent "banalization" of radiological interpretation as a simple product of consumption to be delivered. This intrusion by the computer must not truly make a "screen", where the doctor, who has become "virtual", will not be listened to as closely by the patient and, conversely, the doctor's empathy must not be lessened toward a "virtual" patient. When medical actions are exchanged, the responsibilities of each of the healthcare actors increase, rather than responsibility being shared;

– must ensure the skill of the healthcare professionals who will be taking care of patients;

– must ensure the securitization and confidentiality of medical data against any fraudulent use when these data are archived, such as during their transfer on computer networks;

– senders must[2] ensure that the receiver guarantees protection for the data received, that is, data are "adequate" or "equivalent" to what they were in the sender's country;

– must create a pricing protocol, controlled if possible, defining various situations in telemedicine;

– the singular colloquium between various healthcare professionals and the patient must constitute the pivot of the care support system [LUC 13].

In addition, with "Medicine 2.0", the mentalities, approaches and practices of medicine are evolving due to access to information, community exchanges and the comparison of experiences. According to a new worldwide survey, *Emerging mHealth: Paths for Growth*, conducted by the Economist Intelligence Unit (EIU) for PricewaterhouseCoopers (in 2012), the widespread adoption of mobile technology in the field of healthcare, or m-health, is today considered to be inescapable.

By definition, m-health consists of the use of modern mobile, smartphone and tablet technology in particular to deliver, reinforce and improve healthcare services. m-health is therefore a subcategory of e-health that pursues various goals, particularly easier access to care and information related to health; an increased ability to diagnose and monitor diseases; the ability to launch large public health information campaigns and continuing access to education and medical training for healthcare professionals. Given the aging of the population, the steep increase in chronic illnesses, and the increasing cost of healthcare, the development of m-health services may represent a concrete response to the expectations of patients and healthcare professionals.

m-health applications include the use of mobile devices in the community; collection of clinical healthcare data; dissemination of healthcare information for practitioners, researchers and patients; the real-time monitoring of patients' vital parameters and the direct provision of care (via mobile telemedicine) [GER 05]. Smartphones are constructed to include a certain number of sensors [BEN 13]: an accelerometer, gyroscope, proximity detector, magnetometer and photoelectric proximity switch, and the new generation of sensors, which are more specialized, less costly and have high performance. They are integrated into various types of objects: smartphone

---

2 According to the computer and liberty law of 1978 and according to European Directive No. 95/46/CE of October 24, 1995, completed by Directive No. 97/66/CE of December 15, 1997.

peripheral devices, bracelets, helmets, sporting accessories and even in the form of patches applied directly to the skin. The current trend is toward the development of biosensors (sensors used in the medical field) capable of recording biological parameters such as temperature, heartbeat, blood pressure, weight, stress, calories burned, sleep, health practices and respiratory exchanges with the skin.

It is feasible today to imagine a true at-home healthcare solution, which is a necessity given the lack of doctors in some regions. Sensors and wireless measurement devices (glucometers, spirometers, pedometers, geolocation devices, scales) are available commercially and make it possible to relay monitor information on the daily life of an individual and the possible progression of an illness.

Thus, we are witnessing a veritable explosion in the number of connected devices. Combined with mobile applications that collect these data and present them in a user-friendly manner, these devices offer a precise image of our state of health. The success of current m-health applications with professionals as well as the public at large reveals a real desire for richer solutions. Approximately 17,000 m-health applications are currently available in the principal stores of the market, even with a specific category dedicated to them. Alongside applications for well-being (*my pregnancy*, iSleep), there are more and more applications for the prevention and monitoring of pathologic conditions (diabetes, obesity, etc.).

Healthcare professionals are also the users of mobile services: access to medication databases, official recommendations, medical encyclopedias, etc. In 2010, according to a Kalorama study, more than 50% of physicians used a smartphone or a tablet regularly in their treatment activities.

With the new generation of mobile devices that rely on the datasphere of the Internet (sensors, connected devices, mobile applications, etc.), we consider the practices of the Quantified Self to constitute a symbiotic system of transformation enabling individuals not just to shift from an analog to a digital mode of monitoring via digitalization but to shift from a "quantified self" to a "qualified self" and, thus, to broaden the possibilities of self-action (i.e. of change). For users, the objective is to collect behavioral data, share them and analyze them in order to acquire knowledge about themselves and to make changes in their daily lives.

In this context, the advent of the Quantified Self makes it possible to monitor the personal health indicators on a daily basis: connected health, life hygiene and body upkeep, monitoring of the development of a disease, etc. But, Big Data also disrupts the research practices and the perfecting of new treatments.

Using correlations, digital tools have made it possible for persons to regulate their weight through sleep, stress and the reduction of restrictive treatment with medications. By producing and reclaiming their own data, these persons create a personal informational system, enabling them to recategorize their behaviors. Over the long term, this experience will have enabled them to move from "curative" health practices to "preventive" health practices.

Moreover, after the digitalization of all of the human knowledge accumulated over the centuries, digital services, social networks, mobile devices, and connected objects and sensors are endlessly producing new data – the storage, diffusion, management and usage of which are becoming more and more a part of people's daily lives.

This "metadata", or Big Data, represent the fuel driving today's economy and early 21st Century knowledge. The volume of medical data created each day by our civilization is increasing exponentially. When we connect to the Internet (social networks or various Internet sites), our navigation leaves numerous clues about our personal life, such as our needs, our behaviors and our illnesses. Thus, this "metadata" represents a volume of information that we leave behind us unsuspectingly as soon as we connect to a digital device. These massive quantities of digitized data are stored and archived in data warehouses.

The volume of digital data is increasing exponentially: 90% of all the data available today were created in the past 2 years [BRA 13]. In 2013, people stored more than 2,000 billion gigabytes of new digital data. It is estimated that the volume of data stored worldwide doubles every 4 years [BLO 13]. The data collected are often noisy and imprecise, and must be processed to extract useful information from them; this is done using simple inductive statistical processing algorithms to infer profiles (patterns or models of behavior). This information on information then feeds a very high-value understanding of individual behaviors. Owing to Big Data, each and every person is in a position to compare his or her own data with those of other users to situate himself or herself in relation to the rest of the population. This metadata holds the promise of customizing our medical treatments.

Consequently, the volumes of data recorded and liable to be compared and used, under the cover of anonymity of course, to extract meaning for a healthcare professional are already immense and multiplying quasi-exponentially. These data come from research institutes, epidemiological centers, pharmaceutical laboratories, imaging centers, hospital reports, insurance companies, client files, etc.

For several years now, the digital giants (Amazon, Facebook, Google, Apple) have used these data to improve the quality of the services they offer as well as to sell them back to commercial enterprises. They turn these data into private goods, which are then resold. Today, this target marketing is done solely for business purposes. In these conditions, businesses and institutions are surrounding themselves with "data scientists" able to process the noisy whirlwind of Big Data on a large scale. The objective of these digital marketing specialists is to pick information on the behaviors of the Internet users out of this enormous flood and to anticipate their desires to offer individualized content adapted to their specific needs.

The diffusion of TICs and the arrival of Big Data in healthcare-related sectors, whether pharmaceutical industries, healthcare professionals or care institutions, will, in 2025, pose "as many ethical challenges as scientific and industrial ones" [AUB 09]. The quantity of raw knowledge is continuing to increase exponentially, but the knowledge that results from its processing is progressing much more slowly. The study of this metadata in the service of healthcare gives rise to specific ethical and technical problems and reflections, such as:

– what scientific value can be given to this computer-processed medical data?

– what role will the practitioner's judgment play in this new technological setting?

– will the development of personalized decision trees endanger respect for the human dimension of the doctor–patient relationship?

– the interoperability of data and the security of medical data hosted in different parts of the world.

– medical data published in scientific journals do not necessarily reflect the reality of medicine, because they relate to patients corresponding to specific study criteria;

– rethinking storage infrastructures;

– training healthcare professionals on these NTICs;

– the redevelopment of reading, translation and operation tools for these databases constitutes one of the major challenges for research in years to come.

We can now see that the possible side effects of the secondary usage of our personal data via predictive algorithms have as much to do with the concept of protection of private life and confidentiality as with the risk that we will end up analyzing people based not on their real behavior but on their propensity to display the behavior that the data assign to them. It is clear that this permanent connection generates a digital footprint both through the data we diffuse voluntarily via social networks and through our own conduct.

Thus, the activity that we generate by navigating permanently on the Internet constitutes a flow of information that invades our daily life and disrupts the boundaries between the public and private spheres; we are entering the universe of "permanent connection". The advent of Big Data has destabilized our concept of private life and modified the character of risks related to surveillance. Big Data facilitates the re-identification and reuse of secondary data to such an extent that all of the strategies ensuring the protection of private life – anonymization, prior consent and opt-out – seem ineffective. Now, it is vital to reinvent the protection of private life and to cause the normative and legislative framework associated with this protection to evolve and change. The process of "notification and consent" to guarantee confidentiality seems outdated, and it is impossible to imagine Google contacting all its users to ask their permission to use their searches to predict the flu epidemic.

The "Quantified Self" and other healthcare applications on smartphones are developing exponentially as well. Usages such as this bring up the question of the exploitation of confidential data that may result.

We must not let Big Data entrap us in a social world predefined by probabilities, thus imperiling the potential of each individual. Our human capacity to build our own futures is running the danger of being altered by algorithmic technology that would analyze all of our personal data (social and academic environment, medical history, circle of relationships, etc.). One of the risks would be judging people solely on contextual data and no longer on their actions.

Finally, Big Data risks magnifying the phenomenon of categorization, classification, discrimination and their by-products within society, as the data become more and more closely associated with the person.

Now, with the emergence of Big Data fed by a multitude of technologies to measure and recover various types of information, the world of the readable is progressively being transformed into the world of the predictable, in which Auguste Comte's maxim "*Savoir pour prévoir, prévoir pour pouvoir*", which means "knowledge is power", takes on its full meaning and importance.

Big Data has the potential to change the way in which companies exploit their data. With the increasing volume, diversity and speed of data, companies must adapt their data management practices as they recover and analyze all this information. These efforts to make the most of Big Data start with:

– the use of software that simplifies the integration and manipulation of this metadata;

– the growing need to apply data quality procedures;

– not applying the principles of project management and governance from the beginning.

In the field of healthcare, Big Data can be very promising, notably as part of technological approaches intended to integrate, process, analyze and put in perspective large volumes of medical data. This approach improves the process of considering data. Previously, owing to technical, conceptual and human limitations, most statistical studies were conducted on the basis of samples claiming to be representative. The interpretations drawn from this were certainly not erroneous, but they were sometimes approximative. Now, with the processing of large volumes of data, we can see a tangible improvement in terms of the precision of studies compared with analyses of data samples.

Today, we also know the principal risk factors for disease. We should know how to correlate them with behaviors. In the near future, we will be able to extrapolate data on behaviors and predispositions via social networks, smartphones, e-mails, etc., and study the probability that a person will have a particular disease at a particular time. We can see that this process is already being applied to the world of finance, in which computer devices centralize information from all of the stock exchanges in history, cross-reference it and develop targeted interpretation models to establish refined predictions for traders or insurers. In these conditions, we may imagine a scientific analysis studying, on a very large scale, the Internet behavior and habits of people with chronic illnesses such as diabetes, to target and note possible correlations between risk factors and navigation habits. This metadata would result in the large-scale non-commercial diffusion of public health messages in order to prevent the risk of chronic diseases worldwide.

In addition, the permanent geolocation of applications and supports (smartphones, tablets, computers, etc.) may make it possible to better understand the lifestyle behaviors of the Internet users and to suggest to them the downloading of applications motivating them to take physical exercise, messages informing them about the often-underestimated calorific value of foods, etc.

In this context, Big Data can be used to analyze and exploit the behaviors of thousands of people via cross-referencing of complex correlations to create a predictive algorithm to anticipate certain medical events such as a flu epidemic. This was the case in 2009, when Google Flu established, using its software and mathematical model, a combination of 45 search terms resulting in "a correlation between predictions and official numbers" [MAY 13] for the H1N1 flu epidemic.

Moreover, Twitter, with more than 500 million tweets per day, is also collecting a considerable amount of metadata that can be the subject of processing and analysis, notably for scientists. Free access to the archives of public data on the site made it possible to follow the spreading of the flu virus in January 2013.

For its part, Facebook has enabled researchers to develop a map of the Americans most prone to obesity. This type of large-scale research would be very expensive if it had to be conducted on millions of individuals. Owing to Big Data, this was possible at a much lower cost. In fact, according to the latest McKinsey report on Big Data, the United States saved more than 17% of potential healthcare costs. This saving of 450 billion dollars out of 2,600 billion dollars is the consequence of the large-scale use of Big Data NTICs for the American healthcare system; these savings involve five areas of healthcare:

– prevention with monitoring of healthcare users;

– cost control by making reimbursements and fraud detection automatic;

– "ventilation" of medical personnel with the making available of professionals best suited to the patient's case (choice of a GP or a specialist);

– innovation for improved exploitation and diffusion of knowledge;

– diagnostics aiding healthcare providers to choose the most appropriate treatments.

In these conditions, it is apparent that these digital giants have acquired, because to these algorithms, an extremely in-depth and refined knowledge of the expectations and needs of their Internet users. Therefore, it seems possible to imagine the prevention of health risks using informational messages, targeted advertising, etc. Approaches such as this will make it possible to modify the behaviors of individuals with an interest in prevention. This includes better monitoring and improved knowledge of the impact of the various parameters and factors made possible by a consolidation of medical data emanating from Big Data. IBM has estimated a 20% reduction in the mortality rate of patients owing to the ongoing analysis of their data. These NTICs thus mark the shift from curative medicine to long-term, more personalized preventive medicine; this is "disease management". Thus, behavioral prevention represents a powerful public health lever, improving care support upstream. In addition, PMFs and the codification of medical actions in the clinical research sector are making it possible to conduct precise studies of the best combinations of therapeutic treatments without the establishment of long and costly full-scale experimental protocols.

Finally, tools to aid medical decision-making in the form of computer, reference and statistical databases are available to practitioners when seeking a diagnosis. These tools are unfortunately limited in their capacities to integrate, summarize or update large amounts of medical data. Now, Big Data technologies may be able to make up for this deficit by rapidly exploiting various types of data and medical information coming from multiple sources.

On the basis of these observations, we can emphasize the fact that measuring a person's state of health via smartphone applications may have the consequence of reducing travel and overcrowding of medical offices on the one hand and the "white shirt effect" on the other[3]. The question of

---

3 Increased blood pressure during medical visits.

medical desertification may also find answers in these new technologies. In the medium term, this self-measurement over a longer duration may encourage increased awareness and greater daily responsibility on the part of healthcare users, via the self-regulation of their own behaviors. Now, m-health and e-health may help patients to be more informed and knowledgeable, and more able to manage their own illness and state of health so as to be better prepared for their exchanges with their physicians. Thus, every individual is in a position to compare his or her own data with those of other users, to situate himself or herself in relation to the rest of the society. This is why associations and federations of patients with chronic diseases such as high blood pressure or diabetes have a great deal of interest in mobile-connected healthcare. New blood-sugar readers used as a part of diabetes treatments can be used not only to measure patients' glucose levels but also to regulate insulin injections via regular checks supervised by healthcare professionals. In matters of clinical research, it is now possible to take medical tests without requiring the "guinea pig" to spend several days shut up in a healthcare establishment: measurements of blood pressure, heartbeat, body temperature, etc. can be taken remotely using mobile healthcare technology. This makes patients more comfortable and may even render the clinical study more realistic as people can continue to live without changing their habits.

In addition, the use of medical Big Data includes the promise of personalized medical treatments. Devices can be used to recover, store and study data and present it intelligibly by cross-referencing these medical data with other medical data. This enables us to detect possible anomalies and malfunctions, while improving analytical models and algorithms as time passes. Therefore, Big Data is conducive to prevention, with better patient monitoring, medical diagnosis aiding healthcare professionals to select the most-effected and best-suited treatments, and innovation with better exploitation and diffusion of information.

The study of this metadata enables us to create predictive algorithms. The large-scale processing of Big Data makes it possible, for example, to anticipate a flu epidemic. This was the case for Google Flu, which cross-referenced search words in the Google search engine in correlation with existing health predictions. In these conditions, we can follow in real-time an epidemic of gastroenteritis, 'flu or dengue fever using Google requests. The source that feeds Big Data is not always complete, totally precise or definite, but the law of large numbers delivers reliable and effective final data, particularly in epidemiology and public healthcare.

Ultimately, the dematerialization of medical data is conducive, respecting confidentiality and regulations, to sharing and thus to a better understanding of healthcare practices and optimal patient support in the long run. There is also necessarily the challenge of an economic objective, in the imperative context of limiting healthcare expenses. The challenge of prevention is also a considerable challenge. Understanding ourselves better makes it possible to know the risks to which we may be vulnerable. The medical challenge is to make the best diagnoses, optimize the care path and encourage therapeutic innovation.

However, this metadata cannot fully guarantee accurate interpretation. The protection of personal data means that users must be more responsible for their actions. Finally, perhaps we should draw inspiration from monetary exchanges between banking organizations, which use a money-sharing system called SWIFT. This "trust network" ensures the confidentiality of monetary data. We would point out that this system of exchange has inspired open-source networks for researchers, such as OpenPDS and Open mHealth.

On the basis of this, we can envision introducing similar trust networks for personal medical data, integrating an official contract specifying the possibilities and ethical rules of use of these data. The proper functioning of this secure system of exchange would require these personal data to have an ethical label specifying what can and cannot be done with them.

1.3. Medical secrecy in the face of the computerization of healthcare data

Although modern medicine has gradually distanced itself from classical medicine, questioning some of its erroneous dogma and knowledge and basing itself on rigorous and scientific objectivity grounded in knowledge, it does still claim a part of the Hippocratic legacy[4]. The question of accessibility of information has progressively become a highly structuring part of our society. This is a major issue within which access is likely to replace ownership as a structuring commodity [RIF 05]. Now, the asymmetry of information in the doctor–patient relationship is progressively being reduced.

---

4 See the Code of Ethics and Deontology, the basics of which were laid down by Hippocrates, and in which doctors agree to keep secrets confided to them during consultation and to do nothing that is not within their capabilities.

Faced with a modern democratic society that puts the accent on communication and the diffusion of information at any price, we are right to ask ourselves if the concept of medical secrecy has become outmoded and obsolete. With the launch of the Vitale 2 and then the DMP cards, Geert Lovink [LOV 08] believes that anonymity has become nothing but a nostalgic idea, and that the protection of medical data is in peril.

Before returning to the core of the debate surrounding medical secrecy and the computerization of medical data, it is important as a preamble to define and characterize this concept of medical secrecy in legislative terms.

1.3.1. *Regulatory characteristics of medical secrecy*

Generally speaking, the right to respect for private life and privacy and, by extension, to medical secrecy in matters of healthcare must be considered one of the fundamental rights of human beings. According to Louis Portes, president of the *Conseil National de l'Ordre des Médecins*, "professional secrecy is, in France at least, the cornerstone of the medical edifice and it must remain that way, because there is no medicine without trust, no trust without confidence, and no confidence without secrecy"[5].

Historically, medical secrecy is an ancient concept based on respect for the individual, in this case the patient. Confucius was the first to advise all honest people to avoid gossip by being discreet. But it was another century before this idea achieved recognition with its inclusion in the famous Hippocratic Oath. According to Littré's translation[6], medical secrecy was reworded as follows: "Whatever I see or hear in society during the exercise or even outside the exercise of my profession, I will keep silent about what does not need to be divulged regarding discretion as a duty in such cases". According to the *Bulletin de l'Ordre des Médecins*, published in March 1998, these Hippocratic values are still topical. According to Laurent Selles [SEL 02], "the intimacy of private life is the primary and vital fundamental element of the concept of secrecy". The term "secrecy" comes from the Latin *secretum*, meaning "separated" or "put aside". According to the author, secrecy is "knowledge hidden from others that is characterized by shared knowledge on one hand, and protected knowledge on the other". Secrecy

---

5 During his statement to the *Académie des Sciences Morales et Politiques*, June 5, 1950.
6 Hippocrates, *Œuvres complètes*/Littré; Vol. 10, Paris: J.-B. Baillière, 1861.

thus begins with communication. Its primary function is to protect a feeling, value judgment or opinion. It assumes a relationship of trust [DRA 08].

This medical secrecy is neither a defense nor the right not to answer questions the doctor may ask but rather a constraint that weighs upon him. In other words, secrecy is not a prerogative given to the doctor but an obligation to be discreet and to respect the private lives of others, which is imposed by the law under penalty of legal sanctions. This means creating and maintaining a relationship of trust between the doctor and the patient who confides in him or her [SAR 04]. Situated at the crossroads between the public sphere and private life, it protects the private life of the patient while guaranteeing, by means of a rule of public policy, the trustworthiness of the medical profession. Medical secrecy is the condition necessary for the patient's trust. It represents a symbol of the respect that the doctor owes to the patient, and through its criminal impact, it is also a symbol of society's respect for the individual [MAL 04].

According to Jean-François Mattei [MAT 05], respect for medical secrecy falls within the jurisdiction not of ethics but of deontology; it is not a question of reflection but rather a question of application. The deontological code is by definition a system of obligations imposed categorically by the fact that they determine the very survival of the practice of medicine. Ethics appears "in the cracks of deontology" and is revealed when the deontological code and standards are no longer sufficient to clarify the medical situation.

Medical secrecy is emphasized in three articles of the French medical deontological code:

– Art. 4 Paragraph 1: "Professional secrecy, imposed in the interest of patients, is required of every physician in the conditions established by law;"

– Art. 72 Paragraph 1: "The physician must ensure that the individuals who assist him in his practice are instructed in their obligations with regard to professional secrecy and that they comply with these obligations;"

– Art. 73 Paragraph 1: "The doctor must protect against any indiscretion medical documents concerning individuals he has treated or examined, whatever the content or format of these documents".

When all is said and done, a deontological breach of medical secrecy is a criminal infraction. Indeed, the principle of professional secrecy is included in Article 226-13 of the French criminal code, in the chapter entitled *Harm to the personality*, which is as follows: "The revealing of information secret in nature by a person who is the holder of this information by virtue of situation or profession, due to a function or temporary mission, is punishable by one year in prison and a fine of 15,000 euros". Note that certain ideas are very similar, such as the duty of reserve and the obligation of discretion[7]; these should not be confused.

However, by the very nature of medical practices and of the healthcare establishment, which is considered to be a multidisciplinary structure, healthcare professionals are often obliged to share a certain amount of information and to compare it, comment on it and discuss it with their colleagues. Thus, most of the time, patient support is of a collective and interdisciplinary nature.

It is in this context that jurisprudence recognizes the concept of "shared secrecy". This is the case in the Crochette judgment, in which the French Council of State ruled that when an individual turns to a healthcare structure, it is to all of the medical staff, barring specific instructions from the patient, that a medical secret is entrusted. This situation was ratified in the law of March 4, 2002[8], which stated that "When a person's care is undertaken by a healthcare team in a healthcare establishment, the information concerning this person is considered to have been confided by the patient to the entire team". The concept of shared secrecy itself has also been the subject of legal recognition. Now, the law, and more particularly Article L1110 fourth paragraph of the Code of Public Health, states that "two or more healthcare professionals may, however, barring opposition from the duly informed individual, exchange information pertaining to a single person being cared for, in order to ensure continuity of care or to determine the best health support possible". In summary, the law of March 4,

---

7 The expression "duty of reserve" designates the restrictions of freedom of expression that may exist for military professionals and some civil service officers, particularly judges, police officers and some high-level government officials. The objective is to guarantee neutrality and impartiality of administration and not to harm its reputation. Those who are subject to it must, in particular, abstain from allowing their personal opinions to affect questions relative to their activity or to behave in ways incompatible with the dignity, impartiality or equanimity of their duties. "Obligation of discretion" (including professional secrecy and professional discretion) prohibits agents to reveal information brought to their attention by users or other agents of the government in the course of the exercise of their duties. In other words, if in the exercise of these duties, a healthcare professional is given knowledge of private or confidential information, this healthcare professional is required not to express this information publicly. In conclusion, obligation of discretion is different from duty of reserve, which is aimed at protecting the secrets of individuals.
8 Art. L1110-4, third paragraph of the Code of Public Health.

2002, authorizes the sharing of information only between healthcare professionals.

No one considers medical secrecy to constitute the noble face of opaqueness any longer. What then remains of it today, even though transparency and right to security seem to be becoming imperatives more and more exclusive of any individual freedom that accompanies the right to oblivion?

The importance of medical secrecy lies in the fact that it constitutes "a fundamental value of any society desirous of ensuring the protection of the dignity of its members" [MAS 04]. It goes back to the principle of respect for the individual and for his or her private life, and must be one of the rules and the basis of medical ethics. Without medical secrecy there would be no more medicine; therefore, it is no longer a simple question of non-respect for human dignity, but one of the ends of the medicine.

It is for this reason that we assign it the qualities of general and absolute law, to guarantee its inviolability. But these characteristics also constitute an obstacle to the defense of other imperatives. In these conditions, one of the major challenges of healthcare information systems is to guarantee the trust of users, more precisely, to respect the patients' free choice to define their own compromise between "loss of opportunity" and "level of control" for the access of healthcare professionals to personal health data that sometimes encroaches on medical secrecy. In the interest of the patient, to ensure consistent care for him or her, medical secrecy must be able to be "partially" shared, but the whole problem of sharing lies in this "partially".

Thus, with the right to medical secrecy, a necessary conciliation must take place between the protection of individual interests and the general interest [ASI 09]. The protection of health constitutes a legitimate limitation to freedom of information (i.e., inform and be informed). But health also concerns the general interest. The French law of March 4, 2002, pertaining to patients' rights and the quality of the healthcare system reaffirmed the principle of medical secrecy and instituted direct access to files for the patient.

It institutes, for the benefit of the patient, the right to transparency of the information held, granting "direct access for any person to all information concerning his or her health held by healthcare professionals and establishments" (Art. L. 1111-7 CSP). The patient now has a choice of the mode in which he or she will consult his or her medical file. This information can be in the form of test results, consultation reports, therapeutical protocols and prescriptions or correspondence between healthcare professionals [LAU 05]. This right to transparency from which the patient benefits is intended to remove opacity in the event of the breakdown of a therapeutic relationship and the occurrence of an injury (Art. L. 1142-4 CSP)[9]. If we regard the law of March 4, 2002, more philosophically, a growing unease emerges from the relational context existing between law and medicine as technology disrupts practices.

How can we manage medical "secrecy" and "transparency" in a democracy as they are by definition contradictory concepts? Secrecy is a source of silence, discretion, privacy and opacity. It risks imperiling democracy, which serves transparency, truth and clear policy. It would be dangerous if the implementation of personal medical files and the multiplication of the actors sharing the information recorded in them harmed the confidential nature of the information. The accessibility of these computer data, for both the patient and the healthcare professional, as well as healthcare data-hosting service providers and health insurance companies, risks causing real difficulties for the protection of medical secrecy. The benefit of access to his or her medical file for a patient may pose various risks for this patient:

– risk of communication to third parties who are not intended receivers, for example, to a spouse who may then use the information in divorce proceedings;

– risk of facing excessive demands from an authority (an employer, an administrator, etc.) who would require knowledge of its employee's medical file;

– an even more serious risk from insurance companies evading the obstacle of medical secrecy.

For this reason, Article 29 of the French law of January 6, 1978, guarded against these risks by emphasizing the fact that "computer technology must be at the service of each citizen … it must not harm human identity, the rights of man, private life, or individual or public freedoms".

It is also necessary for every healthcare professional to be able to grasp this computerization effectively, particularly in the context of data shared

---

9 French law of August 13, 2004, pertaining to health insurance modified the computer data of the Vitale card while creating a personal medical file for each insured person.

through networking, while remaining responsible for the medical secrecy of which he or she is a guardian. Medical secrecy endures, but its expression in the digital universe assumes that it will be processed in a modern manner in order to be even more effectively protected. This is the essence of section 1.3.2.

1.3.2. *Protection of healthcare data*

The title of this section itself gives an immediate idea of the substance of the question: is the development of computer systems in the healthcare system liable, despite the considerable progress it represents, not only to be damaging to the quality of information transmitted, but above all to its confidentiality?[10]

In 2010, cyber attacks on e-commerce increased by 10 times [LEI 11]. In these conditions, the securitization of an IS requires a study of the risks to which it is exposed and of the available technical or organizational solutions that would guarantee its confidentiality, auditability, integrity and availability.

On the whole, we can group the risks incurred by an IS into three major categories depending on their origin:

– *Accidents* may correspond to partial or total destruction or to the malfunction of devices, software or the IT equipment in which the information system is located.

– *Errors* may occur during the capture of data, its diffusion by the information system or the manipulation of its exploitation functions, or it may be the result of its incorrect use.

– *Malicious acts* are always associated with human nature. They include the theft or sabotage of computer devices or the misappropriation or deterioration of intangible assets.

Major risks also include transmission of information via the Internet with divulgence of nominative data or data linked to the use of a single identifier, specifically a social security number, which can lead to wholly reprehensible

10 The concept of confidentiality means that an item of information or a resource is accessible only to authorized users (creation, diffusion, backup, archiving, destruction). Thus, this consists of making the information unintelligible to people other than the actors involved in the transaction.

discriminatory practices, notably on the part of mutual health insurance plans, which are then able to select their own clients according to their medical histories. Other risk factors that have not yet been imagined may also appear as time passes and the system gains scope.

The problem of data security is all the more significant because companies regularly approach practitioners to "computerize" them for free in exchange for the office's health data. Thus, practitioners anxious to improve their information technology (IT) violate medical secrecy without being aware of it.

According to Professor Bernard Rüedi [RÜE 03] in his article entitled *Le secret médical est-il en danger?* (Is medical secrecy in danger?), "the threat of confidentiality or medical secrecy is becoming greater with computerization and the evolution of medical practices". Thus, computer technology facilitates much greater rapidity and ease of access and transfer of data. Partners concerned in these data are numerous, which causes an increased dispersal of information, part or all of which will be and remain in the custody of various depositaries. The response to this questioning is not self-evident, as some people – perhaps even many – believe, conversely, that IT is a means of bringing additional security to sensitive areas. With the rule of medical secrecy having been reaffirmed, a number of protective elements[11] have been put in place, thus erecting a considerable number of

---

11 On one hand, the French law of January 6, 1978, relative to computer technology, files and liberties provides a number of guarantees. By its very objective, it is aimed at "framing computer applications in such a way as to avoid harm to identity, private life, and individual or public freedoms". To do this, it requires parties responsible for files in Article 19 "to ensure the security of secrets protected by the law", and medical secrecy is one of these types of secrets. Two vital means are specified by the legislative provision to preserve the concept of secrecy: these are the obligation of security imposed on the parties responsible for files in Article 29 and the specific provisions it makes in defining the recipients of the information contained in these files. It is self-evident that the more recipients there are of a file, the greater the risks of breaching confidentiality [MOU 01].

On the other hand, the French *Commission nationale de l'informatique et des libertés* (National Commission for Data Protection, CNIL), which, through its interventions, contributes in a particularly vigilant manner to the preservation of medical secrecy. The CNIL requires group security, often expressing the feeling that it reinforces medical secrecy by giving it concrete content. It is interesting to note that, even though the law gives CNIL the authorization to decree security regulations, it has preferred to operate via recommendations, such as, for example, with regard to the Sésame-Vitale system. The concerns of the CNIL are in no way contradictory to those of medical establishments, which have developed ways of reflecting so that ethical parameters are taken into account when determining how healthcare networks would best function [MOU 01].

security barriers, but a minimum of realism makes it necessary to remain cautious as potential risks of the violation of medical secrecy, which are intrinsically connected to the very structure of computer systems, still exist.

In the case of hospital computer systems, the risks and undesirable effects that have occurred have had mainly to do with the excessive number of responsible parties of all types and with their lack of competence in the domain of computer technology. The CNIL seems to believe that increased knowledge in this area will make file management more responsible and thus minimize the dangers. For this reason, it has developed specific measures intended to ensure the confidentiality of medical data. These measures may be implemented on various levels and they are of various types: separation of data pertaining to individual identity and strictly medical information, "thinning out" of data and the use of encryption systems. In this context, recourse to "anonymization" techniques at the source is able to fulfill these confidentiality requirements [VUL 10]. These techniques, based on so-called "hash algorithms", are used to encode the first and last names and birth dates of patients, that is, to formulate a meaningless and non-identifying number based on these three items of data. This means that information about a single individual can be matched without this individual's identity being known.

Moreover, the fears generated by the computerization of medical practice on data protection are healthy, because they remind us of the fundamental rules of confidentiality that physicians are obligated to follow and encourage us to compare them with the involuntary negligence that often results from ignorance, carelessness or opportunity. Independent of any computerization, this observation should motivate us to search for better medical data-processing procedures than the procedures applied today. In this way, we could put the following basic ethical principles of medical data protection at the forefront:

– Data that are personal in nature must be treated honestly and lawfully.

– Data that are personal in nature must be used for determined and legitimate purposes and not to be processed subsequently in a way incompatible with these purposes [RUO 03].

– Technical and organizational measures should be taken to prevent any unauthorized or illicit processing of personal data and against the accidental loss, error, abuse, destruction or misappropriation of these data.

– Responsible processing of personal data must be proven.

– Consent necessary for data processing must be given freely [RUO 04a].

– Personal data must not be transferred to the whole country because this does not guarantee a degree of protection sufficient for the whole territory.

– Security and the protection of confidentiality must be planned [RUO 10].

– Personal data must be sufficient, relevant and non-excessive in relation to the end purpose for which they are processed.

– Personal data processed for end purposes must not be preserved for longer than necessary for these end purposes [RUO 04b].

– Medical information issued by a prescribing physician must be transmitted neutrally without the interference of any private industry (medications, prostheses, home-care workers) with its content.

We may count four principles applicable in the domain of confidentiality and private life concerning medical information [NEA 08]. On the one hand, the patient must be able to control who can see his or her file. If the patient is unable to participate in this action, a plan must be put in place so that the patient can have the necessary control. In addition, the principle of minimum divulgence must be applied to all of the data supplied by analysis. Next, personal data can be used only after authorization from the patient. However, this information should also be available without prior consent of the patient in the event that they involve a significant risk to a third party or to the public at large. Finally, the consent and authorization mechanism should be easy for patients and healthcare professionals to manage.

On the basis of this, it is our responsibility to foresee future and possible dangers, remembering that the gravest dangers are the dangers we underestimate, because they become reality one day without us being aware of it; to increase awareness on the part of the healthcare professionals who minimize them; to not allow the constitution of databases whose possible subsequent usages have not been researched and analyzed; and to rapidly require effective measures for current data processing to prevent their deviant use in the future.

Consequently, computerized management of healthcare data calls for increased vigilance and can only be imagined in accordance with certain conditions. Patients will have to be clearly informed of the details of the collection, updating, use and conservation of their medical data, as well as of the conditions in which they can access their data. All healthcare professionals managing medical files on the Internet must have the necessary equipment and must have received appropriate training on it. They must also be previously informed of the conditions of use of these files so that the integrity, security and confidentiality of the data will be fully guaranteed. The healthcare data-hosting service provider must have specific security conditions and must strongly encrypt healthcare data that are circulated on the Internet. The decryption of data must be carried out only by healthcare professionals with specific rights of access to these data.

This leads us to ask ourselves questions about the protection of healthcare data and medical secrecy. Has the concept of medical secrecy become obsolete and outmoded, a relic from another age and anachronistic in a modern democratic society, which gives top propriety to the circulation of information, any information, at any price? Under the cover of the argument for protecting the private life of the patient, is it possible that secrecy has become the armed wing of a redoubtable medical paternalism that might return in a new form? From another perspective entirely, is it not possible that this mad drive toward transparency, rejecting the slightest confidentiality, might in the long term involuntarily turn against the interests of the patients, creating a cold, dehumanized society in which there is no longer any place for the warmth and subtlety of human relationships?

It is always a very delicate matter for a society to place itself in a medial position. Perhaps ethical reflection will contribute to this, helping to preserve a place for confidentiality, especially for confidence and for trust, which remain fundamental to every human relationship.

1.4. Cultural evolution of mentalities surrounding legitimacy of information

Historically, our society developed a culture of assisting others. But under the influence of northern Europe, for several years we have witnessed a true shift of this culture toward another culture more oriented toward individual liberty, giving rise to new rights. Information plays a significant role in these new prerogatives and has even become a requirement. This lawfulness of informing the individual leads us to ask ourselves some questions on the subject. The problem is not the problem of informing but rather the problem of knowing how to inform and who to inform. In fact, it is not really the legitimacy of information that is being called into question here but rather the rightfulness of addressing this information to all ill citizens.

For several years, medical information has had more and more to do with the loved ones of the ill person. This goes back to the core of the proximological approach[12], which claims the preeminence of relationships in the care process. This brings to light the preponderant role and impact of the presence and accompaniment of a close person on the quality of care. In most cases, the doctor–patient relationship is part of a representative familial and friendly surrounding group on which the care-providing team can rely. Dominique Maraninchi [MAR 05] characterizes the people close to the patient as "natural helpers" who participate indirectly in the therapeutic process.

On the one hand, this triangular situation can cause ethical problems when demands made by the patient's entourage differ from those made by the patient himself. In these conditions, it is preferable to apply the ethical principle of respect for the patient's autonomy, as it would be inconceivable for the principal person concerned to be kept out of any discussions regarding healthcare decisions and thus his or her therapeutic and human future. Thus, this principle must induce the patient's right to be informed about the nature of his or her illness.

On the other hand, it may occur that well-informed loved ones request the stoppage of the patient's therapeutic treatment, seeing that the cancer is not diminishing and that the patient's health is declining further and further. It has been noted that the first request for euthanasia or discontinuation of treatment is often made by the patient's loved ones, who protest that there is a certain pointless therapeutic determination on the part of the doctor. Even under this pressure from the family, practitioners must devote all their energy and medical knowledge to caring for their patients.

This is why communicating does not consist solely of delivering precise information but also of evaluating all the interactions engaged in by the patient and the systems that accompany him or her (family, social environment, carers). In this specific context, the significance of medical information can be considered to be

---

12 By definition, proximology characterizes the science studying the demographic, medical, epidemiological and financial evolutions contributing to the necessary rediscovery of the role and place of the loved ones of ill individuals. It is at the crossroads of other sciences including sociology, medicine, ethics and anthropology.

– a subject for sharing;

– an intersection between relationships and care processes for patients;

– a fundamental right of individuals being cared for or caring for or accompanying a patient;

– a challenge to have an active and responsible attitude for more effective care.

The issue of access to medical information no longer concerns the patient alone but also the people around him or her: family, close friends and colleagues. From the moment an illness is diagnosed and throughout its treatment, a complex interrelationship is established around the patient between his or her family, the treating physician, specialist physicians and caretaking staff. The end purpose of proximology thus consists of believing that a better understanding of the exceptional relationship between the patient and the people surrounding him or her must be used to facilitate the task of the entourage to achieve greater quality in the treatment plan.

Our society is now facing several types of legal, reparational and medical problems pertaining to new requirements in terms of information. In fact, informing to inform would be a response to a legal problem, informing to indicate the responsibility for medical errors would be a response to a reparational problem and informing to help a sick person recover more effectively would be a response to a medical problem [PAL 03].

1.5. Processing of personal data in law

For many researchers, as soon as you leave pure science you enter the domain of politics or law. The ethical approach is thus confused with political choices or legal decisions. Of course, this sort of detailed ethical reflection influences political decisions, and all of this interacts to a great extent as it evolves through time. Ethics is closely related to sociology, legal matters, economics and politics, but is distinct from them and must have a personal space for reflection. According to Jean-Michel Cornu [COR 08], in his book *ProspecTIC, nouvelles technologies, nouvelles pensées?*, "ethics is often confused with legal study. However, where ethics call on what Emmanuel Kant called *goodwill*, legality intervenes in cases where this is not enough or is not present, and puts labels on the actions of men in society".

The author is careful to distinguish between:

– the ethical approach, which implies voluntary choice by the individual and value judgments (possibly with rules that put self-regulation above all) and

– regulation imposed by the power of a sovereign government that supervises behavior under threat of sanctions.

The objective of the latter is to ensure values, but it is based on outside arbitration that can be based only on judgments of facts.

Although they are very different in nature, these two approaches interact with one another and are complementary; ethics requires a deliberate personal choice and the law is limited by the ability to judge values from the outside. According to Emmanuel Kant, in *Les fondements de la métaphysique des mœurs* (1785), "law has to do only with concrete relationships between individuals, with their exterior duties, while ethics also concerns the deep beliefs of individuals, their interior actions" [KAN 93]. Thus, ethics is the representation of a personal belief or the belief of a group of individuals whereas law is based on a legislative and legal mechanism designating a place of compromise between the various economic, political and ideological pressures of society. However, individual ethics cannot skip over collective law, as it is drawn from principles that apply to everyone. The political life that determines the law can be inspired by our ethical attitudes, but it is ethics on which law and politics are based and never the reverse. A person may be law-abiding regarding the legislation, while being in the wrong from an ethical point of view. When applied to intentions, this situation acquires a specific dimension with the emergence of NTICs and the virtual world we live in, where the line between action and intention has become blurry. It seems that law must now rely on ethics to judge what happens in the virtual world, where it is necessary to take into account the fact that what is expressed there often consists of intentions.

Moreover, when we look at reality and the development of practices, a reverse trend emerges. Connected objects (*Quantified self* [GAD 12]), game consoles and smartphones offer usages that can be voracious consumers of sensitive data, and the use of this technology in the field of healthcare has given rise in particular to the problem of protecting patients' medical data. This is also the case with medical information websites, social networks, mobile applications, etc. Telehealth applications increase in number each day, and we cannot help but note the rapid emergence of one of the most dynamic sectors in the healthcare industry; these are more and more new uses that cannot be controlled by traditional regulations.

Thus, it is a question of knowing how these new practices to existing regulations should be adapted. The question of regulation is also being asked at the European level; it appears that with the development of the market and new ways of adding value to personal data, public authorities are no longer able to frame and implement an effective system of regulation that works with the new uses. This causes new issues and "brings up new challenges for data protection authorities" [LES 13]. It seems appropriate to hope for an evolution in the law, as well as the development of ethical reflection on the adaptation of present designs to the development of constantly evolving uses.

Finally, it seems that, depending on the culture, the mentalities and morals of a country or a continent and regulations relative to personal medical data are not the same. We believe it is of interest to establish an overview of the legal aspect surrounding the processing of these data, to focus on the differences and common points. To do this, we will now give descriptions of the European, North American and Asian legal frameworks.

1.5.1. *European regulations concerning the processing of medical data*

The early 21st Century should see a change of paradigm in matters of healthcare data protection, a major theme in medical law, if we take the word of Petra Wilson, jurist, ex-European Commission, director of Internet solutions for professionals in the healthcare domain at Cisco. As we have previously seen, patients used to be considered passive actors in their own healthcare and wanted their doctors to be the holder and protector of information concerning their health. With time, and due in part to technological advancements, mentalities have evolved, and now patients want this information to be able to be shared by various participants when needed. It is no longer solely a relationship between a healthcare provider and a patient, but that between a team and a person who is informed and, in theory, made responsible. But exchanges necessarily mean the securitization and regulation of data.

In truth, apart from healthcare professionals, healthcare users do not want their data be made available to everyone, especially their insurers or bankers. It is not so much the sharing of information that is problematic at a time when digital technology has simplified information transfer, but rather it is an issue of knowing to whom and above all to what the patient actually wishes to give access. The theme of this regulatory challenge concerning medical data was the central subject of the 16th Global Congress on Medical Law held in Toulouse in 2006.

For Roberto Lattanzi, a member of Italy's Data Protection Authority, *habeas corpus*, the literal right to have one's body has been transposed into medical law following the principle of informed consent. The evolution of recording the healthcare data into digital form means that a *habeas data* now exist as well. In addition to his or her physical dimension, the patient has now taken on a virtual dimension. A transition has occurred between simple medical secrecy and the protection of medical data, which is an entity much more vast, covering everything from the collection to the exploitation of virtual information not only by healthcare professionals but also by the organizations responsible for conveying, storing or exploiting these data. If the exchange of "sensitive" data within networks has existed for several decades, even before the appearance of the Internet, the fact that this information concerns healthcare has humanized these transfers.

The global aspect of these exchanges worries the patient, while it opens up possibilities for researchers that were unimaginable even 15 years ago. This revolution has caused the legal framework proper to these exchanges to evolve by requiring legislators to regulate new disciplines such as telemedicine, for example. It seems necessary, therefore, to seize this opportunity to sketch out – without claiming exhaustiveness – a comparative study of the European, American and Asian systems of personal data protection, covering the activities of justice systems and internal affairs.

1.5.1.1. *Directive 95/46 CE of the European Parliament and Council*

In terms of European legislation, Directive 95/46/CE[13] relative to the protection of natural persons with regard to data of a personal nature and to the free circulation of these data pursues a double objective in its plan to harmonize legislation among the member states of the European Community; it is aimed at allowing the free circulation of personal data, which is confirmed as necessary to the creation and functioning of the

---

13 "By oneself".

common market while also guaranteeing respect for the fundamental freedoms and rights of (natural) persons. According to Christian Hervé *et al.* [HER 07], the directive prohibits the processing of sensitive data[14] for the reason that data susceptible by its nature to harm fundamental freedoms or private life should not be the subject of processing[15].

According to these authors, seven situations make it permissible to lift the interdiction on using medical data:

– obtaining of the express consent of the person concerned to this effect[16];

– processing is necessary to respect the specific obligations and rights of the processing officer in matters of labor law, provided that he or she is authorized by federal legislation including adequate security[17];

– processing is essential to the defense of the vital interests of the person concerned or of another person in the event that the individual concerned is physically or legally unable to give consent[18];

– processing is carried out as part of legitimate activity and with appropriate security by a foundation, association or any other non-profit structure for political, philosophical, religious or union-related ends, subject to the condition that this processing relates only to members of this organization or people with regular contacts with it related to this end purpose and that the data are not given to a third party with the consent of the persons involved[19];

– processing involves data deliberately made public by the person concerned or necessary for the reporting, exercise or defense of a legal right[20];

– when the processing of data is necessary for the purposes of preventive medicine, medical diagnoses, the administration of care or treatments or the management of healthcare services[21];

---

14 Art. 8.1. D95/46/CE.
15 Cons. 33 D95/46/CE.
16 Art. 8.2.a D95/46/CE.
17 Art. 8.2.b D95/46/CE.
18 Art. 8.2.c D95/46/CE.
19 Cons. 33 D95/46/CE.
20 Art. 8.2.e D95/46/CE.
21 Art. 8.3 D95/46/CE.

– data can be processed on the condition that the reason for this processing is an important public interest, which supposes the effective demonstration of the existence of this reason in each case by the member state[22].

In addition, on December 7, 2011, the European Commission unveiled a new plan of action anticipating the development of the e-health problem over the period 2012–2020. The objective of this plan is "to face up to the constraints limiting a mass use of digital solutions in European healthcare systems".

The plan of action sets a series of objectives requiring a clarification of the legal framework. Today, one observation is manifest: "the healthcare situation is in a situation comparable to that of banks or industrial groups for which IT is an essential service" [BIC 10]. The field of healthcare is a massive producer of information [VEN 13] and new technologies can provide decisive aid to physicians.

However, although it is undeniable that telehealth offers the very strong likelihood of drastically improving public health, the digitization of medicine involves certain risks that must be taken into consideration.

The defining feature of TICs applied to the healthcare sector lies in the existing normative framework. In this field, we can see the coexistence of one set of regulations pertaining to IT and communications and another set pertaining to healthcare, existing mainly within the code of public health. What emerges from the observation of this "legislative and regulatory stacking" [BIC 10] is the necessity of respecting a certain number of principles: confidentiality, respect for private life, security, etc. Today, these principles are being sorely tested by practice (outsourcing, the cloud, connected objects, etc.).

Although it is necessary to regulate the use of healthcare data with the aim of preserving a number of principles, particularly a minimum of confidentiality, it is also necessary to think about the development of information systems and the sharing of healthcare data in harmony with the evolution of these usages. In this sense, it seems crucial – because the ethical and societal challenge is a major change – to find a balance between the rights of the individuals concerned (be they patients or not) and the needs of healthcare professionals (treatment or research).

---

22 Art. 8.4 D95/46/CE.

In addition, the question of the definition of personal data is vital to put the legal framework in place. This definition makes it possible to determine the material field of application of the protection offered by regulation. Consequently, for Directive 95/46 CE, data of a personal nature represent:

> any information concerning an identified or identifiable natural person (person concerned); a person is considered to be identifiable who can be identified, directly or indirectly, particularly by referring to an identification number or to one or more specific components proper to his or her physical, physiological, psychic, economic, cultural, or social identity.

The provision for regulation of January 25, 2012, includes a major modification of the 1995 directive; the term "personal data" is no longer defined *per se*[23] but by reference. In fact, the proposal for regulation (Article 4) provides for the definition of personal data as "any information of which the end purpose is to identify the person concerned". It also specifies that the term "person concerned" translates to:

> an identified natural person or a natural person who can be identified, directly or indirectly, by means reasonably likely to be used by the person responsible for treatment or by any other natural person or legal entity, notably by referring to an identification number, location data, an online identifier, or one or more specific elements proper to his or her physical, physiological, genetic, psychic, economic, cultural, or social identity.

For Professor Rochfeld [ROC 13], "the proposition of regulation may seem, by linking the definition of data and that of the person, to have made an ideological choice in favor of a personalist conception of data and to have diverted the path of its total reification".

Finally, the ownership of data is a central subject in the debate around the balance between protection and freedom of processing of data. The question on the appropriation of personal data is directly related to the commercialization that results from it. Thus, patrimonialization, that is, the likelihood of "assigning a monetary value to this data" [COR 10],

---

23 Directive 95/46 CE of the European Parliament and the Council of October 24, 1995, "relative to the protection of natural persons with regard to the processing of data of a personal nature and to the free circulation of this data".

is becoming a phenomenon of the highest importance. The personal data market has become a market in its own right. The circulation of these data, and their subsequent commercialization, require some legal clarifications. Personal data are linked to a fundamental right. Any commercial exploitation of data represents a potential violation of a fundamental right and must be justified by legitimate interest, consent, the execution of a contract, etc.

Directive 95/46 CE of the European Parliament and Council of October 24, 1995, evokes the "free circulation of this data", a point that leads us conclude that, in the context of commodification, data must circulate as freely as merchandise, assets, capital, etc. These data are also likely to come from the private sphere of the individual, and therefore it is necessary to reconcile the circulation of these data and the protection of private life. The phenomenon of commodification is disturbing this balance between protection and freedom of data processing. Thus, it appears to be of primordial importance to reflect on the fundamental tenets of a new harmonization between the protection of private life and the freedom of circulation of these data.

1.5.1.2. *European and EU instruments protecting private life*

Europe has several legal texts and community tools designed to protect the private life of its citizens. In fact, respect for private life has been guaranteed since the 1950 adoption by the Council of Europe of the *Convention de sauvegarde des droits de l'homme et des libertés fondamentales* or Convention for the Protection of Human Rights and Fundamental Freedoms (CEDH): "every individual has the right to respect for his private and family life, his residence, and his correspondence" (Article 8). In substance, the concept of "the right to private life" included in the CEDH can be described as a right preventing public authorities from taking measures constituting an intrusion into private life unless certain conditions are present. Emphasis is placed on protection against intrusion by public authorities and not by private organizations.

Moreover, Article 17 of the December 16, 1966 United Nations International Covenant on Civil and Political Rights specifies that "No one shall be the subject of arbitrary or illegal intrusions into his or her private life, family, residence, or correspondence, or to illegal attacks upon his or her honor and reputation. Every individual has the right to the protection of the law against such intrusions or attacks".

We may also cite the European Charter of Fundamental Rights[24], which indicates that:

> Every individual has the right to respect for his private and familial life, for his residence and his communications. (Art. 7)

> Every individual has the right to the protection of data of a personal nature concerning him or her. This data must be treated honestly for predetermined purposes and on the basis of the consent of the person concerned or on the basis of another fundamental reason provided for by the law. Every individual has the right to access the data collected concerning him or her and to correct it. (Art. 8)

Note that this charter also includes the express right to protection of data of a personal nature. Respect for private life and the protection of personal data are closely linked but are treated as separate and distinct fundamental rights in Articles 7 and 8 of the EU Charter of Fundamental Rights, adopted in 2000 and proclaimed again in 2007.

Although, effectively, the concept of protection of "data of a personal nature" is linked to that of the protection of data concerning private life, the protection of personal data provides more extensive protection than the protection of private life.

The right to protection of data of a personal nature is established in Article 8 of the Charter and in Article 16 of the Treaty on the Functioning of the European Union, as well as in Article 8 of the CEDH. In fact, the history of data protection begins with Article 8 of the European Convention on the Rights of Man. This provision defines private life as the "right to be left alone", related to the right of private life for individuals. The right not to be subject to the revelation of information related to the "private sphere", whether it is physical (as in the familial residence) or the expression of a relationship to another person (as in secrecy of correspondence), can be defined as the "right to be left alone" [WAR 90].

Thus, as we have just seen, European regulations around personal medical data are currently a major theme of medical law and law concerning

---

24 The European Union Charter has been legally binding since the Treaty of Lisbon.

new technologies. The importance of the subject lies in the increasing exploitation of information and communication technologies in the healthcare sector and the new risks this causes for the rights and freedoms of citizens.

This is why this regulation of medical data represents a major issue to be resolved on the subject in years to come, to ensure the protection of citizens with regard to the processing of medical data. This regulation involves in-depth reflection on the legitimacy of use of these data, as well as on an analysis of legal texts addressing this subject in a precise manner.

1.5.2. *American legal framework surrounding personal healthcare data*

Under the influence of North American debates, the recognition of a right of ownership of personal data has been advanced [DÉT 09][25]. The attribution of a right of ownership to personal data would be seen in Europe as a regression of the current protection founded on individual rights, whereas in the United States its objective is to strengthen the protection of personal data collected and processed by private individuals, which is currently ensured by self-regulation and criminal responsibility and lacks general federal regulations.

Some North American regulations suggest giving individuals the right of ownership over their personal data. This type of right would enable people to better control the obtaining and use of their data, in particular their resale to third parties by the processing agent, by giving them ways to act concretely on a market that has so far developed without taking their interests into account. To this end, Professors James Rule and Lawrence Hunter [RUL 99] proposed the creation of a new right of ownership over personal data. According to these American authors, the right of ownership and the logic of the market would make it possible to better apportion both data, conceived as a good endowed with its own economic value, and private life, perceived as a rare resource that is worthy of protection. This is a deft manifestation of the prevailing American adage that "privacy is your business". In these conditions, aside from certain data collected by banks or hospitals, which benefit from greater protection, businesses are free to exploit data as long as they do not commit "dishonest practices".

---

25 Senate information report pertaining to respect for private life in the era of digital memory.

The principal document in American legislation covering the processing of data by governmental agencies was adopted in 1974. The Privacy Act (law on the protection of private life) is the main legal framework protecting personal data held by the public sector in the United States. It protects files held by American governmental agencies and requires them to apply fair information practices. It is composed of five legal principles:

– Principle of transparency (e)(4): "Any agency maintaining a system of files must […] publish in the federal register, at the time of setup or revision, a notice of existence and the nature of the file system…;"

– Principles of access and correction (d) on "access to files;"

– Data security, which is addressed in the section on "agency requirements" (e)(5)(10);

– Principle of end purpose limitation (e)(1), stipulating that each agency must "keep in its files only information concerning an individual that is relevant and necessary to accomplish an end goal of the agency, which must be executed by law or a presidential decree".

Thus, it is in the United States that the right to privacy was born. This right, which is a result of the development of the press and its indiscretions regarding the private life of individuals, was only given this name following an article written by Samuel Warren and Louis Brandeis, attorneys in Boston in the late 19th Century. These authors notably developed the concept of privacy against threats of snapshot photography in major newspapers. Brandeis, who was a justice of the US Supreme Court, vigorously defended the trend of common law to extend the protection of individuals and goods (logically implying recognition) to the particulars of a new right, the right to privacy. It should be clarified that these authors did not invent the expression "right to privacy", which was not new, but they did conceptualize a theoretical mechanism to legitimize this right and help it to take root in substantive law. All that Warren and Brandeis ever claimed to invent was a legal theory that illuminated a "right to private life", a common denominator that was already present in a wide variety of concepts and legal precedents in numerous areas of common law. According to Professor Glancy, this is why their article reads as if the authors had literally pillaged all the traditional domains of common law they could find, such as contracts, goods, deeds of trust, author's rights, protection of commercial secrecy and infractions, to uncover the existing legal principle underlying all of these various parts of common law. This fundamental legal principle was the right to private life, and their new legal theory shaped and gave form to this principle [GLA 79].

In the United States, the right to privacy protects both secrecy and freedom in an extended sphere of individual life. This right is inspired by the idea that this sphere belongs to every person, or, more precisely, since it does not involve ownership, that each person must be sovereign in this sphere in relation to others, who must respect its secrecy and freedom, and sovereign in relation to the government and all public authorities, the laws of governments or federal laws themselves.

Moreover, after the Privacy Act of 1974, federal legislators developed a series of laws framing the protection of personal data in the private sector, including

– HIPAA (Health Insurance Portability and Accountability Act) on the protection of healthcare data;

– GLBA (Gramm–Leach–Bliley Act) on the protection of financial data;

– COPPA (Children's Online Privacy Protection Act) on the protection of data concerning children;

– FCRA (Fair Credit Reporting Act) on the regulation of solvency profiles of individuals;

– ECPA (Electronic Communications Privacy Act) on the protection of telecommunications data;

– VPPA (Video Privacy Protection Act) on the protection of data regarding video rentals;

– Cable TV Privacy Act on the protection of data on the choices of individuals regarding television programs;

– Can-SPAM Act on the prohibition of advertising messages.

It is also important to note that federal constitutionalism coexists with state constitutionalism and that it is completed by the latter. Constitutional law on the respect for private life is directly guaranteed in the constitutions of certain states. Of these, Californian constitutional law on the respect for private life is also applicable to private parties.

Article 1 (sec. 1) of the constitution of the State of California stipulates that "Every individual is free and independent and possesses inalienable rights. These include the possession and defense of life and liberty, the acquisition, possession, and protection of goods, and the pursuit and acquisition of safety, happiness, and respect for private life". An Office of Privacy Information has also been established in California, and a new data security law is in the process of being developed, which would amend the law on notice of violation to require those who are subject to it, government agencies and individuals or companies operating in California, when they inform individuals of a violation of their personal data, as defined, to inform the Office of Privacy Protection as well. This would only be applicable in the case of notifications made via the "substitution" method, which uses means of mass communication rather than individual notifications [BEL 09].

Note that the absence of comptrolling authorities responsible for the protection of independent data in the United States undoubtedly constitutes, from a European point of view, a weakness in the system, especially in this period of rapid technological advancement.

Finally, the protection of private life was recognized in the 1969 American Convention on the Rights of Man. According to Article 11, "No one can be the subject of arbitrary or abusive intrusions into his or her private life or the private lives of his or her family, in his or her residence or correspondence, or of illegal attacks on his or her honor and reputation (...)".

1.5.3. *Laws pertaining to personal data in Asia*

After analyzing the various legislations pertaining to personal data in Asia, we have concentrated our study mainly on five large Asian countries or cities, specifically Japan and China, with a focus on Hong Kong.

1.5.3.1. *In Japan*

Because Japan is a member of the Organisation for Economic Co-operation and Development, its legislation on private life is influenced by the regulations of this institution. The country ratified an international convention on civil and political rights (PIDCP) in 1979 and also Article 17 relative to private life, which is an integral part of Japanese law.

Article 13 of the Constitution of Japan (1946) specifies that "All people must be respected as individuals. The right to life, liberty, and the pursuit of happiness is, provided that it does not interfere with the public well-being, the supreme consideration in legislation and in other governmental affairs". This article indicates that the freedom of citizens in private life must be protected against the exercise of public authority, … each individual has the right to protect his personal information so that it is not divulged to a third party or rendered public without good reason[26].

In addition, on April 22, 1999, the Japanese Ministry of Health and Social Affairs proposed the electronic preservation of all clinical files. Deliberations on legislation and the divulgence of personal data took place at that time.

Japan currently has a sophisticated and unique system for the protection of data, notably in the private sector; this system is applicable to the domains of telecommunications, financial services, transportation and medicine. This law covers the protection of personal information (PPI) that can be used to identify an individual (name, date of birth or any other description of the individual).

Finally, the law on the PPI[27] governs the collection and use of personal data in Japan. All forms of data processing are covered, but the PPI law is applicable only to situations involving the personal information of 5,000 or more people.

1.5.3.2. In China

China does not have a complete legal framework for data protection. Chinese regulations are based on a multitude of general and specific laws applicable to various sectors of industry. The right to private life is generally recognized and protected by the Constitution and the general principles of civil law in China.

The seventh amendment to the criminal law of 2009 mentions a criminal infraction for employees of governmental institutions or private organizations in the domains of finance, telecommunications, transportation,

---

26 See 1965 (A) No. 1187, judgment of the High Bench of the Supreme Court of December 24, 1969, Keishu Vol. 23, no. 12, 1625.
27 PPI Law: Act No. 57 of 2003.

education or medicine, in the event that they sell or provide illegally to third parties the personal data of any citizen that have been obtained in the exercise of their duties or services.

Moreover, the permanent committee of the National People's Congress has published an initial series of laws at the national level specifically regulating the confidentiality of online data and handing down a decision on the reinforcement of the Information Protection Network, which became effective on December 28, 2012.

Finally, since February 1, 2013, the General Administration of Supervision of Quality and Inspection has imposed specific requirements for each stage of the collection, processing, transmission and deletion of personal data. These directives specifically prohibit the outsourcing of personal data barring the express consent or approval of the personal involved, the appropriate competent authorities or the law. Note that the divulgence and transfer of information may potentially fall under the auspices of the law on the protection of state secrets.

Hong Kong, officially the Special Administrative Region of Hong Kong of the People's Republic of China (PRC), is the largest and most populated of the two Special Administrative Regions of the PRC. It has a complete legislative system that is in overall compliance with the directives on data protection of the European Union and regulates the manner in which a data user must collect, conserve and use personal data.

The Personal Data (*Privacy*) Ordinance imposes the notification of and consent to a growing number of requirements for data users seeking to sell, use or supply personal information for direct marketing. Penalties are specified if users do not comply with these requirements. This ordinance thus protects information relating directly or indirectly to a living person, which makes it possible to identify that living person.

The Commissioner for private life is also authorized to provide legal assistance to wronged persons who may appeal in this direction to request compensation.

2

Ethical Modeling: From the Design to the Use of an Information System

For many years now, diagnostic investigation via medical imaging has been accused of widening the breach in the doctor–patient relationship. The development of computer and digital applications meant for the collaborative search for information among healthcare professionals does not adequately take into account the nature and real needs of the therapeutic act [MEN 09]. For some, IT in healthcare is contributing to the "mechanical assimilation of the human body, which sidelines the flesh-and-blood reality of mankind" [LEB 99]. Its use by the practitioner leads to a reductionist, dualist and mechanical vision inherited from the Cartesian tradition.

Today, human–machine communication constitutes a major technological, industrial and social challenge. The difficulty is no longer only of further extending these performances, but of improving exchanges of information with human users and adapting to their expectations and skills. All technologies define a relationship between human beings and their environment, both human and physical; indeed, one of the great lessons of Hippocrates is to study humans in their biotope in order to be useful to them. As this environment is now largely digital, it is advisable to observe it from an ethical point of view.

No technology can be considered purely instrumental. The human factor, and thus the human–computer interaction, is primordial. In a multidisciplinary context, this inter-relationship is even more significant in the context of the doctor–patient relationship. For this reason, the evolution of IS in healthcare is based on human interactions, which underlie the design, setup and use of technological tools. This situation assumes the necessity of increased dialogue and of human assessment between the doctor and his or her patient.

Now, linguistics, ethics and cognitive and social psychology must be incorporated in the same way as the computer culture in IT models. From this point of view, the collaborative search for information appears as a technological system with social, psychological, sociological and ethical characteristics.

The objectives of this chapter are (1) to describe the evolution of data in practical wisdom, (2) to understand the way in which the methodology of our research was established, (3) to present our ethical analysis space and (4) to present the framework of our resulting ethical model, which are essential to carrying out our field studies on the subject.

Before going into the detail of the subject of the method used, we believe it is crucial to provide a short preamble on the subject of our study; that is, the IS in its current form. The IS, as we understand it in this case, corresponds to a system constituted by the definition of business processes and those of the stores and flows of information illuminating these processes. It is an organization of resources[1] used to gather, classify, process and diffuse information on a given phenomenon.

The IS represents the vehicle of communication in this organization and possesses a digital system composed of:

– computer workstations and servers (data, images, etc.);

– applications (operating systems, office software applications, professional software, etc.);

– communication and telecommunication infrastructures (local networks, intersite links, telephone networks, Internet access, radio links, etc.).

The engineering of an IS is concerned with the incorporation and use of information in social or technical systems. Information has multiple functions within an organization: it enables this organization to attain its objectives and contributes to the maintenance of its unity. A real system is known only through the information it causes to circulate inside and outside of itself. Information creates and maintains the system insofar as it plays an essential role in communication between the elements of the system and between the

---

1 Hardware, software, data, personnel and procedures.

elements of the system and its environment. Thus, throughout its entire lifecycle (development–use–transmission–archiving), medical information is dematerialized in order to be transmitted or preserved in a digital format within an organization.

Two types of IS constitute our study:

– IS patient management supports for the production of reports, in particular, IT management;

– decision-making assistance IS used by (information) managers in their decision-making activities, via the development of the decision-making system. Depending on the performance, this technological tool can aid the decision-maker in activities of intelligence[2], modeling[3] and choice[4].

The question underlying our study is the identification of the ethical principles surrounding the design and use of an IS in healthcare, and particularly in medical imaging. The essential challenge of this part is to link this procedural ethical challenge, based on the ethics of communication and dialogue, to a moral content capable of giving meaning and an end purpose to the management of treatment, and more globally to medicine.

It is a matter of understanding how these ethical concerns addressed by actors interact in decisions, in the behaviors they are led to adopt and in the use of IS at such instances. This question has given rise to numerous questions around this theme in the analytical questionnaires that we consider the very bedrock of our study. These analytical questionnaires have enabled us to study and compare the ends and means involved in the production of an IS.

2.1. Info-ethics: data on practical wisdom

The development of communication systems in our organizations is undoubtedly the primary cause of the current acceleration of exchanges, sharing and the resulting complexity. It is not always easy to distinguish between the concepts of data, information, knowledge, communication and organization because these concepts simply cannot pass from one to another in a more or less harmonious sequence [VAC 09]. A real system is known

---

2 Gathering of data on a specific problem, preliminary statistical processing, etc.
3 Search for models, generation of alternatives, etc.
4 Calculation via simulation, sensitivity analysis, etc.

only through the information it causes to circulate inside and outside of itself. Information has multiple functions within an organization: it enables this organization to attain its objectives and contributes to the maintenance of its unity. It creates and maintains the system insofar as it plays an essential role in communication between the elements of the system and its environment. Some information must be shared; other information must be exchanged, and still other information requires no transfer, although it is vital to the concretization of actions or to the activity of an organization. Information becomes an object through perspective, shaping or simply the memory of a situation. This object has no existence except through human interpretation. The communicational approach of organizations [BOU 03, BOU 07] proposes a framework integrating the communicational dimensions of organizations by observing activities that produce meaning. It seeks to keep together three levels: organizational, political and operational, wherein communication results. This communication is included in information and is "a relationship, uniting subjects via the intermediary of material and intellectual mediations" [JEA 04].

It took many years for the IS to be the subject of research on fundamental philosophical principles, particularly in the conceptualization and study of data, information and knowledge. It was not until the studies by Floridi on NTICs within the functioning of organizations and his concept of the "infosphere"[FLO 04] that human beings, data, information, knowledge, information technologies, society and the interests of individuals were compared with an ethical point of view [FLO 07a, FLO 07b]. In these conditions, a description once epistemological, anthropological and ethical of the progression of data toward a practical wisdom dear to Paul Ricœur [RIC 90] seems essential to the development of a deeper understanding of the way to assess the theoretical and practical implications of communication within organizations.

2.1.1. *Epistemological illumination around the pyramid of knowledge*

The diffusion of information constitutes a process of communication involving epistemological elements[5], ethical values and universal norms necessary to agents of information. In an epistemological and ethical context, there is a conceptual relationship between data, information and true

---

5 These epistemological criteria include objectivity, independence, reliability, exactitude and sources generating information.

knowledge [DRE 99, FLO 05]. To better analyze these concepts, it is vital to have a thorough understanding of the deeper nature specific to each of them.

Generally speaking, computer specialists use the term "data" more often than "information". This arises from the fact that an item of data is defined principally by its type, which can be digital, alphabetical, temporal, binary, alphanumeric, etc. Data have only content and a type; they are not significant in themselves but are something objective and real. They are composed of facts, observations and natural elements, and have little meaning if not processed. For this reason, data are at the very bottom of the pyramidal hierarchy of knowledge.

For its part, information is characterized more by its meaning, and its acquisition and understanding lead naturally to knowledge. This knowledge is what allows us to situate information and to contextualize and globalize it; that is, to place it as part of a whole. However, does the term "information" have a precise meaning? Does it constitute a universal scientific concept attesting to unified knowledge?

Etymologically speaking, information provides knowledge that the recipient does not have or cannot predict. It reduces uncertainty.

From an ethical point of view, information provides meaning, coherence, intelligibility and direction for the development of a relationship of trust between doctor and patient.

This definition stipulates that the value of information is linked to the decisions it enables people to make. Thus, its end purpose is to model the framework of future actions. This information must be incorporated into a system. It is defined as being a process by which a human or social entity is transformed. According to some scientists, it corresponds to a fundamental physical value, just like time, weight or energy, meaning that it can be quantified according to context. Information is a proteiform concept that cannot be easily understood. According to the systemic approach, information disappears for the benefit of communication. The system theory of communications models an organization using the links that unite its elements, considering information as the lubricant that enables the system to reveal representations of its various parts. Information thus constitutes the intermediate stage of the pyramid. The understanding of initial data generally involves the knowledge of other connected data constituting a coherent context for "a mechanism of successive deductions called inferences" [TOU 04]. It is on the basis of this hierarchical modeling that many tools and methods have been developed.

For its part, knowledge answers questions of the type "Why?" and "How?" Knowledge is possessed by an individual, which is not the case for information or data. It is internalized by the person, who formats it according to his or her experience, background and perceptions of the moment. In this sense, knowledge is eminently subjective and personal. Even though collective knowledge exists, it is nothing but the sum of individual knowledge. It can be materialized in products (technology) and multimedia supports (books, films, etc.). Thus, it occupies the upper levels of the pyramid.

Each stage of the pyramid, thus, corresponds to a series of means used to capture, manage, diffuse and exploit elements (data, information or knowledge). This pyramidal ascension, starting from data and rising to knowledge and thus finally to practical wisdom[6], can be illustrated through the words of the English poet Thomas S. Eliot, when he asked: "Where is the wisdom we have lost in knowledge? Where is the knowledge we have lost in information?"[7]. This wisdom, located at the very top of the pyramid, is considered to be the ultimate stage of cognitive evolution. According to Spence [SPE 10], the concept of wisdom is understood as being a kind of "meta-knowledge" and "meta-virtue", placing it at the crossroads of epistemology, axiology and eudemony[8].

In summary, we can state that, much like genotype versus phenotype, data constitute the base support for information. Their nature is both raw and pure. Data represent the "DNA of information". If we continue with this train of thought likening information to genetics, we can suggest that information corresponds to a phenotype: all of the observable characteristics of an individual. In this context, the expression of data (in part) produces information, as the genotype does the phenotype. Data are not the only sources of information;

---

6 Practical wisdom, where duty itself must pass the test of wise and prudent decision-making in the face of singular concrete situations.

7 In his play entitled "The Rock" (1934).

8 It is in terms of eudemony that Waterman [WAT 93] defines well-being. He draws on the classic Aristotelian concept according to which people live more or less in harmony with their "true self", or daimon. It is the daimon that gives direction and meaning to a person's action; if he or she lives in harmony with his or her daimon, he or she experiences eudemony, which Waterman describes as being self-realization, or optimal psychological functioning. From this perspective, self-realization is possible for a person if he or she seizes opportunities to better him or herself, seeing them as life challenges that he or she feels able to confront [LAG 00]. Eudemonism seeks precisely what is "fundamentally good" for human nature and the psychological needs that stimulate human development and the fulfillment of which procures wakefulness and vitality. Literature inspired by the theory of self-determination deals with the idea that there are forms of pleasure that have nothing to do with psychological well-being [DEC 85, RYA 97, RYA 00].

the environment also plays a significant role, as with the environment's effect on phenotype (see Figure 2.1).

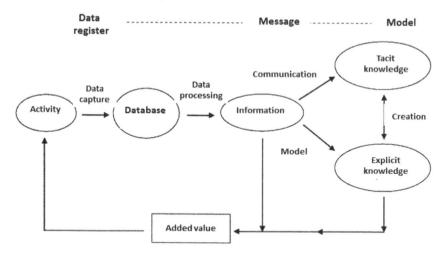

Figure 2.1. *Structural analogy between genetics and information*

Genotype and *phenotype* are terms invented by Bateson in the early 20th Century. It was this same Bateson who, in 1905, proposed the term *genetics* to designate "the science of heredity". An inheritance is nothing more than the transmission of these material assets but, from a human point of view, it is also the transmission of the physical and moral characteristics to their descendants. In these conditions we can conclude that, like genetics, information designates the "science of communication". The data–information relationship, despite its apparent simplicity and the extraordinary rise of NTICs, remains a central problem in modern communication. Knowing all information – meaning all the information contained in the infosphere, or "infonome"[9] – would require observing it with all possible analytical tools and in every possible external and internal circumstance and environment, which is impossible! This creates the complexity of communication, which cannot anticipate (and consequently master) the entire flow of a variable stream of information, which is in perpetual mutation in an unstable and dynamic environment.

9 Neologism constructed on the model of a "phenome", which represents all the phenotypic traits of an individual. Thus, the "infonome" corresponds to all information.

For this reason, the equation *Information = Data + Environment* translates the fact that the composition of a piece of information corresponds to the sum of the intrinsic value of the data and of the environment in which this information is expressed. By nature, data are pure values that are fixed in time and do not vary, unlike the environment, which is in perpetual movement. Thus, the only way of more effectively framing and thus understanding information is to better understand and know the environmental parameters of reality.

In these conditions, the proper use of knowledge necessarily involves an ethical support for information, such as bioethics for genetics.

It is in this context that our model of ethical analysis applied to an environment can contribute to a better grasp and understanding of information. An understood environment is a more ordered environment with weaker entropy. In these conditions, so-called "ethical" information can be translated into knowledge. This confirms the theory of Luciano Floridi [FLO 02] around "the ethics of information". According to the author, "an action considered to be fair or considered as ethical would lead to reduced overall entropy (degree of disorder), and to an increase of the knowledge we have of it".

2.1.2. *From data to knowledge through an information system*

A detailed description of the progression from data to knowledge seems vital to the development of a deeper understanding of the manner of evaluating the theoretical and practical implications of information within the doctor–patient relationship via NTICs. On the basis of this observation, Spence [SPE 09a,SPE09b] created a universal model of normative evaluation of the quality of digital information. According to him, theoretical and practical knowledge have impacts on medical decision-making. The diffusion of information is a communication process involving epistemological elements[10], ethical values and universal norms necessary for information agents. Knowledge is what makes it possible to situate, contextualize and globalize information; that is, to place it in a whole. Each stage of the pyramid corresponds to a series of means used to capture, manage, diffuse and exploit elements (data, information or knowledge).

---

10 These epistemological criteria include objectivity, independence, reliability, exactitude and sources generating information.

According to Nonaka and Takeuchi [NON 11], we can distinguish four modes of knowledge conversion:

– *Socialization*: this is an interactive process by which the members of a team construct representations and forms of shared experiences. It is based on the sharing of experiences. Meetings encourage the sharing of knowledge for the development of a project in the process of completion. Members also socialize tacit knowledge via observation, imitation and practice. Interactions with users are also a source of socialization.

– *Externalization*: this consists of transformation of tacit knowledge into explicit knowledge. It is based on dialogue and collective reflection using metaphors, analogies and models.

– *Combination*: this corresponds to a process by which the members coordinate and elucidate their own knowledge to create a common knowledge. It is based on the theory of information processing. Individuals combine and exchange knowledge using documents, meetings, telephone conversations and computerized communication networks.

– *Internalization*: this is based on the application of explicit knowledge to enrich the user's own tacit knowledge base. It is closely related to organizational learning. Documentation or verbal dialogue facilitates the transfer of explicit knowledge to other people. It relies on resources aiding the members of an organization to access the experiences of other members[11].

In these conditions we can see, when it comes to knowledge, the existence of "paradigm" thought structures; that is, principles and logical connections between the primary concepts that determine the mode of knowing. Anything that does not fit into a schema of thought will be set aside as insignificant. Concretely speaking, comprehension is possible only inside a single thought structure or paradigm[12]. This context must be comprehensible for the recipient. This becomes of primordial importance for the qualification of data, but the value of information is manifested and expressed in their end purpose.

Moreover, the comprehension, perception and idea of usefulness of a piece of data involve the five human senses in order to be effective and must

11 Internalization and externalization are processes constituting the key stages of the knowledge spiral.

12 Magoroh Maruyama prefers to call them "mindscapes" or "mental landscapes" within which we absolutely do not communicate with one another [COL 94].

thus require the smallest possible amount of intellectual translation. Data are transmitted naturally, throughout consultations between a patient and his or her doctor, in order for his or her care to be effective. These data can be of various types: medical, socioeconomic, religious, sexual orientation or behavior, HIV positivity, etc. It is a matter of supporting the patient in the appropriation of particularly sensitive knowledge, and the doctor must ask himself or herself what the patient desires and can hear. He or she may exploit or filter certain information and know how to manage his or her concerns from his or her end.

The IS must guarantee reliability and homogeneity of data, which must be concretely manifested by the setup of a computer system that, once data are recorded, categorized and organized, creates added value by producing information that is reliable and legible and can be processed; that is, comprehensible as a result of being placed within a framework that gives it meaning or chosen in a contingent and useful context. The IS is considered to be a subsystem of the establishment, located at the interface between the operating system used in production and the guidance system that sets objectives and choices.

This IS also supplies intelligence to the decision-maker, in the sense that the latter has access not only to data illuminating his or her decisions but especially to the understanding of the data gathered inciting him or her to action; the raw data are successively transformed into information and thus knowledge. This evolution of the status of data toward knowledge can be illustrated by a pyramid whose base corresponds to data, the middle to information and the peak to final knowledge. The design of an IS imposes the acquisition, storage, processing and diffusion of information, which is converted into knowledge that can be understood, digested and controlled by the user.

Upstream, the IS requires a certain negotiation within the structure regarding the constitution and management of data. An agreement must be reached between the various participants on the information to be collected based on the data and objectives pursued. To do this, it is especially necessary to take into account the sociological and cultural contexts of the structure. It is clear that the majority of researchers emphasize the relationship between data and information, but this is less true for questions concerning knowledge [ALA 01]. We can establish an initial schema interrelating data, information and knowledge (see Figure 2.2).

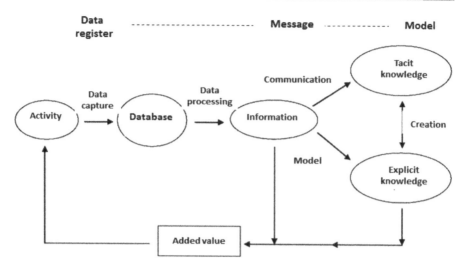

Figure 2.2. *Information systems and knowledge*

According to the authors, data concern the medical file, information constitutes the proper message and knowledge forms the model. The whole corresponds to the IS of data reception, thus to the processing of these data into information, ending with the knowledge resulting from the model [WIL 09]. We can now establish another, more advanced schema of the earlier representation influenced by Boisot and Canals [BOI 08] (see Figure 2.3).

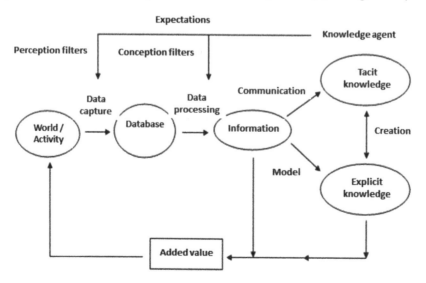

Figure 2.3. *Developed information systems and knowledge*

In this new representation, we can see that the expectations of the knowledge agent are expressed by the presence of two filters through which data pass. The first filter, called the perception filter, converts people and activities into data, while the second filter, called the conception filter, transcribes these data into information. This information can now be communicated[13] or incorporated into a knowledge model[14] that will have the effect of having actions and added value on the physical world and its activities [BOI 08].

In their books on the subject, Collins and Kusch [COL 98] and Collins and Evans [COL 07] established a categorization of actions that can be performed by machines and those that remain fully within the human sector. They used the term "action" and differentiated it from behavior, which they designated as "a sequence of bodily movements" [COL 98]. Actions are always associated one way or another with intentions and correspond to the sum of behavior and intention. Thus, a direct link exists between knowledge and action via the intermediary of intentions.

Ultimately, users have logical requirements, notably that of having access to reliable, pertinent data that are available when they need it. Above all, they want these data to be useful and understandable. According to Tourreilles [TOU 04], good IS ergonomics involves the mixing of numerical and textual elements, as well as visual, auditory, tactile, olfactory and gustatory elements. This evolution is significant technically and must be part of a guiding computer schema.

However, it is even more important at the cultural level, as it implies a shift from a culture of measurement of an objective past that does not give a great deal to a culture of projection that provides real guidance, on the administrative level and on the medical and healing levels.

2.1.3. *Quality and choice of medical information*

Quality is not a unique objective concept. It can be defined, when considering things more completely, as the factor that will result in the satisfaction of the healthcare user with regard to the product or service consumed, depending on expectations, needs or wishes, which vary naturally from one type of product or service to another, as well as from one person to

---

13 Referred to as tacit knowledge.
14 Referred to as explicit knowledge.

another and may even, for a single person, vary from one circumstance to another. With regard to medical information, quality designates the fact that, during processing, conservation or diffusion, data do not undergo any alteration or deliberate or accidental destruction and retain a format that allows them to be used. In other words, quality is defined as assurance that the content of the information has not been modified during its transmission[15]. It influences the reality of the free and informed consent of the patient with respect to the healthcare professional.

Given the immense daily production of information, it is helpful to take an inventory of the information that requires conservation. It seems necessary to retain only what is essential. Information that is retained does not just require storage; it must also be accessible and refreshed at regular intervals. Finally, it is essential to transfer this information from support to support as technology evolves. Thus, it is advisable to establish digital archives with clear rules appropriate to a field in perpetual mutation. Ideally, the individual must be able to determine himself or herself what he or she wants to keep, thus contributing a distributed solution to the problem of choosing which data to conserve.

To make wise decisions and reasonable choices on the subject of healthcare, both the public at large and the healthcare professional need, and have the right, to expect that hospital IS will provide them with precise, up-to-date information that is easy to understand, as well as high-quality products and services.

With regard to overall patient support and the quality of information transmitted, ONCORA (care network in oncology in Rhône-Alpes, France) advises the following [FOU 08]:

– medical information must circulate with a guarantee of confidentiality and in a good-quality process;

– information transmission tools must be effective;

– all healthcare actors must have the same amount of information on the patient being cared for;

– each healthcare actor must be a vector of information in his or her field of expertise;

---

15 For example, following a transfer or a transfer via a network.

– every actor involved in the treatment and possessing information transmitted by the patient must record this information in the patient's file;

– medical information is always progressing and yet to be completed;

– information is revalidated (ability to revalidate a diagnosis, therapeutic strategies, etc.);

– information is confidential within the treatment team (city hospital);

– consistency of information requires coordination time.

For this reason, the quality of medical information can be characterized by five clearly determined elements and criteria:

– integrity;

– accuracy;

– precision;

– validity;

– authenticity.

The development of the quality use of public healthcare information relies on shared trust, induced by prior ethical debate involving mainly technologies, morals, rights, deontology and the analysis of practices [LER 04].

2.1.3.1. Indicators of data quality

To evaluate the quality of services, we believe it is crucial to begin by translating quality objectives into measurable indicators of information. A complete system of quality control uses various types of indicators, each of which measures a different aspect of quality and brings out complementary information. There are various ways of conceptualizing and defining these indicators. By definition, an indicator is a piece of information intended to aid an actor to take a course of action toward the achievement of an objective or to enable this actor to evaluate the result of this action.

One of the numerous definitions of a quality indicator is that it is an evaluation tool, and it must, therefore, possess certain properties, specifically:

– pertinence:

- true,

- fair and stable,

- precise and sensitive,

- useful;

– operational character:

- easy to establish (simplicity),

- easy to use,

- communicating,

- useful to prevention;

– consolidable character:

- quantifiable,

- accruable;

– nominal character:

- is never unique,

- limited in number;

– relational character:

- recognized/acceptable,

- motivating/federative/mobilizing [PON 04].

In summary, for Gilles Duhamel[16], information delivered to patients, unlike communication, must be at once objective, adapted to the patient, based on scientific proof, up to date, reliable, understandable, accessible, transparent (sourced), pertinent and in compliance with legislation.

The indicator must have operational and strategic relevance and cognitive effectiveness in terms of the knowledge it contributes. Indicators are used to inform various types of decision-making, strategic, tactical and operational, regarding the information to be diffused. It is a piece of informational data vital to the spatial, temporal and typological characterization of the action being assessed.

---

16 *Inspecteur Général des Affaires Sociales* or Inspector General of Social Affairs.

2.1.3.2. *Criteria for improving the quality of medical information*

Part of making sure that the healthcare information supplied by IS is of good quality involves consideration of the actions and indicators they should put in place to achieve this quality.

On the basis of this observation, several measures are necessary and in line with this objective of quality of medical data:

– supplying information that is consistent and based on medical evidence arising from medical sources and references in order to guarantee the credibility and soundness of the data;

– evaluating information rigorously and fairly, including that used to describe a product or service;

– indicating clearly whether the information is based on scientific studies, expert consensuses or personal or professional experience or opinion;

– ensuring that medical opinions or advice are given by qualified practitioners;

– indicating when products (medications or medical devices) or healthcare services are subject to government regulations and have been approved by appropriate certification organizations such as the U.S. Food and Drug Administration, the U.K. Medicines Control Agency or the French *Agence Française de Sécurité Sanitaire des Produits de Santé* (French Agency of Sanitary Safety of Healthcare Products);

– recognizing that certain subjects are controversial. If this situation occurs, it is vital to present all reasonable parties in a balanced manner. For example, informing the healthcare user that there are alternative treatments for a particular health condition, such as surgery or radiation therapy for prostate cancer;

– making information more accessible to the patient or non-specialist healthcare professional so that he or she can understand it and use it in the best possible conditions. To do this, the products or services used should be described in language that is clear, easy to read and appropriate for the users targeted;

– clearly indicating the date of transfer or of hosting of data to ensure that information is current and up to date.

This non-exhaustive list of criteria for information quality is necessary for the users of this information to form their own opinions. Individuals must be able to judge for themselves the quality of the healthcare information they use via communication tools.

2.2. Identification of method used to develop the ethical analysis model

Our analysis model was created based on the convergence between Platonic dogmatism and sophist empiricism. For Plato, universality, conception and generalization in the development of knowledge as a collective construction of stabilized knowledge were important. Without the hypothesis of universality of concepts and cognitive organizations, science is not possible. The basis of the issue of knowledge is transcendental. This model of thought constitutes a general operator of truth, allowing us to analyze reality and to interpret both its universal essence and its uniqueness. Mathematics, the science of numbers, the "divine science", is a universal language that enables us best to express the essence of phenomena. This whole intellectual movement was at the heart of the epistemological reflection of Aristotle, Descartes, the Vienna Circle and Kant.

Parallel to this, the sophist Protagoras emphasized that it is in action and movement that the intentions and meanings of things become known. Human intentions cause the revelation in situations, in the same movement and context, of the intentions and resources for these intentions, the meaning and pragmatic conditions of interpretation and evaluation of the appropriate action. The challenge of this sophist position is to combine knowledge and action at the moment of the emergence of meaning. This stream of thought was developed by Leonardo da Vinci, G.B. Vico and contemporary constructivists. On the basis of these two models of thought, we have developed our own ethical model applied to medical communication, constituting a process of mediation between social theories and practices and concepts and the empirical equivalent. This new model thus constitutes a theoretical perpetual adjustment system of emergence in a context of action and movement. According to Sinaceur [SIN 99], "a model always acts as a mediator between a theoretical field of which it is an interpretation and an empirical field of which it is a creation". It always manifests a simplification either of empirical events or of a theory it desires to put forward. It can, therefore, perform multiple functions depending on the way in which it has been developed and the end purposes of its use [MUC 12].

Moreover, to model is to design, construct and learn to use instruments, or to orchestrate [LEM 98]. The modeling of a complex system translates mainly as the fact of modeling a system of actions. This modeling of complex action represents the general idea of a process, which is translated by its exercise and its result. On the basis of this observation, we use the basic concept of systemic modeling, which is the action taken to construct our own ethical analysis model. It starts from the question: "what does that do?" The characterization of an action involves the concepts of process and system. Thus, any complex system can be represented by a system of multiple actions or by a process that can be an enmeshment of processes. In this systemic modeling, the concepts of organization and information are closely linked. Concepts suited to systemic modeling include plan or process, active unity, system, design, conjunction(or articulation), organization, balance, intelligence, effectiveness, projection, pertinence, comprehension and teleology.

Our model thus illustrates a systemic approach of exchanges between individuals and considers the interdependences between organizational structures, organizational exchange systems, culture and relationships of power between actors and context.

This systemic modeling refers to three concepts:

– energy, which expresses what is produced;

– the game, which expresses the action of the game and the result;

– organization, which expresses the action of organizing and the result of this action [LEM 99].

We have decided to base our model on an analysis framework composed of three axes of interpretation: the actions, situations and intentions that form an ethical event. Intention[17] is associated with human values and the four universal ethical principles. Because of our tendency to intend to act out ideal concepts, some of these may become ideal models of our activity and can guide it, meaning that they can be presented as values. On the basis of this realization, the subject of our research, in this case "the design, setup and use of an IS in healthcare" representing the event in this analysis model, is therefore not a simple spontaneous action. It takes root in a situation, with

---

17 It represents the possibility of representing a state of things that is only ideal, which is not materially present, but which can be created by what is often called our symbolic "activity".

an intention that incorporates universal human values and in a defined social framework, as illustrated by Figure 2.4. This analysis model can translate an evolutionist algorithm, the objective of which is to obtain an approximate solution to an optimization issue when no established method exists. This modeling thus belongs to the family of stochastic algorithms because it iteratively uses random processes. It is used to "reproduce the result of a succession of events" [GRA 03].

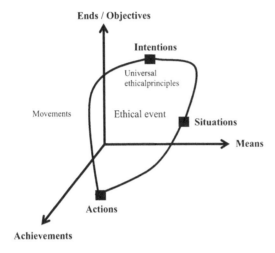

Figure 2.4. *Construction of an ethical event*

In light of these reflections, we can confirm that we have constructed a model that can be characterized as systemic and neo-Platonic in nature.

The construction of the various facets of our ethical model is based on a progressive and iterative approach. It can be divided into five phases:

– initialization, dedicated to the identification of needs of various types, or to the taking note of sources of information and creating a plan of action to follow;

– inventorying of existing elements in the environment: tools, materials, actors and organizational structures;

– study of what is recommended. Taking note of actors' missions and assignments;

– analysis of effective technological tools and materials (final or intermediary). Actors' real activity is also noted by questioning them and accompanying them during their activities;

– restructuring of elements identified in the preceding phases to form the basis of our model.

On the basis of this intellectual approach, our model may describe its environment statically and in detail, and its activity flows and especially interactions dynamically [BEL 04].

Under these conditions, we led a field study on the various healthcare IS, by performing targeted interviews with people in charge of these IS and their users. This approach of going into the field and surveying IS designers and users, and of observing and interacting with them, seems self-evidently effective for understanding the conditions in which these individuals use medical information on a daily basis. This manner of proceeding uses qualitative or empirical–inductive methods in its approach[18]. The comprehensive interview method, which is a part of these qualitative methods, proposes inverting the mode of construction of an object by starting with the situation and thus constructing only a theoretical mode. This collection work took place fairly early in our research, which made it possible for our readings and the direction of our work to be based on designs and issues coming straight from the field and not on purely theoretical ideas. Direct contact with other information-gathering practices allowed us to anchor ideas revealed by various readings in the literature of numerous books addressing the subject.

This work carried out in the field corresponded to three objectives:

– observe actors as they carry out their daily duties;

– conduct interviews with them;

– understand the context, their expectations and the difficulties they encounter in the manipulation of their IS.

During the second phase, we conducted these field studies via the intermediary of questionnaires based on the ethical model crossed

---

18 These methods seek to establish a complete comprehension schema of a phenomenon based on data collected from various actors and by exploring the links between this phenomenon and other connected phenomena.

with the "environmental parameters of real life", established on the basis of our interviews combined with bibliographic research (see Table 2.1).

Fundamental ethical principles of the theoretical architecture of an IS	Environmental parameters of real life			
	Structural and technological	Strategic and methodological	Organizational and regulatory	Relational and cultural
Principle of autonomy				
Principle of beneficence				
Principle of non-malfeasance				
Principle of justice				

Table 2.1. *Support on which analysis questionnaires are based*

To reflect on the nature of an IS tool, we must reproduce it in the game of interdependence that it imposes on us; this makes it necessary to consider not only the technical instrument and its end purpose as such, but also the condictions and impacts of the object's existence. In this sense, the positioning of the technological aspect occupies an existence midway between the tool and the environmental milieu. A system is composed of a group of elements in relation with one another in such a way that the development of any one of them causes the development of the whole and that any modification of the whole has an impact on each part.

These multisectoral "reading keys" of real life thus hinge on one another and make it possible to give an applicative and concrete value to the ethical framework.

According to Dherse and Minguet [DHE07] in their book entitled *l'éthique ou le chaos?* (Ethics or chaos?) and according to Ponçon [PON 09] in his presentation *Une éthique de l'usage du SIH* (The ethics of HIS usage) during HIT 2009 (Health Information Technologies 2009), the history of IS covers four successive eras:

– *technical era*, corresponding to the era of mass production;

– *organizational and regulatory era*,composed of the organizational era with more in-depth research regarding a better contribution of TICs to the performance of industry processes;

– *behavioral era*, representing the relational era and the era of trust, requiring healthcare professionals to act in the best interests of the individual and to report on this action afterward;

– *era of end purposes and ethics*, corresponding to the era of increased responsibility on the part of the professional involved in ethical principles. This is the point at which mutual trust attains its full importance.

In addition, throughout his book, Abbad [ABB 01] emphasized hospital management based on strategic and technical tools, participatory management, financial management, an organization based on communication and the paying of particular attention to the sociological and cultural aspects inherent to actors in the establishment.

According to Breton and Proulx [BRE 02], the emergence of NTICs has contributed to the creation of a "digital paradigm"[19] representing a homogeneous whole in which four dimensions mingle: a basic technology (electronic in this case), a methodology specific to the processing of information, a system of representation to a coherent and universal world (extolling the values of ethics) and a strategic and economic challenge. The power of this new space tends toward a synergy operating between dimensions that were previously splintered in a world where technology, economics, politics and philosophy interfered with one another. This paradigm thus constitutes the cultural and ethical product of a technological development or a digital convergence, putting TICs at the forefront. In these conditions, designing a technological product has become a strategic act that not only has economic and technological dimensions but also political, ethical and social dimensions.

Moreover, we can emphasize the case requesting approval of the hosting of healthcare data of a personal nature instituted by the Ministry of Health[20], composed of six forms[21] that cover a multisectoral perimeter, such as:

---

19 From the English "digital".
20 Decree no. 2006-6 of January 4, 2006.
21 These six forms are composed of the detailed introduction form of a candidate; the detailed introduction form of a subcontractor; the form describing the clauses of a model contract; the

– description of technological provisions for the hosting service;

– security policy;

– compliance with regulations on individual rights;

– organization and strategy of the hosting and archiving service;

– identification of the individual responsible for the hosting service, the doctor, the subcontractors and the operator in charge of implementing the service or categories of people with access to medical data;

– information pertaining to the financial situation of the candidate and his or her subcontractors;

– provisional reports of hosting activity.

Finally, the communication of information is a process that depends on the environment; that is:

– spatial, physical, sensory and temporal contextualization;

– positioning and structuring of human relationships;

– development and emergence of norms and codes;

– identity expression of actors;

– establishment of relational referents or qualification of relationships.

For this reason, in light of the information available in these books and others in the same line, we have been able to distribute the environmental parameters into four precise domains whose order is as follows:

– structural and technological;

– strategic and methodological;

– organizational and regulatory;

– relational and cultural.

Our theoretical framework is thus based on these four environmental parameters, which must not be static or isolated from one another so that the complexity of real life may be taken into account. It is our belief that good analysis and rigorous deliberation have everything to gain by being

---

form introducing the hosting service; the form introducing the results of risk analysis and the form describing security provisions.

considered as parts constituting a whole, all from points of view interpretative of an incommensurable complexity, with these parts feeding into one another and in constant interaction.

2.3. Development of the ethical analysis space

Any IS must be based on a clear and precise end purpose that determines the moral and social needs of the tool in relation to its situation and context. This end purpose develops a strategy and recommendations to fulfill these needs. It evolves with the adapted strategy. The end purpose of an action is its "why", the meaning in opposition to its "how", to the mechanisms or functions it puts into play. It is seen as self-evident when a person undertakes to do something that a result will be obtained. This obviousness leads to the interpretation as "purposeful" of the action observed by another person; what does he or she want to do? What is the meaning of his or her act? We think we are observing the end purpose, not simply in the action of a person but in the behavior or the structure of an organization, even supposed to be involuntary, if we can see in it a certain adaptation of means to an end. Where do our ethical considerations come from? How does the distinction between good and bad operate? These questions lead us to examine the ends. Ends do not simply guide human activities; they also find orders and adapt human efforts to their appropriation. Because of this, these ends also define states and duties attached to these states and qualities to the virtues required to achieve them successfully.

However, an IS is not just a tool that can be analyzed in isolation. It is intrinsically connected to the whole organization and to the policy and strategy of the structure using it. An ethical approach must seek balances. It makes it possible to put forward facts such as human challenges that are also aimed at better patient support, while maintaining the quality and motivation of caretaking teams and updating of what is available technologically.

In this context, we believe it is impossible to address an IS without discussing all the environmental parameters of real life that exist in the functioning of an establishment (see Table 2.1).

Any rigorous analysis requires creation and application of a precise framework, a space, in order to begin with coherent and fair fundamental principles on the subject. The philosophical approach of Emmanuel Kant in his *Critique de la raison pure* (Critique of pure reason) [KAN 81] expounds in depth on the position of the space he considers necessary to the thought process. All reflection imposes is a form of exteriority that can be constructed from this space [LAC 06].

From this perspective, the idea of "space" proves conducive to expression and debates, the sharing of experiences and the acquisition and appropriation of knowledge, beginning with scientific and technical knowledge. It favors critical judgment and the assumed exercise of liberty in the face of the truth of others. The purpose of this space is to become a place of convergence or "crystallization" of all ethical initiatives applied to healthcare in relation to the IS. This concept of space symbolizes the freedom of speech and openness of spirit illustrated by

– multdisciplinarity and plurality of opinions;

– favoring of a system of questioning rather than the search for a consensus.

For this, we have relied in part on the cindynic approach[22] founded by Georges Yves Kerven in *Eléments fondamentaux des Cindyniques* [KER 95], which presents ethics within organizations as

– a "technology for structuring cindynic hyperspace" ;

– a basic questioning of end purposes, values and rules;

– a strategy of common agreement on the fields of activity and the rules of behavior of members of the company in their relationships with each other and external actors;

– a tactic for the addressing of delicate problems;

– a self-referential mechanism constituting the ethics of conviction and a relational mechanism corresponding more to the ethics of responsibility.

Next we move on to the concept used by Höffe [HÖF 91] applied to the analysis of justice according to three "levels". These levels were used by him to qualify more precisely the levels of assessment and legitimization of obligations and duties. For this reason, our ethical space is composed of three distinct dimensions applied to the IS system and its hosting structure:

---

22 This approach proposes concepts essential to practical ethics through the study of the sciences of danger.

– an *axiological dimension* including values;

– a *teleological dimension*[23] describing end purposes;

– a *deontological dimension*explaining rules, norms, laws, codes, standards and limits.

As we indicate in Figure 2.5, this three-dimensional space causes three plans with different natures and challenges to appear:

– An *organizational and technological plan* bringing together structural, technological, organizational and regulatory aspects, similar to Mintzberg's models and Shannon's information theory, as well as that of Floridi, which we will discuss.

Figure 2.5. *Ethical space*

This space goes back to "practice" and is devoted to the application of rules and usages. It must concretize the end purposes established by the teleological dimension. This involves the means, procedures, provisions and approaches established to accomplish the "effectuation" of the objectives.

– A *strategic and political plan* composed of strategic and methodological and relational and cultural criteria, as well as laws, legal texts and deontological codes.

---

23 The concept of acting teleologically was broadly developed by Habermas in *Théorie de l'agir communicationnel* [HAB 87], in which he achieves a goal or causes the appearance of a desired state by choosing and using in an appropriate manner the means which, in a given situation, appear to ensure its success. "This model of action is often interpreted in a utilitarian sense; thus we assume that the actor chooses and calculates means and ends from the point of view of maximum or expected usefulness".

This space can be characterized as "pragmatic". It brings objectives to light that were already presupposed at the forefront but without being clearly expressed in a "normative" way. This plan also involves deontology, the function of which is the regulation of practices.

– An *ethical plan* representing the characteristics of the four fundamental ethical principles [BEA 01] and the ethical challenges specific to the nature of the structure being studied. This space is "reflexive" in nature, and its mission is to provide the "legitimization" for any practice or norm, thus giving it a certain seminal connotation. This plan is oriented by values that serve as both normative and critical governing bodies.

This conception of an ethical space is also shared by Paul Ricœur[24], who divides moral problems into three sections, specifically

– *ethics*, which plunges a person into "the desire for self-accomplishment", in which satisfaction is found. It corresponds to the "ultimate core of the moral problem" illustrated by values;

– *morals*[25], in which ethics must undergo the "test of moral obligation". The individual encounters prohibitions and duties represented by rules, codes, norms and limits;

– *practical wisdom*, in which the duty itself must pass the test of wise and prudent decision-making in the face of unique concrete situations. This can be manifested by the means and procedures put in place to achieve the desired end purposes.

We can see that the first two plans constitute the environmental parameters of reality, based on human exchange and sharing. This anthropological vision turns toward relationships between individuals.

Finally, with regard to the ethical plan, this will be broadly described during the first three parts but is also found throughout our research as a background framework. Ethics are thus continually required "to stay alert in its mission of legitimization, and led to mobilize its reflexive capacity in relation to values" [HÖF 91]. Considering all these definitions enables us to better situate the different aspects of informational ethics and the levels

---

24 An exchange of views between the philosopher Paul Ricœur and Professor Yves Pelicier, a psychiatrist. "Ethics, between the bad and the worse". Interviewed by Christian Ballouard and Sophie Duméry.
25 Morals, from the Latin *mores*, designate all the rules of behavior that define the norm of a society.

of sectoral study connected with them. This can be summed up in Table 2.2, illustrating a model of ethical analysis.

Levels of analysis	Plans	Content	Forms	Functions
Descriptive ethical	Organizational and technological	Means, procedures, provisions and approaches	Practice	Application and effectuation
Normative ethical	Strategic and political	Norms, codes and rules	Deontology	Regulation
Reflexive ethical	Ethical	Principles and values	Questioning on fundamental principles	Legitimization

Table 2.2. *Model of ethical analysis*

In addition, by picking up and applying the principal cindynic concepts, that is, the representation in five dimensions of the "hyperspace of danger", we have been able to associate our ethical space with a plan called the "informative plan"[26].

This plan is the result of the combination of two dimensions (see Figure 2.6):

– a *statistical dimension* composed of historical memory facts and statistics. This is the information used to populate our databases for study;

– an *epistemic dimension* incorporating representations and models based on facts. This is the knowledge bank that supports calculations. According to Piaget, epistemology can be defined as "in the first approximation as the study of the constitution of valid knowledge" [LEM 07].

This plan enables us to question ourselves as to which data are likely to be of interest for our study. Every researcher is led to ask himself or herself fundamental questions about the information being sought, the way in which to recover it, modes of data protection, the validity or value of these data, their form, their foundation, their evolution, etc.

This stage thus constitutes a fundamental preamble to any research project. For this reason, this plan involves the field of raw, unprocessed information, which we have added to our field studies and to the bibliographical research to which our ethical model will be applied. The collection of these data – effected

26 According to disciplines of the cindynic approach, this plan is called "experience return".

via individual questionnaires, semi-directed interviews and the reading of literature – has concretely and numerically fed our ethical analysis space.

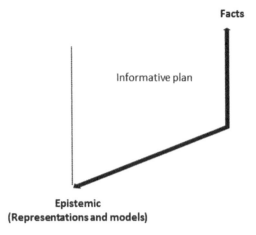

Figure 2.6. *Informative plan*

The joining together of four plans of study and five dimensions connects to form our "ethical analysis space", which is vital for the analysis from an ethical point of view of raw data concerning the IS of a healthcare establishment (see Figure 2.7). It is on this analytical framework that our ethical model partially rests.

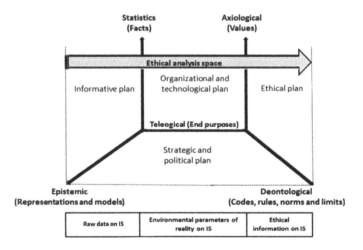

Figure 2.7. *Ethical analysis space*

Finally, our ethical analysis space uses the three levels of modeling of classical antiquity as part of a study of the events, specifically

– the "given state of being"[27], represented by the informative plan;

– the "perceptible world"[28], illustrated by the grouping together of the organizational and technological plan with the strategic and political plan. It constitutes the environmental parameters of reality based on human relations;

– the "objective reality"[29], characterized by the ethical plan.

With these three spaces being formed, the scientific method can be summarized by:

– the observations in the perceptible world of the given state of being (see empiricism);

– a development of theories in the context of objective reality in order to model the phenomena analyzed;

– an addition of associated mathematics to render the evolution of phenomena in time predictive;

– a permanent pursuit of the collection of data for modeling to be dynamic and evolutive commensurate with new situations.

2.4. Presentation of the ethical model

A model is a simplified, quantified and rationalized representation of reality. It can be used to simulate, explain and/or predict reality. Its objective is to replace the study of a concrete phenomenon by that of an object constituted by its definition; that is, by the analysis of an abstract object. The model corresponds to a representation of the phenomenon that is at once simplified and complete. It exists only through its definition and cannot be worth more than that. As an abstract object correctly defined, a model offers us the resources of a logical reasoning between concrete, real and supposed facts. By nature, the construction of a model enables us to avoid difficulties

---

27 The whole of everything that constitutes the world to which human beings have partial or indirect access through their senses.

28 The world of sensations, which is the sole source of data that can be used to obtain information on the real world of the given state of being.

29 A space wholly conceived by the human mind. It consists of constructing explicative models, which translate data issuing from the perceptible world.

concerning introduction. It is posed in a derisory manner and hypotheses do not have to be justified by considerations drawn from experience. There are no true or false models but only good or bad models according to a field of questions. It constitutes the basis of our "logico-mathematical analysis" [LÉV 54] translating a language common to the various actors involved in our study.

2.4.1. *Ethical cube of an accepted contingency*

The application of a model and of concepts leads to a rational and quantitative analysis of the principles to be implemented, which is attractive in its approach but relatively complicated to put in place [ALP 86]. The first approach to be used to understand a phenomenon is first to isolate it precisely. Thus, there is a division from reality, a pertinent framework that it is necessary to construct. A model helps to frame an analysis, targeting the actors, issues and dimensions of the phenomenon. Once the framework is completed, the elements to be studied appear. These must thus be put in relation to one another. This conceptual model constitutes a simplified representation that provides individuals with different ways of understanding what they are creating, their organization and the environment that surrounds them.

This exposure to a pre-established model gives the possibility of modifying our conception and attitude toward NTICs in healthcare, both individually and collectively, in a context of organization of treatment support. Modeling acquires the value of an objectification of reflection. It is presented as a clarification of the parameters involved in reasoning and constitutes the "link that exists between understanding and acting" [NOU 02].

This model-based approach seeks to give intelligibility, that is, meaning, to a phenomenon. In the context of our thesis, we have relied on the ethical analysis space constructed by us for the occasion and on the models by Beauchamp and Childress [BEA 01], Massé [MAS 03] and Vézina [VÉZ06], which we will examine later, in the development of our own model and theoretical ethical context.

For this, we have studied the design, setup and use of an IS in healthcare by investigating precise and concrete sectors. These constitute "justifications of reality", true keys to examining reality represented by various domains such as structure and technology, organization and regulation, strategy and methodology and the relational and the cultural. It should be noted that these justifications have been constructed based on bibliographical research on the subject and on semi-guided interviews with certain individuals referred to as "experts", including reflection groups on the subject and with IS actors (designers and users).

This model will be observed according to three aspects in interaction:

– the first point of view, called the ontological (or structural aspect), considers the IS in its structure. This is the view of the "being" of the apparatus;

– the second point of view, which is functional in aspect, considers the IS in its function. This is the view of the "doing" of the apparatus;

– the third point of view, called the genetic (or dynamic aspect), considers the IS in its time evolution. This is the view of the "becoming" of the apparatus.

However, the choice of a set of ethics starts with the relationship to the subject matter, with the relationship to the meaning we give it in our encounter with and approach to the other and, finally, with the perception of the dimension of the inner person. The absence of ethics results in chaos, illustrating a "universe in which no Word comes to give meaning" [DHE 07]. We are facing a limited reality, which in philosophical terms is called a "contingency"[30]. It is not itself its own definition or sufficiency; it could just as well not have been. We are not experiencing a fullness of meaning rather we are in search of meaning. This contingency is thus a decisive stage in the progression of a set of ethics. It confronts human beings on the meaning of life and their actions, and on the very meaning they give to the world that surrounds them. This interpretation of contingency profoundly affects all the environmental parameters of real life. Our attitude toward contingency thus has ethical issues. If ethics are defined as the search for meaning, for fair action, the manner of understanding contingency will guide the set of ethics put in place.

---

30 From the Latin *contingere*, meaning "touch". *Contignit* means "happening by chance"; thus the word "contingency" can take on the meaning of an eventuality or "something that can be otherwise".

Consequently, we can use this questioning as a tool of discernment and diagnosis for action. This instrument enables us to evaluate our sense of direction and to predict the internal logic resulting from this. The progression of this contingency route necessitates making a choice at every moment, avoiding a certain immobility in solutions where nothing is fixed. Ethics are revealed and developed according to the contingency model recognized and accepted. For this reason, we can reposition the concept of "accepted contingency" in our three-dimensional ethical space in order to end with the creation of an "ethical cube of accepted contingency" illustrating the path of ethical thought (see Figure 2.8).

In addition, we can emphasize a bond of kinship between model and metaphor: "metaphor is to poetic language what model is to scientific language" [RIC 75]. Better still, the model is the most profound part of a metaphor. Thus, modeling would be the very essence of metaphor. On the basis of these considerations, ethicists can see in this cube the cultural metaphor for the process of psychic evolution of every human being; the force pushing us toward knowledge and the meaning of things. This is reminiscent of another sort of cube, proportions and all; a stone dear to alchemists, the Philosopher's Stone, which represented for them the stone of real and absolute knowledge.

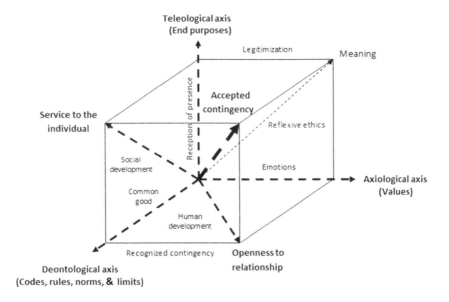

Figure 2.8. *Ethical cube of an accepted contingency*

The openness that recognizes the accepted contingency becomes an openness to the presence of the other with whom we are united. The way in which an individual reflects on existence, on the meaning of things and enters into a contingency will contribute to his or her entry into reflexive ethics based on values and end purposes. This acceptance of presence and openness to relationships enables us to be aware of the value of the things that surround us and opens us up to responsibility and to interdependence with our fellow humans. This contingency, recognized and thus accepted, becomes a capacity for wonderment and for service to the individual, leading to the legitimization of our ethical reflection.

Finally, human and social development progress through the daily act of ethical thinking by each person in his or her decision-making, more and more aware of "his universal shared responsibility for choosing ethics, which in the end makes him both the gardener and the fruit" [DHE 07]. Thus, based on questionnaires 1, 1' and 2, we can note the respective scaling of:

– the teleological axis;

– the deontological axis;

– the axiological axis;

– orientation toward service to the individual;

– orientation toward openness to relationships.

These measurements, incorporated into the modeling of our three-dimensional "ethical cube", will enable us to use a value to quantify the direction and thus the accepted contingency that results. The scaling of this accepted contingency translates an "ethical score" in the analysis surrounding the IS in medical imaging. One of the ultimate objectives of this model is thus to constitute an algorithm for the solution of ethical problems that can put this "ethical score" of the accepted contingency in numerical terms. This modeling will be applied as a part of the study of objectives and the production of an IS. Means will be designated as "good" or "insufficient" depending on an average that we have chosen arbitrarily based on the gathering of the data supplied by questionnaire 3.

2.4.2. *Ethical model of information system in the doctor–patient relationship*

Our analysis of ethical issues concerning IS in cancer care has led us to reflect on the major objectives of an IS in healthcare and thus more globally on the ethical challenges of a healthcare structure combined with health information that has become "multiform, which dematerializes and does not remain confined to one area" [TAB 10]. In this analytical context, the overall concept of "information" considers three dimensions that interfere with one another:

– its physical and structural form and presentation;

– its content, which is necessarily structured according to the meaning it conveys;

– its usage, related to its communication.

Thus, a complete analysis of an IS tool is impossible without an in-depth study of the environment that makes it function, in this case healthcare actors and, more globally, healthcare structures. This goes back to questioning ourselves about the place and role of the IS within the carer–patient relationship. The interest of this model is to facilitate a complete analysis of an IS and of the human–machine interface, or infosphere[31], which brings together both technology and ethics.

Given that the IS tool does not necessarily include a guarantee of trust[32] for the people who use it, it is important that each participant be clearly identified and, at best, recognized as a correspondent. These observations imply the setup of an IS that considers these human and technical aspects. Technologies combine and interact with human beings; it is not technology that changes society but the appropriation by society of certain technologies.

For this reason, in order to be effective and consistent with reality, this model must be configured according to:

– the content and services used and the sensitivity of information and operations;

– the users of the IS, taking into account their situation and role;

– the system, in relation to its functionality, morphology and behavior.

The objective of the infosphere paradigm lies mainly within the perspective of defining this model, which thus represents a tool to translate

---

31 This word was invented by Dan Simmons and was also used by Floridi to designate the environment in which information develops. This space is represented by the red zone in Figure 2.11.
32 This degree of trust is proportional to the quality of the human relationships previously established between the correspondents.

technical language into ethical language and vice versa. It facilitates the convergence of the "info-signal" of technology and the "info-significance" advocated by ethics. There is a triangulation of the doctor–patient relationship with a technological device that becomes a full partner in care management.

During the treatment of the patient by the doctor, the lifecycle of medical information is counterbalanced between the fundamental ethical principles characterized by social values and the environmental parameters of real life represented by rules and norms.

According to Bruno Charrat, director general of the *Centre National de référence Santé à Domicile et Autonomie* (French National Reference Center for At-Home Health and Independence):

> ...technological innovation is above all the successful convergence of a user's desires (or needs), what it is possible to do thanks to technology, and what it is viable to design. Without this convergence, the solutions developed are not generally good ones; the products are obsolete technically, or difficult to appropriate by the user, or even inaccessible to some, and a potential source of discrimination.[33]

In these conditions, the ethical modeling of an IS "with a human face" necessarily involves this convergence, and this exchange of types for which we start from the universal, the abstract and the general[34] to move toward the practical, the concrete and the specific[35]. This approach reflects both the environment in which the actors are involved in care management work and their social organization. All are seeking balance and harmony between the antagonistic forces of the universe. As emphasized by the Canadian anthropologist Constance Classen, "the human body (the singular) serves as a model of the cosmos (the general) and becomes a mediator between cosmic forces" [CLA 11].

In other words, we begin this model with a set of so-called "reflexive" ethics of legitimization expressed by a questioning of fundamental ethical principles[36] for actors, then continue with a set of so-called "normative"

---

33 Interviews published in the industry magazine *Electronique et de ses Innovations* [CHA 11].
34 Illustrated by the blue zone in Figure 2.11.
35 Represented by the yellow zone in Figure 2.11.
36 Values and principles.

ethics of regulation, which consider deontology[37] in the production of the IS, and end with a set of so-called "descriptive" ethics of application and effectuation in the form of practice[38] with the means used.

This means a triple compromise: in the reflection between ethical values, in the production of an IS between rules and norms and in the setup and use of an IS between the means and procedures contained in the "justifications of reality". This idea of compromise comes into play when multiple justification systems are in conflict. According to the book *De la justification* by Luc Boltanski and Laurent Thévenot [BOL 91], the basic hypothesis is that no society has a single system of justification of what is fair or unfair. Each person perceives justice and injustice in light of his or her interests (depending on whether he or she is religious, a unionist, an ecologist, etc.). The problem with compromise is that the common good cannot be obtained through unitary justification, but only by intersecting multiple values. The compromise is thus essentially linked to pluralism of justification; that is, to the arguments that people put forward in conflicts. It therefore falls between rival requirements arising from these different values. Conflicts are resolved within a homogeneous order, a closed-off space in which individuals recognize one another and speak the same language. According to Ricœur, this resolution is linked to "practical wisdom" [RIC 90]. Ultimately, it seems that the common good is characterized by a compromise between the rules and rival values that cover various sectors of activity and worlds of action.

Thus, our ethical model can be populated as well in a more materialistic sense by computer specialists and information technologies as in the opposing, more spiritual sense by healthcare professionals, philosophers or moralists. To function and harmonize these two domains, which are utterly opposite at first sight, our analysis framework must fulfill a single major and fundamental prerogative: it must place the interests of the patient at the center of all recommendations and actions that are technical and ethical in nature, while also considering the expectations and requirements of the healthcare professionals and the IS designers, who use the IS and cause it to function. The IS tool must correspond to the real needs and expectations of users. The actors or subjects involved in the design of an IS come from different disciplinary and cultural universes, hence this necessity to turn to mechanisms of comprehension.

Moreover, information used in design is generally unstructured. It is sometimes difficult for the IS designer to have access to information that is

---

37 Codes, rules and norms.
38 Means, devices, routes and procedures.

both complete and pertinent. Interaction with other actors is, therefore, of the essence in order to make up for this lack of cohesiveness. In this context, it is clear that the role of cooperation is of primordial importance in the process of designing IS tools to develop a mutual and interdisciplinary language between these individuals.

We will thus translate these different expectations by applying them to an ethical reflection based on the four universal principles. This ethical reflection results from a lack of satisfaction, and a desire, and thus an expectation. In this, we have also drawn inspiration from the concept by Roland Barthes [BAR 70], which translated communication by introducing a transmitter with ethics (composed of values, "ethos"), which transmits a meaningful message (endowed with meaning and semantics, "logos") to a receiver, which receives it with emotion (endowed with sensitivity, "pathos") [RIG 03].

In these conditions, information must be the subject at all times from its transmission to its reception and subsequent diffusion, to the rules of ethics, even if these are sometimes obscure.

> I see, at the bottom, the development of ethical norms from a concrete and practical point of view, with these norms being themselves the result of enlightened discussion not based on preconceived notions or prejudice. They are, as Descartes wished, provisory and always able to be reexamined [CHA 98].

For this reason, these expectations and requirements can be expressed throughout the modeling of information[39] by establishing three types of filters, arising from the doctor–patient relationship as well as the IS designer, and vital to medical decision-making based on an ethical IS:

– *perception filters*, acting on the capture and storage of data[40];

– *design and implementation filters*, impacting the process selection for the conversion of data into information[41];

– *utilization filters*, targeting direct communication and the modeling of information leading to knowledge[42].

---

39 Ranging from data to knowledge.
40 With questioning on the nature, authentication and storage conditions of data, etc.
41 With reflections focused on the choice, form, clarity, ranking of data, etc.
42 With questions focused on the diffusion, use and framing of knowledge on the part of the patient for medical decision-making, etc.

These filtering processes[43] are strengthened by the fact that the transmitter and the receiver rarely have the same focuses of interest and concerns. What is said by one is not necessarily heard by the other. Research in cognitive psychology has shown that individuals are never neutral. They filter, decode, select and reinterpret what they receive. In this context, epistemology is used to design an anthropology, which is a primary condition of ethics and becomes part of a loop in which each stage is necessary to the others. By applying our ethical analysis space in the infosphere, we can follow the conversion of data into practical wisdom (see Figure 2.9).

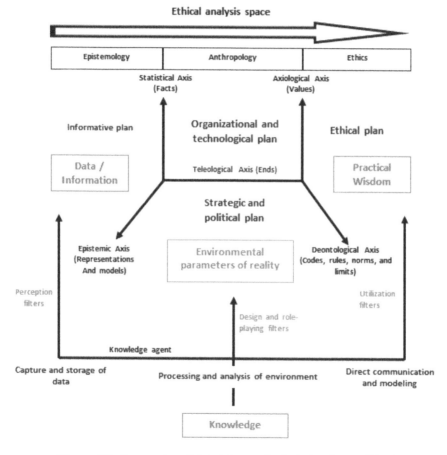

Figure 2.9. *Conversion of data into practical wisdom in an ethical analysis space in the infosphere*

---

43 This modeling and these filters were influenced by the works of Boisot and Canals [BOI 08] and of Willcocks and Whitley [WIL 09].

Moreover, this direct communication supplies the so-called "tacit" knowledge[44], which is highly personal in nature and difficult to formalize. This knowledge includes a technical dimension that corresponds to personal aptitudes, "*savoir faire*" and a cognitive dimension encompassing the ideals, beliefs, perceptions, values and models of thought rooted within us. Although this knowledge is subconscious and difficult to communicate verbally, it is possible to acquire and communicate it through shared experience or observation.

We can distinguish the two dimensions of this knowledge: the technical dimension, which deals with the aptitudes and talents encompassed by the term "*savoir faire*" or "know-how", and the cognitive dimension, which refers to mental models, beliefs, perceptions, ideals, values and emotions.

For its part, the modeling of information will contribute to knowledge referred to as "explicit"[45], which is expressed in words or numbers and will be more easily shared between individuals by verbal or written means. It maintains a complementary relationship with tacit knowledge. There are two subcategories of explicit knowledge: "codified explicit knowledge", which is found in documents or databases; and "personalized explicit knowledge" or "practical knowledge", which is not recorded and is transmitted verbally. Knowledge is constructed, which requires frequent interactions between the members of an organization. In other words, the organization develops knowledge on the initiative of individuals and the interaction that takes place within a group of people. Knowledge can be amplified and crystallized in this group through dialogue, discussion, the exchange of experiences and observation. Groups provide the shared context in which individuals can interact with one another.

According to Takeuchi and Nonaka, the individual interacts with the organization through knowledge. The development of knowledge takes place at three levels: the individual, the group and the organization. The dynamic of the development of knowledge is a spiral process in which the interaction between explicit and tacit knowledge takes place repeatedly (see Figure 2.10). This dynamic facilitates the transformation of personal knowledge into organizational knowledge [NON 94, NON 06].

---

44 This knowledge is embedded in individual action and experience. Impressions, intuition and subjective elements are part of this knowledge, which is highly personal and difficult to articulate, communicate or share with others using formal language.

45 This knowledge can be easily transmitted in a formal manner. It is contained in specifications, good practice manuals and codified procedures. It can be stored in a computer database and transmitted electronically. It is not solely synonymous with codified procedures.

The basic premise of the development of this model is that the dissemination and creation of knowledge is not a linear phenomenon rather the conversion and creation of knowledge that takes place at the organizational level through a process of interaction between the two dimensions of knowledge: the tacit and explicit knowledge of individuals. Nonaka's process of conversion and creation of knowledge takes place, in a specific context, through four conversion processes, specifically socialization, externalization, combination and internalization, as previously seen.

Thus, knowledge is converted through a process of exchanges that follows a spiral route. Although knowledge is initially created by individuals, it becomes organizational knowledge due to the conversion process described in Nonaka's theory. However, conversion and creation also take place within a specific context, Ba, which corresponds to the space (space–time) facilitating the creation of knowledge. According to Nonaka [NON 94], this is a space (physical, virtual and mental) that makes interactions possible.

Moreover, to contribute to the understandability of a complex organization, Shannon's model will represent a sort of reference schema based on which various theories of organizing and autonomizing information can be formulated and usefully interpreted. This is the case with the concept of entropy of information in which the movement toward knowledge contributes to the reduction of entropy, that is, the degree of disorder of the informative system. This knowledge contributes to the acquisition of "practical wisdom" [RIC 90] through which medical decision-making takes place causing effects on the therapeutic act on the patient (see Figure 2.11).

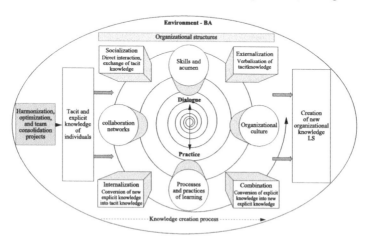

Figure 2.10. *Nonaka's model of organizational learning*

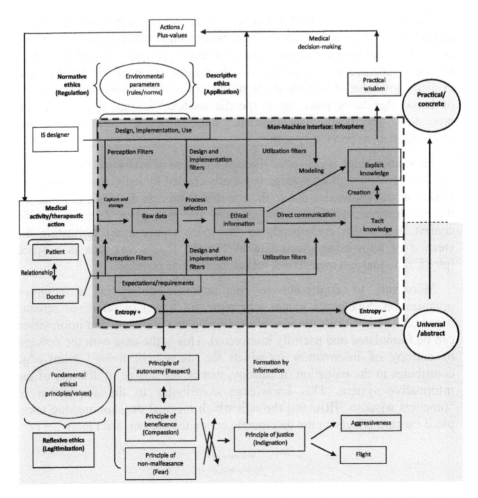

Figure 2.11. *Ethical modeling of information system in the doctor–patient relationship. For a color version of the figure, see www.iste.co.uk/beranger/ethics.com*

In these conditions, we can define our ethical model as being an ontological analysis[46]. The etymology of ontology goes back to the "theory of existence;" that is, a theory attempting to explain the concepts that exist in the world and how these concepts overlap and organize themselves to give meaning. Unlike for human beings, knowledge for a computer system is limited to the knowledge that it can represent.

46 In philosophy, ontology (from onto, taken from the Greek ὤν, ὄντος "being", which is the present participle of the verb εἰμί, "to be") is the study of the nature of being, that is, the study of the general properties of what exists.

By analogy, we have taken this term and applied it to our analysis of the architecture of knowledge as a form of representation of knowledge on the subject of a world. In this context, ontology constitutes the structured group of terms and concepts representing the meaning of a field of information, whether via the metadata of a space of names or the elements of a field of knowledge. Ontology in itself constitutes a data model representative of a group of concepts in a domain and the relationships between these concepts. Its objective is to model a set of knowledge in a given domain, which can be real or imaginary. It is used to reason with regard to objects in the domain concerned. In simple words, "ontology is to data what grammar is to language". According to Gruber [GRU 93], it is the specification of a conceptualization that is an abstract and simplified view of the world we wish to represent. It is the basis for a formalization of knowledge. It belongs at a certain level of abstraction and in a specific context; it is also a representation of a shared and consensual conceptualization, in a specific domain and in pursuit of a common goal. It classifies the relationships between concepts into groups. To construct an ontological model, it is necessary to:

– determine passive or active agents;

– describe their functional and contextual conditions;

– indicate their possible transformations toward limited objectives;

– break them down into categories or other subjects;

– group together a set of concepts describing a precise domain;

– rank and graduate concepts and fields of study;

– predicate in order to understand adjacent transformations and head toward internal objectives;

– put things into perspective in order to embrace concepts.

A technology-centered approach cannot provide reliable results if we do not extend our gaze to include the people and processes involved in this IS. Thus, the purpose of this ethical approach is to bring out more or less graduated balances involving a certain compromise between the multidisciplinary actors involved in care management. Our reflections intermingle ethical principles and rules as well as the conditions of exercising medical "practical wisdom" in such a way as to incorporate the various dimensions that compose it. The objective is to develop a set of ethics of medical information capable of addressing the universe of healthcare data, information, knowledge and communication as a new environment: that of the ethical medical infosphere. It is with an eye to this that we have combined a system of values with this digital space in order to define a "digital governance" based on an axiology in the ambient space. These ethical values will be used to define the objectives of this space, which are propagated in all infospheres interacting with one another. From this perspective, the quality of an IS is a determining factor in its acceptability. It must be studied in particular depth ergonomically, making it possible to use the system in normal work conditions. Its use must be simple, and the time needed to learn it reduced to the shortest possible amount. It must lead "internal" users to assess the daily exercise of his or her profession both in technical terms and in the design of patient treatment, at the center of the ethical medical infosphere, and healthcare professionals must necessarily appropriate this development and act to use it.

It is our belief that this modeling of decision-making and the ethical concepts connected to it are themselves a force capable of influencing reasoning and causing sustainable changes in the process of medical decision-making.

Consequently, this model serves to remind us that new technologies and processes surrounding information are designed to be used in the service of the people who use them, and not the other way around – which often seems to be the case. It is on this basis that we are seeking to lay the groundwork of a set of ethics proper to healthcare IS. Our objective is to reconcile the medical world with that of NTICs by contributing a humanist dimension of medicine to the IS.

2.4.3. *Ethical modeling of medical communication*

The fundamental question we have asked ourselves during the creation of our ethical model applied to the doctor–patient relationship is as follows: What approach is best suited to equip healthcare professionals and decision-makers in their analysis of the morally acceptable limits of regulations aimed at creating healthy environments or behavioral modification strategies? These are flagship values that guide not only the actions of citizens but also the evaluations made by actors participating in the ethical discussion of the acceptability of these actions, in this case, criteria of judgment.

Computer ethics, far from being a form of informational realism, are in fact a form of informational idealism [FLO 10].

Most communication theorists assign great importance to the influence of time and place on the interpretation and use of information. In other words, knowledge must be made accessible, interpreted and put in relation to a given situation. In the medical environment, this means the work carried out on a daily basis by practitioners. If knowledge represents power, power is most probably attributable to the mastery of information. In other words, the strategic importance of information in a current socioeconomic context arises from the capacity of individuals to appropriate knowledge temporarily and, consequently, to appropriate the advantages that can result from it. Information can be both active (shaping) and passive (taking shape) when an object that is strongly marked socially exercises a direct influence on human behavior. According to Miège [MIE04], information is the cognitive and symbolic content of communication, whereas for Bougnoux [BOU 01] it is also content that, he specifies, is loaded with meaning, communication being a relationship solely capable of supplying sense. According to Wolton [WOL 95], information is the noble part, the "good content" and the values whereas communication is the shadowy part, interests, manipulation and dependence on the economic or the political. Given the unavoidable interferences between these two concepts, how can there be "information" without "communication"? [LOQ 95].

Conversely, communication does not necessarily lead to information. Communication resides more in the continuity and situation of human relationships, the weaving of contact or the organization of the community. Thus, information offers openness and progress to society through its potential for interpretation, whereas communication offers closure for a culture due to the obligation to save others and to its tendency to preserve gains and community replication. Communication and information play an indispensable and incompressible role in the functioning of organizations, and it is largely through IS manipulated by humans that each person is put in relation to others and made part of the world [TIS 99].

In communication, the understanding and interpretation of messages exchanged occurs based on contextual elements such as the existing situation, the appearance of the person speaking, the nature of the human relationship, the intentions of the main players and the reason for the encounter [DES 04]. According to the Knotworking approach, communication places the emphasis on human responsibility between the identified constraints of control and mutual trust. The concepts of data, information, knowledge, communication and organization form aninextricable knot and cannot bypass each other; therefore, they interconnect with one another more or less harmoniously [VAC 09].

This model of organizational communication facilitates reflexivity of the collective action involved in the doctor–patient relationship. It represents scientifically multiple points of openness that are at once epistemological, anthropological and philosophical for the study of medical communication. Its plan or objective may be heuristic, scientific or, sometimes, even pedagogic [CAR 12]. It may have qualities of popularization and mediation. This systemic model is applied to communication based on certain specific rules such as the definition of the framework, the observation of recurring generalized exchanges between actors, the study of strong and constant interactions arising from the context, the immediate schematization of relationships, the explanation of types of exchanges and systemic contextualization.

This modeling thus makes it possible to better understand the simulation, support, forecasting and assessment of communication between caretaker and patient. Its principal mission is to guide the scientific observation of the medical act, to explain it and to anticipate it based on a theory and a reference methodology. We are thus in a logical, pragmatic series of events leading to the success of the action. This model draws mainly on the works of Shannon, Wiener, Morin and Floridi. It is used to study the roles of communicational and informational structures of organizations and the epistemological, anthropological, philosophical and cultural elements in which these interactions take place [VAC 12]. Daily practices surrounding information and communication occupy a structuring role in organizations, that of mutual recognition of work and of actions taken [VAC 97, VAC 04]. The analytical model is neither a scholarly applied ethical tool nor an empirical study aimed at drawing up a portrait of all the ethical challenges raised. Nor is it an instrument offering a complete response to the legitimate questions with which healthcare professionals are confronted on a daily basis in the field with regard to the making of decisions with ethical implications. This chiasmus between an empirical investigation and the concepts proposed by ethical theorists helps to equip healthcare actors so that they can take on a responsibility that has become unavoidable, that of a structured justification of the ends and means underlying the doctor–patient relationship. This approach can be divided into two segments: the conceptual and methodological tools required to create a set of ethics on one hand and the description of the ethical challenges involved in a given situation on the other hand.

This ethical modeling applied to medical communication constitutes the basis of a new approach that is respectful of all actors and is oriented toward thought, conscience and human responsibility [DEV 95], as "the incommensurability that separates saying from doing, and practical writing, involves both the codes of proper conduct and the ordinary things in life" [LEN 95]. The socio-informational analysis model is intended to bring to light a cognitive system relying on ethnomethodology, which explains the relationship between professional practices, communication and evaluation. Thus, it has general functions that are actions of knowledge and sharing (such as theories).

This model of analysis constitutes a tool for the translation of technical language into ethical language and vice versa. It facilitates the convergence of the "info-signal" of technology and the "info-significance" advocated by ethics. It is applied to the infosphere, which brings together technology and ethics at the same time. The doctor–patient communication occurs in five very specific phases (see Figure 2.12):

– *capture*: the objective of this phase is to recover primary data in order to create a base of raw primary data;

– *process selection*: this stage represents the processing of raw data. It constitutes the digestion and targeted refinement of data, keeping only the most useful;

– *modeling of use*: the goal of this phase is to introduce, use and adapt information received in a given situation and environment;

– *development of complex thought*: this stage leads to an ethics of responsibility (recognition of a relatively autonomous subject) and solidarity (linking thought). It leads to an ethics of comprehension, enabling harmony and pacification in the doctor–patient relationship. It is applied at the time of the medical announcement of the diagnosis of the patient made by his or her doctor;

– *shared medical decision-making*: the objective of this phase is to supply a precise response to the treatment planned. It formalizes a decision-making process regarding care, established between the doctor and the patient.

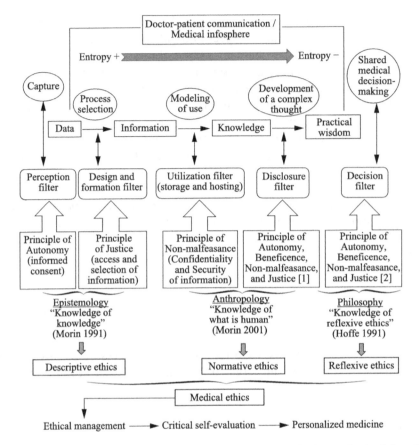

Figure 2.12. *Ethical modeling of information system in the doctor–patient relationship*

Comments on Figure 2.12:

[1]

– Principle of non-malfeasance: what are the ideal conditions in which to tell a person that he or she has a serious illness?

– Principle of justice: what information is necessary to transmit to a patient?

– Principle of beneficence: what should be said to the patient's family to avoid the use of intensive medication on this patient?

– Principle of autonomy: what words and terms should be used so that the patient will understand completely the illness he or she has? What are the questions this patient is asking himself or herself?

[2]

– Principle of autonomy: make the patient participate in the medical decision-making.

– Principle of beneficence: provide well-being to the patient.

– Principle of non-malfeasance: prevent the patient from experiencing harm or useless suffering.

– Principle of justice: share among all patients equivalent available resources (time, energy, listening, money, etc.).

Each of these phases is associated with a specific filter. Among these, we can distinguish:

– *perception filter*: with a questioning of the nature, authentication and conditions of capturing data;

– *design and formatting filter*: with reflections focused on the choice form, clarity and hierarchical arrangement of information;

– *utilization filter*: with questions focused on the usage, storage and hosting of information;

– *disclosure filter*: with reflections focused on the diffusion and framing of knowledge for the patient;

– *decision-making filter*: with a questioning of the medical decision-making shared by the doctor and the patient.

These filters constitute tools of ethical assessment and questioning. This set of medical ethics falls within the intention geared toward the end purpose and meaning of medical acts.

It is composed of the following:

– *descriptive ethics*: this set of ethics applies to the organizational and technological plans. It is a set of ethics of application in the form of practice with the means, devices, routes and procedures implemented;

– *normative ethics*: this set of ethics concerns the political and strategic plans. It is a set of ethics regulating the deontological aspect via the norms, codes and rules put in place;

– *reflexive ethics*: this set of ethics applies to the philosophical plan. It represents a set of ethics of legitimization based on the questioning of fundamental principles and end purposes through principles and human values.

On the basis of this approach, we can associate with it a form of adapted ethical management. It is located in a sort of mediation, of the "between:" placed between the individual and action, between an individual's interaction and its implementation and between a person's professional and personal lives. Its action is, therefore, significant in terms of learning.

For this reason, it contributes to the optimization of the aptitude for change, individual performance and organization of hospital practitioners [PED 04]. This kind of human support is not intended to seek the "why" of things but rather to optimize the consequences and effects of medical actions.

Subsequently, critical self-evaluation results from this ethical management. This process is intended to help individuals make a judgment on their actions and to encourage the acquisition of situational knowledge in order to make good medical decisions. It tells the learner about the mental processes he or she activates in order to act and contributes to the learning of specific and cross-disciplinary skills. It consists of continuous observation of an action by the subject himself or herself, who then compares the activity he or she is in the midst of performing with the goal to be achieved. It calls upon the capacities for anticipation, regulation and self-correction. Evaluation represents a decision-making tool when it is incorporated into the communicational circuit.

Finally, this process leads to personalized medicine based on an ethical analysis model, a validation of adapted management and a self-evaluation of medical practices, composed of a high degree of openness, improvement of performance via the best transmission of knowledge from the healthcare professional and development of his or her autonomy.

Ultimately, as we have shown, human values are omnipresent in every dimension of medical communication between caretakers and patients. Multiple ethical challenges result from the conflicts that arise between these values, and an implicit ethical normality takes hold within this system.

2.4.4. *Process of creation of practical wisdom via neo-Platonic systemic ethical modeling*

Globally speaking, the notion of complexity is based on the principal idea according to which a system composed of different parts forms a whole that differs from the sum of these parts. Complexity falls today within a veritable movement of thought that invites us to restore the intelligence of complexity in our cultures and ways of acting. It poses a key epistemological problem for knowledge and action. Becoming attached to complexity means introducing a certain way of addressing reality and defining a specific relationship with an objective. This implies that the very organization of these components causes developments to occur, meaning that it produces specific properties that are not deductible from the knowledge of each of the parties. Analysis alone of the connections between elements is no longer enough. It now seems of primordial importance to develop new tools of reflection that will allow us to better understand and predict the mechanisms of recursive logic, feedback and phenomena of relative autonomy that make up an organization geared toward the creation of practical wisdom. The complexity of an organization requires three prerogatives:

– central prioritization of the practice, teleology and thought process of interdisciplinarity;

– redefinition of evaluation systems and the taking into consideration of human and social aspects;

– systematic amplification in collective use of scientific auto-reflexivity based on exchange and dialogue.

This is a true challenge for knowledge from a theoretical and practical point of view. Thus, this process of development of practical wisdom makes it possible to shift from a state (A) of complex, disorganized and fuzzy knowledge to a state (Ω) of simple, structured and teleological knowledge (see Figure 2.13).

To achieve this simplification successfully, we must use the correct representation and modeling that consists of substituting a description of process for a description of status. This transformation is made via the intermediary of a neo-Platonic systemic ethical modeling process (Ψ, G, Φ) that includes:

– the reflections of Leonardo da Vinci[47], G.B. Vico[48], P. Valéry, E. Morin and J.-L. Lemoigneon on (ethical (Ψ: Psi[49]), epistemic and anthropological (G: Gnosis[50]), pragmatic (Φ: Phi[51])) modeling;

– the construction of an ethical event (intentions, situations and actions);

– Nonaka's model of the organizational learning surrounding dialogue and practice (socialization, internalization, externalization and combination).

Systemic modeling is used to develop pertinent decision-making and legitimization methods by considering the ethical issues underlying the event being studied. In these conditions, modeling enables us to better understand our experiences of the relationships we have with others; in other words, to "transform our experiences into science with conscience" according to Leonardo da Vinci. This includes considering interactions that are both relational and cognitive with, on the one hand, methodology used to "learn how to do something" and, on the other hand, teleology aimed at "understanding why to do something". Consequently, an improvement of tools of thought necessarily causes an improvement in decision-making.

---

47 According to Leonardo da Vinci, "modeling (the Disegno), is of such excellence that it not only shows the works of nature, but produces an infinitely more varied number. [...] It surpasses nature because the basic forms of nature are limited, while the works that the eye requires from the hands of mankind are limitless" (L. da Vinci. CU, f. SOr, and CU, f. 116 r. Taken from the English translation by McCurdy). We become aware of the importance of a system of representation that contextualizes the plan: what do we want to do, in what, for what?

48 "L'ingegnio (l'ingenium) is that mental faculty that makes it possible to link, in a rapid, appropriate, and happy manner, separate things." G.B. Vico [LEM 90]

49 This Greek letter is often used to designate psychology, psychiatry and psychotherapy, or more generally the sciences of human thought. The symbol means *soul* or *psyche*.

50 This term means *knowledge* in Latin.

51 This Greek letter designates the golden ratio, measuring 1.618. Since classical times, this symbol has represented the divine harmonious proportion. It constitutes the basis of structures in architecture, art, anatomy, music and literature, that is, the concrete and practical aspects of science and the arts.

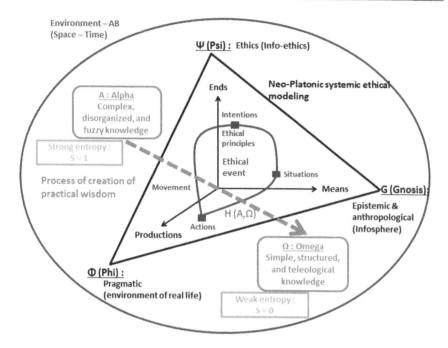

Figure 2.13. *Transformation from alpha to omega via the neo-Platonic systemic ethical prism*

By representing our complex knowledge using models, systems of symbols that we develop, via which we analyze and exchange, we end by mastering this knowledge, by making it simpler and therefore more intelligible. Symbolization is part of the purely formalist tradition of the Pythagoreans. According to Simon and Newell [SIM 71], the device of the symbol represents "the conjunction of form and relationship, answering the question: 'What causes a symbol to symbolize'?" This search for practical wisdom contributes to a tendency toward very low entropy (S)[52]: that is, a degree of disorder that is virtually zero. Thus, we can see the beginnings of the knowledge that humanity has been pursuing since its origins. This process of ethical legitimization of the knowledge of the infosphere combined with the pragmatism of the real-life environment enables us to simplify our knowledge by taking it on both statically, through its environment, and dynamically, through its interactions. In these

---

52 The word "entropy" was introduced by Clausius and is derived from a Greek word meaning transformation. It still represents the complexity and, thus, the possible disorder of a system, structure or organization.

conditions, ethics constitutes, on the one hand, the value characterized by absolute transcendence and, on the other hand, the validity of pragmatic "immanence"[53]. According to Morin [MOR 04], ethics is inseparable from complex knowledge[54]:"knowledge that connects, expresses, and builds on itself as soon as a person decides to a responsible and connected citizen". It seems of primordial importance, therefore, to redefine intelligence in order to face up to the complexity of the world that surrounds us, and of ethics itself.

By nature, a complex system is a dynamic system involving multiple interactions and feedback, within which processes occur that are very difficult to predict or control, which to the classical mind would have been unimaginable [MOR 05]. The complexity of a system takes on its full rigor when its representation becomes intelligible by basing itself on the paradigm of the Constructed Universe (axiomatic–inductive–pragmatic). Thus, this system incorporates a cognitive representation and a projective (or intentional) construction of reactions associated with teleologies we invent. It thus becomes projective or systemic (intention–conception). This open system is composed of an environment, functions, actions, teleology and transformations. Our model attempts to integrate and ensure the endurance of the reflections on this subject by illustrious researchers such as Aristotle, Archimedes, da Vinci, Francis Bacon, Descartes, G.B. Vico, Cl. Bernard, P. Valéry, G. Bachelard, J. Piaget, H.A. Simon, E. Morin and J.-L. Lemoigne. This model was populated in part by the reflections of da Vinci when he insisted that it was necessary "to do in order to understand, and to understand in order to do". According to Blondel [BLO 93], "from thought to practice and from practice to thought, the circle must be closed in science because it is closed in life. Thereby … this double relationship of knowledge and action … is determined". In these conditions, the intrinsic strength of this model lies in its character that is at once interactive, multidimensional, and actively oriented towards the meaning, knowledge, and teleology of an event. It is composed of three separate dimensions that connect and interact with one another (see Table 2.3):

– informative dimension (G): infosphere;

– environmental dimension (Φ): environment of real life;

– ethical dimension (Ψ): info-ethics.

53 This is a philosophical term designating the character of what has its principle in itself.
54 Edgar Morin (1994) uses the term "auto-ethics" to designate the necessity of "complexifying judgment" in action. The word "auto" means, for the author, "fundamental autonomy" (Autos).

Informative dimension (G)	Environmental dimension (Φ)	Ethical dimension (Ψ)
Data/information	Structural and technological plan	Descriptive ethics
	Strategic and methodological plan	Normative ethics
Knowledge	Relational and cultural plan	Descriptive ethics
	Organizational and regulatory plan	Normative ethics
Data/information/knowledge	Four environmental plans	Reflexive ethics

Table 2.3. *Interactions between the dimensions of ethical modeling*

We have chosen to represent the state of complex and simplified knowledge by the Greek letters alpha (A) and omega (Ω), respectively, in relation to their symbolic aspect. In Christian tradition, A and Ω symbolize the eternal life of Christ, with alpha (the first letter of the Greek alphabet) translating the beginning of everything[55] and omega (the last letter of the Greek alphabet) illustrating the end of the world[56]. This metaphor was taken up by the Jesuit Pierre Teilhard de Chardin to represent human evolution from A to Ω. In probability, omega corresponds to the universe of the possible, whereas in Euclidean geometry, it constitutes the center of a similitude, that is, a transformation that multiplies all distances by a fixed constant called its ratio. The image of any figure created by this type of application is a similar figure, intuitively "of the same shape". Finally, traditional physics and chemistry use the symbol Ω to indicate a state of equilibrium in a given system. All this effectively translates the idea of the transformation of an initial complex and disorganized state into a final simplified and ordered state; in other words, an ethical evolution of human knowledge toward practical wisdom.

$f: A \rightarrow \Omega$ (with $y = f(x)$, where A represents the starting set and Ω the final set)$(S \approx 1)(S \approx 0)$

$x \rightarrow y$

This ethical conversion ranging from A to Ω fundamentally transits via our systemic modeling (Ψ, G, Φ), which is manifested by a transit matrix $M(\Psi, G, \Phi)$. According to Quastler [QUA 56], we can see that in the

---

55 See Chapter One of the Gospel according to Saint John.
56 See the Apocalypse according to Saint John.

representation of transmitted information, two systems never communicate directly, but rather, necessarily, via the mediation of a non-neutral third party, the channel, which is included in their communication.

Moreover, based on the description of this transformation of knowledge, we can also represent it via the flows of quantities of information that such a process of conversion involves, according to Claude Shannon's theory of information. "The quantity of information (H) in a system is a measure of its degree of organization", wrote Wiener [WIE 48]. According to Morin [MOR 04], information is a physical reality comparable to energy. The latter is "indestructible" (first law of thermodynamics), degradable (second law of thermodynamics), polymorphous (kinetic, thermal, chemical, electrical, etc.) and transformable (into mass or matter). Information is necessarily linked to the "concept of duplication and of noise" [MOR 77, 3.2I].

On the basis of this observation, the Shannonian measurement of the quantity of information liable to be transmitted or lost in a system suggests in effect an assessment of what seems to be the system's complexity. Complexity assessment includes considering the probability distribution of cases of behaviors or possible states (or of entropy (S)), and thus their relative uncertainty (see Figure 2.14).

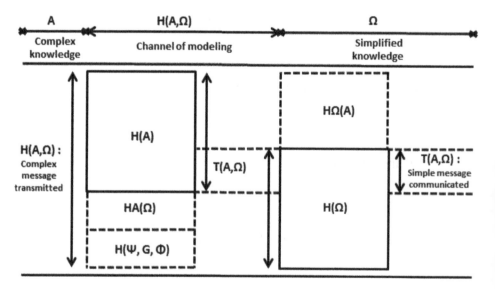

Figure 2.14. *Flow of quantity of information from A to Ω*

$$H(A) \rightarrow H(\Omega)$$

$$H(A, \Omega) = H(A) + H(\Psi, G, \Phi) + HA(\Omega) \text{ and}$$
$$H(A, \Omega) = H(\Omega) + H\Omega(A)$$

with:

$H(A)$ = quantity of Shannonian information in the complex message;

$H(\Omega)$ = quantity of Shannonian information in the simplified message;

$H(A,\Omega)$ = modeling channel with capacity presumed to go from A to Ω;

$H(\Psi, G, \Phi)$ = quantity of intentional information issuing from model (Ψ,G,Φ);

$HA(\Omega)$ = quantity of non-intentional information exogenous to the message, the "emersions" produced by the organization;

$H\Omega(A)$ = quantity of non-intentional information exogenous to the message, the "noise" due to equivocation of reception;

$T(A,\Omega)$ = complex message transmitted;

$T(\Omega,A)$ = simplified message received.

Symbolically, the receiver Ω of an item of simplified knowledge receives both less equivocation or "noise" ($H\Omega(A)$) and more ambiguity or "emersions" ($HA(\Omega)$) of non-intentional information than has been sent by the transmitter A of an item of complex knowledge. At first glance, this loss and this gain of non-intentional information have no reason to compensate for one another. However, insofar as this transmitted information is presumed to be indispensable to Ω in order for the behavior of the knowledge to be in accordance with its plan, we may see the expected behaviors disappear[57] and witness the appearance of unexpected ones[58].

From a mathematical point of view, we can translate this ethical simplification as follows:

---

57 By ignorance of the "noise" linked to the message transmitted.
58 The appearance of the meaning and ethical aspect of the message via the decoding of organizational emersions.

– Let A be a set of complex and disordered items of knowledge endowed with any basis written as BA = (e1, e2, e3).

– Let Ω be a set of simple and ordered items of knowledge endowed with an ethical basis written as BΩ = (Ψ, G, Φ).

– Let M be the passage matrix from the basis BA to the basis BΩ. We use this passage matrix to pass from the complex state (A) to the simplified state (Ω).

Thus, for a complex message $\alpha \in$ A, we associate a simple message $\omega \in \Omega$ such that

$$\Omega = M \times \alpha$$

In terms of quantity of information, this gives

$$H(\omega) = H(M) + H(\alpha)$$

H(M) corresponds to the information contributed by the change of basis (or change of representation). In other words, by the change of representation, we contribute the term H(Ψ, G, Φ).

Note that Ψ, G and Φ constitute dimensions that are by nature independent and that interact with one another. This means that M may tend toward orthogonality (meaning the optimization of its use) without ever attaining it.

We have thus defined the quantity of information carried by the item of knowledge and the change of representation of this knowledge:

$$\boxed{H(\omega) = H(\Psi, G, \Phi)) + H(\alpha)}$$

Note: According to Quastler, the message transmitted and received (common to A and Ω) is a symmetric form. On the basis of this observation, we can state that

$$T(A,\Omega) = T(\Omega,A)$$

$$T(A,\Omega) = T(\Omega,A) = H(A,\Omega) - HA(\Omega) - H(\Psi, G, \Phi) - H\Omega(A) \text{ or}$$

$$H(\Psi, G, \Phi) = H(\Omega) - H(A)$$

$$= H(A,\Omega) - HA(\Omega) - H(\Omega) + H(A) - H\Omega(A)$$

$$= H(A) - HA(\Omega) \text{ or } H(A) = H(\Omega) - H(\Psi, G, \Phi)$$

Thus, we obtain:

$$T(A,\Omega) = T(\Omega,A) = H(\Omega) - HA(\Omega) - H(\Psi, G, \Phi)$$

It is clear that the final message communicated via our ethical model has indeed been simplified and reduced, while still retaining the essence and meaning of the initial message transmitted. In fact, the quantity of information included in the message received ($T(\Omega,A)$) is markedly lower than the amount that makes up the transmitted message ($T(A,\Omega)$). $H(\Omega)$ has incorporated the non-intentional information $HA(\Omega)$ of the organization's emersions and that of the ethical modeling $H(\Psi, G, \Phi)$ in order to summarize a communicated message received ($T(\Omega,A)$), which is ordered, concise and teleological.

NOTE.– The quantity of exogenous non-intentional information in the message ($H\Omega(A)$), the "noise", naturally separates from the final message received. This loss of information, which arises from the equivocation of the reception, is a mechanical phenomenon that occurs with all transmissions of information.

It also suggests that the system should be able to obtain for itself a representation of the user with whom it is interacting, in order to adapt itself to this user. For its part, the user tends toward adapting himself or herself to the system from the moment he or she understands that he or she is dealing with a machine, which has the pragmatic advantage for the designer of simplifying certain aspects of the dialogue.

An organization is active, self-organizing and dependent on and connected to the environment. It also reacts according to the information. Information is a stable configuration of a symbol that is both a sign and signified. It helps the organization to adapt its behavior at all times via regulation, to transform itself and to re-balance itself in order to be in osmosis with the environmental parameters of the infosphere, info-ethics and the computosphere (see Table 2.4).

Thus, information gives rise to a permanent process of adjustment of the organization by channels (the system adapts by accommodation) and codes (the system adapts by assimilation) of communication relative to a plan. To represent the organization, we propose a model composed of a decision-making system, an informational system and an operating system.

Field of study	Infosphere	
	Strategic and methodological	**Structural and technological**
Epistemology: Data/information & *Anthropology*: Knowledge	Applicability Richness Adaptability Order Flexibility Evolutiveness Performance Reusability Pragmatism Consolidation Functionality/operationality	Coherence/meaning Exactness Integrity Exhaustiveness Authenticity Reliability Robustness Legitimacy Nominal/database
Field of study	**Organizational and regulatory**	**Relational and cultural**
Epistemology: Data/information & *Anthropology*: Knowledge	Pertinence Stability/continuity Assurance Multidisciplinarity Systematicity Reference Normativity Maintainability Regulation Auditability Coordination	Security Confidentiality Federation Diffusion Accessibility Friendliness Universality Availability Cooperation

Table 2.4. *Environmental parameters of the infosphere*

In light of this reasoning, we can state that the passage of data (A) to practical wisdom (info-ethics) (Ω) is translated by the equation of the following Shannonian quantities of information: data → practical wisdom (info-ethics):

$$T(A,\Omega) \to T(\Omega,A)$$

$$H(A) \to H(\Omega) - HA(\Omega) - H(\Psi, G, \Phi)$$

This passage is accomplished via the channel of ethical modeling.

In addition, this pyramidal schematization involves control filters for each field of study (see Table 2.5):

– visualization/perception filter and design/epistemological implementation filter;

– cartographical and anthropological usage filter;

– application, regulation and ethical legitimization filter.

Level of knowledge	Nature	Content	Function	Filter
Data: discrete elements	Epistemology	Numbers Codes Tables Databases	Categorize Calculate Collect Measure Gather	Visualization and perception (What is it?)
Information: linked elements	Epistemology	Sentences Paragraphs Equations Concepts Ideas Questions Simple accounts	Contextualize Comparer Order Converse Filter Frame Rank	Design and implementation (How?)
Knowledge: organized information	Anthropology	Chapters Theories Axioms Conceptual frameworks Complex accounts	Structure Understand Interpret Evaluate Demolish	Cartography and use (Why?)
Practical wisdom: applied knowledge	Ethics	Books Paradigms Systems Religions/beliefs Philosophies Traditions Principles Truths Schools of thought	Protect Embody Adapt Summarize Apply	Application, regulation and legitimization (What is best?)

Table 2.5. *Structuring of pyramid of knowledge*

On the basis of this view of the evolution of our information society, we have developed our ethical analysis model applied to NTICs. It should be noted that the idea of using mathematics to describe the "sensitive world" seems to have originated with Pythagoras or the Pythagoreans [DIX 03].

In summary, complex thought binds epistemology and anthropology in a loop. Epistemology makes it possible to understand anthropology, which is a primary condition of philosophical thought that becomes part of a loop in which each stage is necessary to the others in order to result in a set of ethics. Finally, cybernetics relies on info-ethics to develop artificial intelligence or the evolutive knowledge of expert systems using diagnosis. In other words, these four macroscopic stages of society can be illustrated by a microscopic approach of an IS, manifesting as its design, setup, use and development. This type of approach motivates us to re-examine the epistemological perspective in which an organization of production and reappropriation of knowledge is used, as is the case with healthcare establishments in particular.

On the basis of these reflections, we can integrate our process of the creation of practical wisdom via the concept of organizational intelligence (see Figure 2.15).

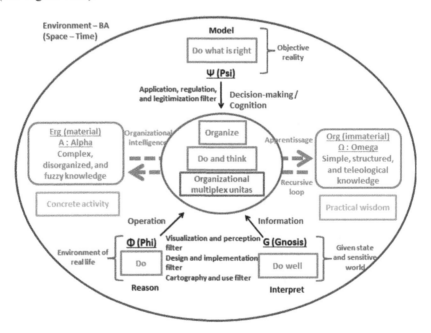

Figure 2.15. *Process of creation of practical wisdom via organizational intelligence*

The passage from concrete activity (alpha) to practical wisdom (omega) can also be characterized by the Erg dialogic (material)[59] and the Org dialogic (immaterial)[60] involved in disorder–order generating interaction. The organizational intelligence that facilitates this transformation includes operation, information and decision-making. The cohesiveness of an organization constitutes the central element of the complexity of an event or situation.

It seems necessary to orient ourselves toward "poietic"[61] knowledge (according to Ménon and Morin), which is intended to be heuristic, functional, geno endogenous and sfumato, that is, which links and opens. This active linking constitutes the fact of relearning to observe, develop, think and act; to compose the recursive loop, always repopulated with knowledge and reflections, with the knowledge of knowledge. Thus, the knowledge of knowledge requires complex thinking [MOR 06], which necessarily requires the involvement and connection of the infosphere (informative dimension (G): information); the environment of real life (environmental dimension (Φ): operation) and info-ethics (ethical dimension (Ψ): decision-making), moving ceaselessly from one into another. The passage from alpha to omega necessarily includes the linking of the pragmatic (reasoning[62]) and epistemic knowledge (interpreting[63]) and ethics (modeling[64]) surrounding an event. If the pragmatic aspect calls for ethical analysis, ethics goes back to epistemological study, which calls upon and activates reflection on experiences, which expresses the pragmatic[65]. The organizational intelligence of complexity brings together separate data, information and knowledge in order to tend toward practical wisdom. This intelligence of reality represents a reconstitution and translation of this reality by a human mind, which is made possible by multiplex organizational units (MOU), a metaprinciple representing a radiant core that centralizes, organizes and links the triangulation (Ψ, G, Φ). This MOU translating

59 The Erg constitutes the energetic activity of the system, in the permanent degeneration–regeneration involved in autonomization and ecologization.
60 The Org represents the negentropic or information activity of the system, which is generative in the organization via the energetic activity of the system by developing three functions: computation, information, and memorization and communication.
61 This is the study of the potentialities of a given situation leading to a new creation.
62 Reason: congruence, cognitive interaction, ingenium (heuristic exploration or deliberative rationality), satisficing (adequacy), deliberation.
63 Interpret: recognition or linking, dialogic, transformation, recursiveness, hologramatic.
64 Model: symbolization, representation, teleology, systemic, multilevel organization.
65 This can be illustrated by the Viaticum of Leonardo da Vinci: "Sapience (science with conscience) is the daughter of experience".

"doing and thinking" connects and integrates the "doing"[66] of the real-life environment with the "doing well"[67] of the given state and the sensitive world, and the "doing what is right"[68] of objective reality.

The intelligibility of an organization's actions possesses the capacity to maintain and to maintain itself (auto-regulation); to connect and to connect itself (auto-reference) and to produce and to produce itself (auto-poiesis). Thus, the formation of practical wisdom via organizational intelligence extends to a decision-making system.

For this reason, in light of this analysis, it seems indispensable to bring to the heart of healthcare organizations in particular, philosophy, sociology and ethics, which are responsible for producing the conceptual tools leading to practical wisdom.

2.4.5. *Ethical inductive algorithmic governance (Ψ, G, Φ)*

A mathematical algorithm is defined by a sequence of stages and instructions that can be applied to data. It generates categories of information filtering and data exploitation, examines models and relationships and, in general, aids in the analysis of information. The algorithm for the ethical management of data evolves with datasets that cross it, with the attribution of different weights to each variable. Placing an algorithm at the center of expert system models, as is the case in the medical field[69], leads to questions about the faithfulness and fairness of the medical decision-making algorithm and filtering mechanisms.

The algorithm will structure medical decision-making, which will give rise to major ethical issues around algorithms processing and analyzing data.

> If an algorithm can inform you before your doctor does, and without completely understanding why, that you have an increased probability of having cancer, why deprive ourselves of this?! In the end, big data analyses are tools that cannot be substituted for the understanding of scientists; they draw

---

66 In what to understand? In what context?
67 To do "why"? For what plans?
68 To mobilize intelligence? For what decision?
69 IBM: Lung cancer (Watson), Genomics: analysis via an expert system, Qualico Google, which will soon replace doctors.

attention to correlations detected so that these scientists can then search for causal explanations [BLO 13].

Those who develop data utilization models must also show the scientific interest of doing so and the difficulties that arise when we wish to make data anonymous and quantify the dangers to which we expose ourselves by sharing the data.

Let us take the example of a type of algorithm used in medical imaging technologies, aimed at representing human and biological structures on a computer in a precise manner to improve the diagnostic or therapeutic perspectives of illnesses. One of the many ethical questions brought up by these algorithms is the risk of producing false-positive[70] and false-negative results[71]. Thus, these algorithms include a vital element of value judgment and, consequently, a set of ethics. The designer is led, thus, to make a compromise between minimizing false-positive results and the number of false-negative results[72]. This compromise will inevitably be based on a value judgment. Generally, designers choose a reasonable value for the threshold or parameter setting of computer software. The user bases his or her decisions on the output of the software results, which have been generated on the basis of a set of parameters based on the ethical hypotheses established by the software designer; hence, the necessity for these ethical hypotheses to be similar to those of the user.

For this reason, the design of an algorithm must help the user to choose the circumstances in which it is located. It is, therefore, vital for the IS designer to allow the user to specify the ethical parameters and, at the same time, to give him or her the responsibility for defining the default status of the software.

Moreover, from a macroscopic point of view, Moore's law supposes that: "the more technological revolutions increase their impact on society, the more ethical problems increase. This phenomenon occurs due to new

---

70 The algorithm triggers a system of counting (cells, symptoms of a disease) in a digital environment that is not really there.

71 The algorithm is not able to identify a structure of the image that truly exists.

72 The algorithm designer faces a decision-making process that is similar in many ways to that encountered by people who design other technological artifacts. This implies that the value judgments integrated into an algorithm are similar to those involved in design processes.

opportunities for actions being enabled, actions for which ethical policies will not have been developed" [MOO 05]. Thus, the more the technological revolutions increase, the larger the quantity of data becomes. The formation of this big data (A) contributes to the increased complexity of algorithms and entropy (S) (degree of disorder) of the data diffused, causing more ethical problems through their use (see Figure 2.16). To counterbalance this phenomenon, we believe it is necessary to apply our system of selective ethical ranking (Ψ, G, Φ) to transform big data (A) into info-ethics (Ω).

Now, the exploitation of big data can effectively be translated as: "an instantaneous search for essential information, its inclusive analysis without prior value judgments, the reproduction of effective mechanisms previously observed, and the production of new information that is directly useful in the current situation" [MAL 13].

It is here that big data moves away from the "traditional" Cartesian scientific knowledge, which advances mainly by deduction: from a hypothesis, we logically deduce a consequence that we then try to test in order to verify. In this context, big data is processed via induction[73] by generalizing a phenomenon observed, even if this phenomenon is observed only once.

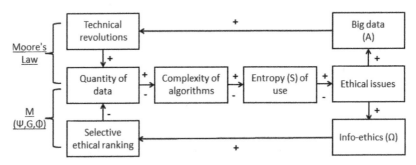

Figure 2.16. *Technico-ethical regulation of data*

Our ethical modeling (Ψ, G, Φ) can be likened to ethical data mining using algorithms intended to cause the emergence of new information, referred to as info-ethics, via the analysis of a large quantity of data.

---

73 Induction facilitates algorithms to reproduce phenomena observed by generalizing them beyond their context as long as they remain effective, without attempting to model them.

Reducing the quantity of information is at the heart of an ethical dilemma. Is it necessary or not to deliberately lose information in order to regulate it and make it functional (info-ethics)?

If we consider the model created by James Clerk Maxwell, who used figures from Willard Gibbs[74] to establish a three-dimensional image of energy (Z), entropy (X) and volume (Y) of the thermodynamic surface, we can see that energy diminishes when volume or entropy increases. On the basis of this, we can put forward the idea that free energy (G) will be high when entropy is negative and volume is small. In other words, we believe that a process of precise transduction (characterized by an efficient reduction of data, filtering out only what is essential and useful) will contribute to the development of an ordered and ethical system in which entropy is negative. In these conditions, it seems of primary importance to reduce the overall quantity of data in a message in such a way as to maintain the usefulness of the data transmitted.

Moreover, the number of operations necessary to process a quantity n of data must not increase too quickly with n. Algorithms acceptable for small amounts of data (e.g. with a variation of n^2) take too much time in the domain of big data. Sampling methods in which all the data are not read enable a variation lower than n. The optimal complexity of algorithms is translated by n log n (2).

We admit by hypothesis that:

$M(\Psi, G, \Phi)$ = sampling = selective ethical ranking

Optimal complexity of algorithms = entropy of use (S)

So, expression (2) means that $n \log n = S = A \times (1 - M(\Psi, G, \Phi))$

If A = all the complex and disordered knowledge transmitted = big data = n (quantity of data processed), then we get:

$A \log A = A \times (1 - M(\Psi, G, \Phi))$

$\log A = 1 - M(\Psi, G, \Phi)$

$A = 10$ showing $(1 - M(\Psi, G, \Phi))$

---

[74] See the second law of thermodynamics.

We saw previously that if entropy (S) tends toward 0, then $M(\Psi, G, \Phi)$ tends toward 1:

$A \simeq 10$ showing $(0) \simeq 1$

Thus, when entropy (S) tends toward 0, the big data (A) processed tends toward 1. This means that the most optimal degree of simplification of an algorithm for the processing of complex data (A) yields a degree of disorder (S) that is almost zero.

This result confirms the fact that our passage matrix $M(\Psi, G, \Phi)$ does indeed make it possible to cause a complex message A to change into a simplified message via selective ethical ranking, without losing the meaning, end purpose and thus ethics of the initial message:

with f: $A \rightarrow \Omega\Omega = M(\Psi, G, \Phi) \times A$ $S = A \times (1 - M(\Psi, G, \Phi))$

Finally, our ethical approach dovetails perfectly with the work that has been done on the inductive algorithms at the center of big data technologies. Inductive algorithms must be combined with a reward (or convergence) function that evaluates the benefits of new inferences and, thus, limits the number of them. As with ethical progression, there is no single and universal inductive solution to a given problem. However, it is commonly the case that a reduced number of processes respond to a particular end purpose. As with an ethical process, the most optimum inductive algorithms are evolutive. They improve by adjusting their ways of processing data according to the most pertinent use that can be made of it.

To develop swift inductive algorithms, it is vital for the processing of data to be anticipatory and contributory. For this to be the case, the exploitation of big data must convert these data as soon as possible into info-ethics that can be exploited during subsequent periods. Thus, our selective and inductive ranking transforms a large quantity of data "in expansion" into information that is "comprehensive" in form, more flexible and less voluminous. Rapidity allows a mechanism to focus on essential and meaningful data while remaining iterative; that is, this processing algorithm can be stopped without losing results. Info-ethics is rapidly accessible and can adjust itself via an ongoing process.

2.4.6. *Toward a selective ranking of medical data*

During this time of exponentially increasing volumes of information – big data, e-health and m-health – the ranking and selection of medical data seem fundamental, necessitating the adaptation of a management strategy for production of databases that distribute data among various storage categories to optimize the performance achieved by the user. This process relieves the management constraints associated with data placement. For this reason, digitized medical communication, in addition to its informative value, now faces the challenge of restoring the trust of the actors involved in the patient's circuit while optimizing treatment support. An added value of medical communication via an IS consists of transforming these data into information by giving them another dimension through which to alleviate, modify and amplify the perception that reception may yield.

Although medical information brings together objective data, with the shift to medical communication including their ranking and selection, as may be the case for initial clinical constants[75], we re-enter the area of subjective knowledge, in which the healthcare professional decides to prioritize and diffuse part of the information on these constants to his or her patient in order to improve the latter's understanding. In other words, a metamorphosis of epistemological data and information takes place into knowledge associated with anthropology and the experiential background of the individual. Thus, the communication of medical knowledge exceeds objective data alone by favoring certain items of data and information above others. For this reason, it seems more precise to use the term "medical knowledge" rather than "medical information" when speaking of medical communication. We can argue for and illustrate these reflections by taking the example of the content of a medical consultation pertaining to a patient composed of the following: relative administrative data, the reason for consultation[76], anamnesis[77], initial clinical constants, initial clinical examination, history/allergies[78], treatments in progress[79], latest constants after the undertaking of treatment[80], diagnosis and final treatment. Potentially, the person responsible for the IS may have the ability to view all of these data (administrative and medical). Only the initial

---

75 Earliest elements observable by a healthcare professional (physician or not).
76 Initial signs and symptoms.
77 History of signs of illness.
78 This is part of anamnesis.
79 This is part of anamnesis
80 This corresponds to data from additional tests (biology, imaging, etc.) contributing to the eventual final diagnosis.

clinical examination, the latest constants after the undertaking of treatment, the diagnosis and the final treatment are the domain of the physician; the rest can be carried out by a paramedical staff member (delegation of tasks). For his or her part, the patient has access only to the reason for the consultation, anamnesis, history/allergies, treatment in progress, diagnosis and final treatment. The billing department should have access only to administrative data pertaining to the patient. However, as emphasized by Dr. Loïc Etienne[81], the fact that the patient considers accessibility to his or her medical data alongside healthcare professionals (doctors or paramedical professionals) as secondary, this reinforces the idea that hospital reports consider only a part of the issue, keeping silent on certain things that the patient would wish noted or investigated.

The ranking of data also calls now for a consideration of the intrinsic value of the information gathered. How should the value of a piece of data or information be evaluated and according to what criteria? To do what, for what purpose and with what objectives? What should be evaluated? [SIM 07]. The value of a piece of data is defined in the context of action. Although this value can of course be judged from the point of view of content, it can also be judged on the basis of duplication, variety and quantity.

The value of data is defined by its use and not by its nature, as well as by the service rendered for its user. It is proportional to the knowledge it includes and determined by the level of sharing, the quality and quantity of the exchanges made. After having estimated and determined the value of a piece of data, its evaluation becomes possible. Evaluating a piece of information also means determining the strategy for its diffusion: giving access to it at the right moment; transmiting it selectively according to the centers of interest and needs of users and determine which piece of data and information the IS designer must make available to them. In other words, what data are necessary in order to decide or to act?

Obtaining a practical balance within the IS between the improvement and an overload of data transmitted also assumes the optimization of the function of ranking and selection based on two variables:

– The frequency of reevaluation of the attribution of data to different overall and specific levels of functional activity on the part of the IS.

---

81 Interview on the subject of the organization into a hierarchy of medical data, Paris, December 16.

Consequently, if this re-evaluation is carried out too frequently, the overload associated with the movement of data in one direction and the other risks canceling out the performance obtained due to the movement of data on storage disks (SSD).

– The volume of data to be included in the minimum storage unit and thus to be managed and moved within the IS. An overly large quantity of data will complicate and slow down the selective ranking function of the IS.

Our ethical approach is always based on the four ethical principles discussed earlier. The solution of the selective ranking of healthcare data seen through this ethical prism makes it possible to better understand the unstable equilibrium between the availability and the protection of data. This counterbalancing can tip one way or the other depending on context. The approach raises a series of questions to be asked beforehand: what are the objectives, challenges and meanings of this stage? What will I use as data? Partial or total data? How will I use it? Where? Among which users? More broadly, how can the heterogeneous mass of medical data accumulated and stored in an IS be exploited? What relevance does it have in relation to the uses, needs and expectations of healthcare professionals and their patients? Will selective ranking impair the initial informative value? Will the integrity of the final message be preserved? Is it part of a better use of the IS, of optimized medical communication and of an improved experience for the patient?

This ethical approach demonstrates that the selection of medical data is an action with a positive effect in terms of at least three of the four principles of Beauchamp and Childress [BEA 01]:

– appropriate diffusion of medical knowledge among users (healthcare professionals and patients) guarantees the soundness and legitimacy of the action. Medical communication, and thus treatment, becomes more effective: *principle of beneficence*;

– clear, precise, adapted and understandable prior information that guarantees the informed consent of the patient, who is able to deliberate, decide and act. He or she carries out an autonomous action: intentional, voluntary and independent, with understanding and without an external influence of control: *principle of autonomy*;

– limited access to medical data depending on the profile and nature of the user improves data security, confidentiality and protection: *principle of non-malfeasance*.

This selective mechanism for medical data does, however, have a negative repercussion for the principle of justice, as the medical information transmitted is not the same depending on the user of the IS. The system imposes different (and therefore unequal) rules of attribution and access according to the type of person. This results, in a certain sense, in discrimination toward individuals, causing an imbalance of medical knowledge that calls into question the transparency of medical information. Healthcare professionals are on the whole favorable to access data but limited to the department in which the patient is hospitalized in the case of caretaking personnel or dependent on the user profile of the data for personnel working within the *Direction des systèmes d'information et de l'organisation* (Information Systems and Organization Management) [RAV 13].

Medical information is not intended to be distributed to all professionals working within a healthcare establishment, but a patient may need to visit several departments during treatment. This means that medical information is shared by a larger number of healthcare providers. To deal with this "potential loss of confidentiality", some suggest the creation of a core data curriculum that would host shared information, with each department able to have access to its own data, which it would not share with other departments. This idea, which implies a ranking of medical data, approaches the limits of an overly fragmented view of the patient's state of health and may have a negative effect on the patient's treatment.

For the Vice President of the *Conseil national de l'Ordre des médecins* (French National Order of Physicians), Jacques Lucas, medical information included in the conclusions of the medical act must be presented in the digitized file for the coordination of treatment and be wholly known to the patient, who is the true owner of it [LUC 13].

In these conditions, the balance between availability, confidentiality and protection of healthcare data is proving difficult to establish. In our opinion, technology cannot provide a full answer to this issue. Deontology and the adoption of behaviors (not hosting nominative patient medical information on an Internet site or platform isolated from a healthcare IS, outside of a workstation and secured equipment; not transferring professional data to the home via unsecured Internet messaging or a removable external hard disk; regularly changing the work session password, etc.) by healthcare professionals are necessary to guarantee the confidentiality of data.

In these conditions, the use of an IS has repercussions for all actors involved in the life of the hospital: staff, patients, families and the publishers of the IS. It makes it necessary for IS designers to reflect on multisectoral questions such as standards, norms, rules and procedures[82]; good practice guides[83]; protocols, implications and important legal texts[84] (conservation of data, hosting, authentication, identification, etc.) and the inter-relations between the daily use of the IS in varied work contexts, as well as its management.

Finally, the data are categorized and sorted according to the importance accorded to them and the questions posed by their use and diffusion. The simplification of the data transmitted results in a more efficient access and use, with better capture and greater security. However, it also causes reduced integrity of data. For this reason, the ranking of data simplifies the work of healthcare personnel but causes greater technical complexity for the IS designer in terms of process. Given that this selective ranking of medical data plays a major role in the level of complexity of the data and in its accessibility to users, it can be made a part of "medical organizational intelligence".

---

82 Round table on telemedicine during the international day of the *Institut International de Recherche en Éthique Biomédicale* (IIREB), March 19–20, 2013. Conference on "Les enjeux et bonnes pratiques éthiques de la télé-expertise radiologique en recherche Clinique" for the conference of Atlanpôle Biothérapie: TIC & Santé, December 10, 2013 at Nantes.

83 DGOS. *Hôpital Numérique: Guide des indicateurs des pré-requis et domaines prioritaires du socle commun*. April 2012. Conference and round table entitled *Vers une éthique de l'usage des systèmes d'information en santé* during the "Ethique and NTIC" colloquium of the *Espace Ethique Méditerranéen*, December 5, 2012.

84 Law 78-17 of January 6, 1978, pertaining to computer technology, files and freedoms; Directive 95/46/CE, pertaining to the protection of data of a personal nature; Law of March 4, 2002, pertaining to patients' rights and the quality of the healthcare system; Art. L. 1111-7 CSP, pertaining to the accessibility of medical information; Art. L. 1142-4 CSP, pertaining to the right to transparency of medical information; Decree no. 2002-637 of April 29, 2002, pertaining to the accessibility of personal information; Code of medical deontology: Art. 4 al. 1, Art. 72 al. 1, Art. 73 al. 1, pertaining to medical secrecy.

Uses of this Ethical Model

3.1. Implementing the ethical model

In the context of our study, we took inspiration from models proposed by Beauchamp and Childress [BEA 01], Massé [MAS 03], Vézina [VÉZ 06] as well as the ethical analysis space that we created so as to build our own model and theoretical framework based on the four universal ethical principles.

For this reason, an analysis of the production and use of a healthcare IS by investigating specific and concrete areas is necessary. They represent "real justifications," veritable keys to interpret reality, characterized by various sectors such as technology, organization, politics, behavior and ethics. Note that these justifications were built from a literature review on the subject as well as from semi-structured interviews with managers, designers and users of IS, as well as with individuals known to be "experts" on the topic.

To all these ethical principles were associated values that these justifications reference. The values implicate all that is subjected to either a supportive or a rejecting attitude, or a critical judgment, by an individual or a group of individuals and that results in conscious or subconscious attitudes, behaviors or stances. For this reason, all contemporary writers of medical ethics insist on the personal values of actors as standards used to approach and understand individual behaviors.

Nonetheless, we can see that healthcare professionals also refer to other systems of values than their own, notably within:

– objectives (therapeutic, preventative, promotional or relational) undertaken;

– intervention methods and used techniques due to the advances of disciplinary knowledge;

– the art of intervention drawn from acquired experience.

This process allows for each doctor involved not only to have an awareness of their personal scale of personal and professional values, but also to distinguish and evaluate the differences between these values and those of their patient, which could become reasons for conflict. According to Reigle and Boyle [REI 00], "the clarification of values does not indicate which decision must be taken or which action should be undertaken, but examines the coherence and compatibility between the different value systems involved. It can notably result in more coherent decision-making and behavior".

Thus, the clarification of personal, professional and institutional values constitutes a prerequisite for all reflective approaches to medical ethics.

Moreover, for clarity and understanding, the creation of this technical and ethical model is based on only four fundamental ethical principles. The ethical rules described in the first paragraphs are not present, even if they are indirectly included in the model through the major ethical principles.

Ultimately, the combination of these different criteria should allow us to highlight locations where ethical issues might lie. The consideration of several justifications on a single parameter of the IS, or the contrast between different principles and resulting moral values, will bring ethical clarity to solutions to the problems and challenges faced by our research (see Tables 3.1 and 3.2).

This model therefore shows ethical principles down the columns and the keys to interpreting reality across the rows. The aim is to identify when one of these justifications can be applied to an ethical principle. Or inversely, to show when one of the ethical principles or social values will be upheld by one of these keys to understanding reality. Supported by this questioning and continuous research of a "human" IS, healthcare establishments will be able to incorporate an ethical methodology and reasoning that will be suggested to managers and users of the IS.

This ethical model is therefore the foundation on which our analytical questionnaire, critical to undertaking our field research, was built. It must not therefore be used as a rigid framework, but rather as a flexible structure to be integrated into the creation, implementation and use of the IS of healthcare establishment.

3.1.1. *Implementing the model on the major aims of an information system*

This model is composed of 40 justifications that constitute the main aims of an IS. These are split equally across two clearly separate categories (see Tables 3.1 and 3.2):

– Justifications of the purposes of the main aims of a healthcare IS (corresponding to the teleological dimension of our ethical analysis space), containing 10 characterizing the principle of beneficence and 10 representing the principle of justice.

– Justifications of the limitations of the main aims of a healthcare IS (corresponding to the deontological dimension of our ethical analysis space), containing 10 characterizing the principle of autonomy and 10 representing the principle of non-maleficence.

These 40 actions composed of the four universal ethical principles have corresponding social values (which refer to the axiological dimension in the ethical analysis space), of which 4 are most significant[1]: respect for persons, preservation of social links, responsibility and social justice.

Thus, we feed these 40 items into our ethical model represented by the three-dimensional construction of the "ethical cube" (see Figure 2.5). The aim is to measure and compare the "unitary ethical score" of each of the four ethical principles with that of the "acceptable contingency" according to the actors and nature of IS in oncology. The challenge is to prove that our ethical analysis via our approach of "acceptable contingency" conforms to that of the four ethical principles considered as being a universal reference framework.

---

1 We consider that the notions of "efficiency", "universality" and "precaution" do not, strictly speaking, represent prominent social values.

Justifications of the purposes of the main aims of a healthcare information system	Fundamental ethical principles	Associated social values
B1: Aiding medical decision-taking as described by the healthcare professional B2: Promoting quality, organization, management and planning of patients being taken into care B3: Working for the good of the patient	Beneficence	Respect for persons
B4: Sharing transparent and accessible information between the patient and the healthcare professional B5: Ensuring the quality and choice of information shared with the patient B6: Improving continued treatment B7: Sustaining monitoring of all healthcare activities		Preservation of social links
B8: Aiding the Ministry of Health to respond to the expectations of patients with cancer and to provide support B9: Establishing legitimacy of rights and data management with the patient B10: Establishing an obligation for the security, integrity, traceability and protection of medical data		Responsibility
J1: Evaluating performance and locating areas in which action is required by investigating existing faults J2: Efficiently directing the healthcare establishment by managing costs J3: Allowing for epidemiological or statistical analyses	Justice	Efficiency
J4: Improving and encouraging interactions with actors outside the healthcare establishment J5: Improving the availability of healthcare professionals		Preservation of social links
J6: Facilitating user access to medical information: reducing social inequalities		Social justice
J7: Respecting equal access and distribution of information rules regardless of the profile or status of the patient: notion of social justice		
J8: Distributing the advantages and disadvantages of a tool fairly within a healthcare professional's workload		
J9: Sharing the same information and assistance to medical decision-making among all healthcare professionals involved in the patient's care J10: Creating and sharing precise information appropriately adapted to all patients		Universality

Table 3.1. *Justifications of the purposes, fundamental principles and underlying social values to the main aims of a healthcare information system*

Justifications of the limitations of the main aims of a healthcare information system	Fundamental ethical principles	Associated social values
A1: Putting the patient back at the center of the decision by giving them more comprehensive and rapid medical information: better patient autonomy A2: Ensuring the consent and compliance of the patient A3: Respecting private life and the right to medical secrecy and confidentiality A4: Respecting the right to prior information, rectification and opposition as described in the "information technology and freedom" law A5: Reducing information asymmetry between the doctors and their patients: better equilibrium of the doctor–patient relationship A6: Reinforcing the transversality of services within the structure	Autonomy	Preservation of social links
A7: Establishing individual and/or collective use of medical information		Universality
A8: Equating use of medical information with the organization of the healthcare establishment A9: Adapting technology to the knowledge and know-how of the healthcare professional		Respect of persons
A10: Institution of a management and guidance policy on the use of medical information		Efficiency
NM1: Following legislative regulations concerning medical data NM2: Respecting storage, hosting and distribution rules as established by the National Commission on Informatics and Liberties (NCIL)	Non-maleficence	Universality
NM3: Maximizing the ethical quality of decisions and the concern for efficiency and organizational effectiveness of the use of medical information NM4: Developing an organization oriented toward collective performance		Efficiency
NM5: Minimizing or eliminating harm caused to patients due to misinformation NM6: Possessing certainty that used methods must not exceed which is necessary to attain desired objectives NM7: Reducing useless or poorly calculated risks NM8: Ensuring the reliability and continuity of medical data collection NM9: Ensuring technical utility and human merits of the tool		Precaution
NM10: Rendering user guidance a process that is accountab the entirety of the healthcare establishment		Responsibility

Table 3.2. *Justifications of the limitations, fundamental principles and underlying social values of the main aims of a healthcare information system*

– *Creation of the unitary ethical score*: this score is composed of the sum of the 40 items corresponding to the four ethical principles: autonomy, beneficence, non-maleficence and justice. This total is out of 100.

– *Creation of the ethical score of acceptable contingency*: this score corresponds to a more refined and detailed quantification of the unitary ethical score.

We must be aware of the values of the five necessary criteria used to evaluate the conditions of acceptable contingency focused on the search for meaning. These indicators are as follows:

– the teleological axis;

– the deontological axis;

– the axiological axis;

– the focus on services to persons;

– the focus on encouraging relations.

This score is calculated from the sum of the 86 items distributed according to the five indicators listed earlier (see Table 3.3).

	Teleological axis	Deontological axis	Axiological axis	Services to persons	Encouraging relations
B	B1–B2–B3–B4–B5 B6–B7–B8–B9–B10		B1–B2–B3–B4–B5 B6–B7–B8–B9–B10	B1–B3–B8–B9	B2–B4–B5–B6–B7
J	J1–J2–J3–J4–J5 J6–J7–J8–J9–J10		J4–J5–J6–J7–J8		J4–J5–J6
A		A1–A2–A3–A4–A5 A6–A7–A8–A9–A10	A1–A2–A3–A4–A5 A6–A8–A9	A3–A4–A9	A1–A2–A5–A6–A10
NM		NM1–NM2–NM3–NM4–NM5 NM6–NM7–NM8–NM9–NM10	NM10		NM4–NM10

Table 3.3. *Distribution of the justification in the ethical cube of acceptable contingency*

The dimension of the acceptable contingency translates the "ethical score of acceptable contingency" of analysis of IS in medical imagery into a score out of 100.

The utility of this model lies in its ability to perform a complete analysis of an IS and of the human–machine interface or "infosphere", which combines technology and ethics. It represents, therefore, a tool used to translate between technical language and ethical language. Ethical modeling of a "human" IS must pass through this transformation and this genre change so as to go from being universal, abstract and general to practical, concrete and specific.

On the basis of this reasoning, we searched for the ideal representation that reconciles philosophy of thought and mathematical rigor so as to construct an algorithm for resolving ethical problems able to quantify this "ethical score" of acceptable contingency.

To accomplish this, we turned to Leonardo da Vinci and his Vitruvian Man (or *Homo Universalis*), which was the result of a study carried out on the proportions of the human body around 1492. This anatomical representation – possessing strong symbolic significance – is the synthesis of anatomic and scientific research. Desiring to show the unity of human proportions, this drawing represents the dual motion of the human body. This mobility allows for the extent of the symbolic value of this diagram. It does not attempt to show the ideal Man but instead displays the geometric model of a "normal" human, which is set within a circle and a square (see Figure 3.1). The circle is the symbol of Nature (macrocosm), infinity, the sky, universality and spirituality. The square represents the ancestral image of the Earth (microcosm), practicality and reason. The Temple is the intermediary between the self and the other, between the top and the bottom. Via the Temple, we obtain the "square of the circle", representing the inseparable union of the spirit and the matter. The Vitruvian Man is within this Temple and he reaches the "square of the circle", therefore, he is the said temple.

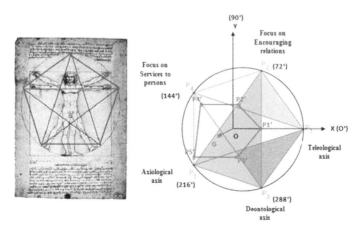

Figure 3.1. *Geometric representations integrated within the sketch of the Vitruvian Man. For a color version of the figure, see www.iste.co.uk/beranger/ethics.zip*

Thus for Leonardo da Vinci, the Vitruvian Man is an innate link between the divine spirit and matter. The balanced proportions and mathematical perfection of the drawing result in a representation of the Vitruvian Man as a pentagram within a circle (see blue section of Figure 3.1).

By joining each of the five points of the pentagram, we obtain a pentagon (see purple section of Figure 3.1). This shape contributes to the creation of a perfect geometric shape or golden ratio. In fact, the ratio between one of the sides of the pentagram and one of the sides of the pentagon is equal to $1.618034 = (1 + \sqrt{5})/2 = Phi = \varphi$, which is the golden ratio[2].

Since antiquity, for many Roman, Jewish and Egyptian researchers, artists, mathematicians and philosophers, this geometric representation has symbolized universal perfection and harmony in the visible world. For the Greeks, and mainly for the Pythagorean school that Plato was a student of, this figure illustrates esthetic, geometric and philosophical perfection. It constitutes the link between abstract reflection and specific practices. Regardless of its interpretation throughout history, it has always been perceived as unifying, synonymous with knowledge, meaning and thus contingency.

Our model is, therefore, based on the geometric representation of a pentagon composed of the five criteria of our model (see the green section of Figure 3.2):

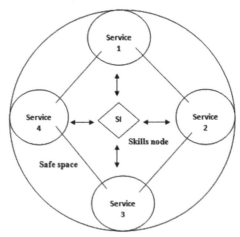

Figure 3.2. *Implementation structure of an information system*

2 The letter Phi can be used in philosophy as in physics. It brings together both fields: in the former describing philosophy and values of perfection, and in the latter describing perfect geometric proportions.

– P1: the teleological axis;

– P2: the focus on encouraging relations;

– P3: the deontological axis;

– P4: the axiological axis;

– P5: the focus on services to persons.

We describe our "ethical score of acceptable contingency" as the average of the sum of the unitary scores of each of the five parameters (P1', P2', P3', P4' and P5'):

Ethical score of acceptable contingency = (P1'+ P2'+ P3'+ P4'+ P5')/5

We calculate standard deviation of this score so as to analyze the spread and possible homogeneity between the five axes.

After having inserted this pentagon into a trigonometric circle and having considered the teleological axis and the center O of the figure to be the *x*-axis, we can therefore infer the presence of a *y*-axis from an orthonormal frame. Using this new geometric reference point, we can calculate the coordinates of P1', P2', P3', P4' and P5' (see the red section of Figure 3.1).

To accomplish this, we use the following formulae:

– *P1'*:

　　XP1' = unitary score of P1' × COS 0°

　　YP1' = unitary score of P1' × SIN 0°

– *P2'*:

　　XP2' = unitary score of P2' × COS 72°

　　YP2' = unitary score of P2' × SIN 72°

– *P3'*:

　　XP3' = unitary score of P3' × COS 288°

　　YP3' = unitary score of P3' × SIN 288°

– *P4'*:

XP4' = unitary score of P4' × COS 144°

YP4' = unitary score of P4' × SIN 144°

– *P5'*:

XP5' = unitary score of P5' × COS 216°

YP5' = unitary score of P5' × SIN 216°

These five coordinates allow us to calculate the coordinates of the center of gravity (G)[3] of the red polygon. We can then calculate how much this point is skewed toward any of the five variables from the distance OG. This corresponds to a uniformity test between the five variables. Specifically, the shorter the distance OG, the higher the equilibrium around the center O. In contrast, the greater the distance OG, the more the point will be skewed toward one or several of the five axes.

Moreover, the argument of the function, which is the angle GÔX (in degrees), describes the direction of the skew toward one or two axes. This represents the direction of the vector OG.

Thus, the coordinates of the center of gravity (G) of the red polygon are as follows:

XG = (XP1'+ XP2'+ XP3'+ XP4'+ XP5')/5

YG = (YP1' + YP2' + YP3' + YP4' + YP5')/5

The distance to the center is as follows: $OG = \sqrt{(XG^2 + YG^2)}$

The argument GOX is equivalent to:

– if YG ≥ 0, then the angle GOX = arg(OG) = arccos(XG/OG); or

– if YG < 0, then the angle GOX = arg(OG) = 360 – arccos(XG/OG).

Note: "arccos" is the function "arc-cosine", which is the inverse of the cosine function.

---

3 This point is the center of the polygon: Either in physics, called the center of gravity G, or mechanics, the mass balance point around which the weight is evenly distributed.

Distribution of the ethical justifications: The 40 ethical justifications can be classed based on the different categories of real environmental parameters, from which we can establish the following (see Appendix 1):

– 11 correspond to the strategic and methodological sector;

– 11 belong to the organizational and regulatory domain;

– 9 belong to the structural and technological domain;

– 9 correspond to the relational and cultural sector.

It can be seen that all the real environmental parameters are represented homogeneously and in a balanced manner. This can be illustrated as shown in Table 3.4.

Fundamental ethical principles	Political and strategic domain		Organizational and technological domain	
	Strategic and methodological	Relational and cultural	Organizational and regulatory	Structural and technological
Beneficence	4	2	2	2
Justice	4	2	2	2
Autonomy	1	3	3	3
Non-maleficence	2	2	4	2
Total of ethical justifications	11	9	11	9
	20		20	

Table 3.4. *Proportion of real environmental parameters within the fundamental ethical principles*

These justifications are crossed with the four fundamental ethical principles and their associated social values (corresponding to the axiological dimension in our ethical analysis space). After putting our model together, it can be seen that the fundamental ethical principles are grouped into two categories (see Appendix 1):

– The principles that serve only to justify the purposes of the main aims of a healthcare IS:

- "Beneficence", which includes:

– four justifications from the strategic and methodological domain;

– two justifications belonging to the relational and cultural sector;

  – two justifications belonging to the structural and technological sector;

  – two justifications from the organizational and regulatory domain.

- "Justice," which includes

  – four justifications from the strategic and methodological domain;

  – two justifications belonging to the structural and technological sector;

  – two justifications from the organizational and regulatory domain;

  – two justifications belonging to the relational and cultural sector.

- The principles whose sole purpose is to justify the limitations of the main aims of a healthcare IS:

- "Autonomy", which includes:

  – three justifications belonging to the relational and cultural sector;

  – three justifications belonging to the structural and technological sector;

  – three justifications from the organizational and regulatory domain;

  – one justification from the strategic and methodological domain.

- "Non-maleficence", which includes

  – four justifications from the organizational and regulatory domain;

  – two justifications from the strategic and methodological domain;

  – two justifications belonging to the structural and technological sector;

  – two justifications belonging to the relational and cultural sector.

Thus, the justifications of the purposes made up of the principles of beneficence and justice are mainly associated with the teleological axis and therefore with the political and strategic sector of our three-dimensional ethical space.

Conversely, the justifications of the limitations including the principles of autonomy and non-maleficence are mainly linked to the deontological axis and therefore to the organizational and technological sector of our three-dimensional ethical space.

In these conditions, it is perfectly reasonable to suggest that the principles of beneficence and justice include 60% of their respective real environmental parameters of strategic and methodological nature, and of relational and cultural nature.

The same can be said for the principles of autonomy and non-maleficence, which also possess 60% of their respective real environmental parameters of structural and technological nature, and of organizational and regulatory nature.

3.1.2. *Implementation of the model in the general creation of an information system*

We will follow exactly the same process as used to analyze the aims. We will use the second questionnaire including 80 items dedicated to the study of the creation of an IS. Two items will be associated with an action linked to an aim. For example, item 1 of questionnaire 1 on the aims will be described by items 1-1 and 1-2 of questionnaire 2 on the creation of an IS, item 2 will be represented by items 2-1 and 2-2, and so on.

3.2. Presentation of the study's questionnaires

Using publications in the field of anthropology, we have put together a maintenance framework that has allowed us to create semi-structured interviews with relevant stakeholders. By interpreting the data obtained from these interviews, we created first drafts of questionnaires that were given to a small number of healthcare professionals.

This, in turn, allowed us to modify and correct our tool before distributing it to the entirety of the stakeholders chosen to participate in our research.

These questionnaires allow for a database on the understanding of medical information ethics not only by healthcare professionals particularly aware of such issues in IS, but also by the creator of the IS, healthcare users and publishers of IT.

So as to successfully carry out our field research, we had to create three types of questionnaires:

– a questionnaire dedicated to analyzing the perceptions of the stakeholders on the main aims of a healthcare IS. It was distributed to almost all[4] the study stakeholders (see Appendixes 2 and 3);

– a questionnaire dedicated to studying the creation and characteristics of the IS. It was distributed to the creators of the IS involved in the healthcare establishment being studied (see Appendix 4);

– a questionnaire dedicated to analyzing the methods and tools put into place to enable the functioning of the IS. It was only given to the creator of the IS (see Appendix 5).

These three questionnaires allow us to see, among other things:

– if there are any discrepancies between the aims and the final IS;

– if the methods used for the creation, installation and use of an IS are real;

– if there are discrepancies in the ethical perceptions of the different stakeholders involved with the IS;

– if the market demand is in line with the ethical demands of the creators and users of IS.

With the law of March 4, 2002, relative to rights of patients and the quality of the healthcare system, legislators dedicate a certain number of questions that now reveal good practices within a healthcare establishment. These are usually based on the use of medical information, decision-making guidance, sharing of responsibilities, etc. Such ethical approaches justify initiative that need to be made while considering the reality of the situation on the ground. This questionnaire was prepared on the basis of a significant amount of literature review on the subject, as well as from information derived fromsemi-structured interviews with various stakeholders so as to provide better understanding and improve its creation.

These research interviews correspond to a particular face-to-face situation, that is to say a technique for the collection of spoken information that is produced during social interaction between the researcher and researched. They can be considered as an exploratory technique because the aim of the interview is to understand how the individuals being questioned live their situation and what the questions they ask themselves are. For the

4 External users, that is, the healthcare users, were given a simplified version of this questionnaire to facilitate their task.

purpose of our study, we will use a reasonably flexible structure containing several themes, which is where the term "semi-structured" stems from. The interview will have its own dynamic and a set of questions tailored to the individual.

As such, the use of a questionnaire aims to explain a certain number of practices, to identify what individuals are thinking and to locate their position within social space. An essentially explanatory approach is adopted in the search of explanatory factors. Social factors must be treated as real. Explanatory factors must always be sought after.

The methods used for the creation and analysis of the survey are as follows:

– The researcher conducts a semi-structured interview and provides a questionnaire to be completed by the stakeholders.

– The main developer identifies the users said to be "internal" to the IS.

– Spaces used for free responses to questions allow these to be refined or specified.

– The interview with the stakeholders on the state of the IS represents the qualitative aspect of the study.

– Responses are recorded anonymously.

– Comments made by the stakeholders are quoted in between quotation marks and in italics.

– The presence of removed sections of quotes is represented as follows: […].

– Words inserted into quotes so as to give context to the statement will be indicated as follows: [author's comment].

– The majority of the questionnaires are numerically weighted and scored based on the following rules:

- The response "Yes, certainly" is worth 3 points.

- The response "Yes, partly" is worth 2 points.

- The response "No, not really" is worth 1 point.

- The response "No, not at all" is worth 0 points.

– This weighting of the answers will be applied for the two questionnaires dedicated to the analysis of the aims of an IS and its creation.

– The third questionnaire dedicated to studying the methods has its responses weighted more simply: "Yes, completely", "Yes, partly" and "No, not at all" are worth 2, 1 and 0 points, respectively.

– The results will be expressed as a total score out of 100 or as a unitary score out of 3 (or 2 for the third questionnaire).

– We consider that a stakeholder takes an ethical principle into account when a score of more than 66.66 of 100 is attained, which is two-thirds of the maximum score. We will use this number as a reference point because the answer "Yes, partly" is worth 2 of 3 possible points.

3.3. Necessary environmental changes for healthcare information systems: recommendations and actions

For about 20 years, constant development of ICTs in the field of healthcare has been contributing to bringing a new access space to medical data for doctors and patients. Doctors are more and more favorable towords the development of computing tools useful to the practice of medicine. As a result, this establishes a new dimension of medical practice as long as each protagonist can access medical information or perform therapeutic and/or diagnostic procedures via an IS. The Internet does pose several security and technical threats, but it is particularly liable to cause cultural shock as the hospital can no longer consider itself to be the center of the world but instead as a satellite provider. These ICTs then result in questions of a societal nature, and these come not only from the ever-growing number of healthcare users but also from traditional creators of health-related information, such as healthcare professionals.

How can healthcare professionals be better prepared to use these new technologies? How can the development of the concept of sharing or co-management of medical decisions be encouraged? Are IS facilitating elements or are they instead an obstacle to the doctor–patient relationship? Will the Internet soon become key to the automatic management of patients, perhaps almost entirely removing the need for "family" doctors [SCH 09]?. Finally, will the very value of medical secrecy, initially created to protect patients, be put into question?

All these questions lead us to logically consider what the necessary environmental changes will be in order to enable an optimal functioning of IS in hospitals.

Most of the methods for organizational change fail because they do not begin at the beginning, that is to say by basing themselves on the very essence of the singular nature of the situation and the initial aims that result from it. The utility of an IS lies less in its concept than it does in its execution. The issue relates to the almost universal difficulty of obtaining continuous performance. The solution therefore lies in the suitable alignment and creation of the aims of the user and the organization, so as to achieve a genuine change of culture and structure, which is based on performance and information.

From this observation, the statement of an aim must be simple, immediately understandable by all and precisely formulated, without ambiguity and such that no confusion may arise in achieving a unique goal. The recommendations made or actions performed in the context of achieving an aim must be quantifiable. The goal must be linked to a specific and precise context. Knowing that a goal is attainable allows individuals to give themselves the means to reach it. All goals considered to be realistic must include internal data (numeric analyses) and external data (economic or financial context).

What will allow me, specifically, to check that I have achieved my objective? What context is necessary to the correct achievement of the said goal? With whom? When? Where? According to what plan? How is the goal even important? What is the price to pay for achieving this goal (money, time, energy, etc.)? What advantages or disadvantages does achieving this goal create?

Having presented the different ethical problems surrounding the lifecycle of an IS from a theoretical perspective, beginning from its creation, its setup and then its final use, it is now time for us to remove this information in order to put together a summary in the form of questions and reflections on the subject.

In this section, we will address a reflection on what an IS that can satisfy our current and future needs should be. This section will include recommendations and strategies grouped depending on the nature of their content, whether from a structural, technological, methodological, organizational, relational or cultural point of view. This will all contribute to projecting us into a reflection on the construction and use of an ideal computing tool created by private software developers.

Finally, we undertook an opinion survey with healthcare professionals from the "AP-HM", the *Assistance Publique – Hôpitaux de Marseille* or Public Assistance – Hospitals of Marseille. This survey was conducted on the recommendation of systems to be put into place as well as on the new perspectives that our publication has brought.

As we have previously seen, ethical questioning must guide humanity in the management of medical information as well as in the research of the behavior most concurrent with the impression it has of itself. Faced with new knowledge, how are new decisions and choices to be made and how are new liberties to be given while also assigning new responsibilities? How is the most just equilibrium between society's demands and the respect of the individual found? How do we settle this conflict of interest and structure common rules for a pluralistic organization that does not always comprehend the same cultural, moral or philosophical standpoints? Who is the actual owner of medical data? In the sense that propriety lies in the ability to possess and use something in an exclusive and absolute manner restricted only by the rules established by legislation.

All these questions will be answered in this section by presenting the preoccupations and aims of the stakeholders involved with the IS.

This suggestion grid allows for a more pedagogical and specific approach. Indeed, the standards and rules determine which actions are undertaken surrounding a decision. The term "rule" suggests something more concrete, closer to the action. The principle of it is often undetermined and allows for various applications. A rule has a precise content. Rules can be numerous and variable.

This grid can be applied prior to beginning a project intent on creating an IS, allowing it to be better integrated within the organization of the healthcare establishment as well as within the definition of technical constraints.

The aim of this chapter is, therefore, to establish recommendations in the form of actions on the implementation, use, methods and means necessary to ensure optimal operation of the IS in a hospital.

3.3.1. *From a structural and technological perspective*

Practically speaking, three elements are important for the success of the digitization of a radiology department: suitable technical characteristics, taking into account the sequentiality of tasks undertaken within the department, and the use of project management techniques for the implementation process. It is essential that an ergonomic tool that does not require much knowledge or training to be recommended for general use.

The creation of an IS depends on technical factors more or less associated with each other, whose complexity requires the need for a "computer scientist–networkengineer" whose role is to respond to the requirements listed below while ensuring their adequacy with the existing computing setup or a setup in the process of being built [COU 04]:

– addressing the procedures;

– security of the computer network;

– adapted topology of the IS;

– number of users;

– applications (intranet, database server, etc.);

– data type (data weight) and flow (data quantity);

– ability to bring together the procedures of different developers.

Globally, the integration of an IS can be achieved via the intermediary of an "integrated" offer proposed by a single developer, or assembling elements from different developers. In the first case, we refer to a single-developer system in which the interactions are regulated by proprietary protocols whereas the second refers to a multi-developer solution, based on the use of standards such as DICOM or IHM (see Table 3.5).

Generally speaking, most developers (notably PACS – Picture Archiving and Communication System) have turned toward the second approach "as indicated by their active collaboration with work to standardize DICOM and IHE" [GIB 05].

		Single-developer approach	Multi-developer approach
For the user	*Advantages*	– Potentially more effective solution	– Liberty to choose suppliers
			– Choice of the best of the generation ("best of breed") for each component
			– Sustainability and scalability of the solution
	Disadvantages	– Disparate levels of quality	– Must manage the issue of integration themselves
		– Difficult to improve the system	
For the entrepreneur	*Advantages*	– Flexibility with regard to technical innovations	– Ability to integrate with a large number of suppliers
		– Captive customers	– Sustainability and low costs of the solution
		– Ability to cover functional aspects not part of their main skill set	
	Disadvantages	– Risks lacking being competitive, or not satisfying customer expectations (who often desire multi-developer solutions)	– All customers are free to choose

Table 3.5. *Advantages and disadvantages of single- or multi-developer approaches*

Moreover, according to "Clusif" (Club for French Information Security), to design a coherent security system, the following are essential [BAL 06]:

– now the entire IT application is organized around the workflow, that is to say the professional work process: welcome, review, interpretation, reporting, dissemination clinicians, archiving, etc. [DEC 06];

– managing security, notably by analyzing incidents and rapidly responding to emergent risks, by adapting to the evolution of threats, etc.;

– being familiar with all the installed hardware;

– identifying all access and communication points of the information system;

– covering a wider perimeter than that dictated by the premises of the organization;

– having a backup system and a continuity plan.

In addition, in the light of different interviews conducted with "internal" users of healthcare establishments, it appears that the structural setup of an IS is a compromise between:

– a decentralized network: location of substantial communication. There is no resulting leader and its layout is not particularly efficient. It usually results in a greater number of errors. For this reason, adding an adapted and high-performanceIS renders this setup most adequate for taking patients into care within a healthcare establishment. This type of structure is appreciated by all its members because they feel involved in actions undertaken; and

– a "combined" model that consists of converting different specific knowledge into a more complex system of specific knowledge, able to be offered to many individuals within and outside the organization. It includes collection, processing, validation, testing and distribution of knowledge. This architecture allows for excellent ICT integration and use.

This new implementation structure will be made up of a "safe space" representing the geographical location where the different services involved in the healthcare establishment interact. The IS will be located at the center of this space. An informal communication system is put in place between the IS and the services that make up this space. The interdisciplinarity is therefore represented by spontaneous and flexible links established between the different skills necessary to the functioning of the formal part of the organization. These links form a "skills node" between the IS and the services involved.

The flows of the operational work of health professionals travel in this space. The data integrated within the organization of this area can be stored and then analyzed in the central IS of the governing body of the healthcare establishment via information reporting. This IS aims to centralize the information such that the activities of the different nodes that make up the healthcare establishment can be regulated and controlled (see Figure 3.2).

The implementation of an IS must be accompanied by the setup of a physical space allowing for the creation of informal networks. This includes installation of intranets, newsletters or any other methods allowing individuals to inform themselves and share their working techniques with the IS.

Ultimately, the recommendations for this sector can be summarized as given in Table 3.6.

20 Actions
– Establish an IT setup that is suitable and coherent with the organization of healthcare
– Have a backup system, an emergency plan and a continuity plan for the IS
– Identify and prepare for potential IT threats
– Be familiar with all installed hardware so as to create a suitable guidance policy
– Cover a wider perimeter than that dictated by the premises of the organization
– Identify and order all the challenges and risks associated with the IS
– Install the IS at the center of the space that makes up the services involved in the management of targeted treatments
– Obtain data with the use of a standardized interface adapted to the user (doctor or patient)
– Use reliable knowledge (business rules, computational algorithms) originating from its own knowledge base or from other known databases
– Be able to communicate the results of applying rules to patient data to the user in the form of alerts, recommendations, reminders, etc. as well as to its applied environment (prescription system, digitized patient records, etc.)
– Construct a technical IS that is comprehensible, useful and easy to use (according to users)
– Embed uniform technological reference solutions that are in line with any regulations in effect (DICOM, HL7, etc.)
– Create a flexible, adaptable and evolving IS
– Insert procedures within the IS that allow patient identity to be kept anonymous
– Include good practice protocols within the IT setup
– Set up supervision and surveillance mechanisms
– Ensure that the IS is monitoredsuch that an alarm can be raised in case of malfunction
– Install a system for exporting data (for the State or its governing bodies)
– Install a system for exporting epidemiologic data of public health (for the State or its governing bodies)
– Add internal human resources charged with regularly monitoring the IS

Table 3.6. *Recommendations for the structural and technological domain*

Finally, such procedures must be accompanied by strategic and methodological modifications and adjustments.

3.3.2. *From a strategic and methodological perspective*

Ethics have become an essential element in the way in which IS engineers approach the creation and use of such a tool. Nowadays, there are many who adopt an approach including the following:

– defining the conditions of sustainability and development of the IS;

– listing the risks, challenges and dangers that the tool might face;

– constructing a system of values unique to the IS and its users;

– creating norms and a code of conduct for its usage;

– promoting and installing the entirety of the IT setup.

The procedure that we will describe here allows for an ethical dimension to be integrated with the use of medical information by a healthcare professional. This methodological aspect is built on interdisciplinary considerations, as they model the reality of patient care most closely. This procedure has been greatly influenced by the article of Saint-Arnaud entitled "The reflective and interdisciplinary approach to healthcare ethics: a tool for the integration of knowledge and practices" [SAI 07].

This is made up of 10 distinct stages:

– *Identifying the ethical and medical challenges faced*: with regard to identifying the challenges in question, the stakeholders involved are invited to describe their perceptions of the problems that they are faced with. Ethical issues are often recognizable due to the emotions they cause. These challenges will be integrated into the learning objectives of the IS for timetable planning, general planning and organizational strategy.

– *Collecting information on the facts of the situation, and identifying those that are relevant to the challenges to be analyzed*: ethical decisions do not arise from facts, but they must nonetheless be built on a correct understanding of the facts so as to be pertinent and realistic. It is therefore necessary to research and synthesize information of different origins (therapeutic, psychological, etc.) that surrounds these issues.

– *Listing the individuals involved, their missions and their goals*: the individuals involved in taking the patient into care must be identified and those that referred the patients to them must be found such that dialogue between the various parties is facilitated.

The proper progress of a project must pass by defining and identifying the roles of each entity involved with the project management and implementation. A project group bringing together the project managers must as such meet when necessary so as to resolve the conflict linked to the requirements of the proceeding or coordination of the project. This description of tasks must be done for the legitimacy of the IS to be recognized.

– *Identifying the different possible options in terms of interventions*: listing the decisions or stages that lead to the issue, but also examining the possible options considering the issue in question. These options are suggested by the parties involved, argued on and discussed in multidisciplinary encounters. During this stage, it is necessary to identify the obstacles to this ethical learning and to develop methods for overcoming them.

– *Identifying the legal, social, deontological, institutional and governmental norms and constraints*: at this stage, the norms and constraints that are relevant to the study context are to be identified. The norms give details on what behaviors are or are not accepted. They represent the institutional memory of standards regulating society's conduct and aid ethical decision-making. Nonetheless, they can also be representative of obstacles to ethical intervention in some cases, when the constraints imposed conflict with requirements of other standards or with the moral obligations created by ethical principles.

– *Identifying the guidelines, case studies, ethical principles and theories that can provide tools for analyzing and reducing the number of errors of the situation in question*: these ethical principles and theories reveal ethical competence that itself arises from the field of philosophy. This is a dialectical approach, which examines the possible options based on the facts and appropriate ethical reference points. In this approach, the beneficiary is associated with reflection and the choice of the solution by defaultso as to suggest path or compromises that respect the ethical norms, principles and views and will to agreement. For us at least, the principles that represent the expression of a deontological theory constitute one of the components of the ethical dimension of decision-making. They must be associated with the ethical issues that correspond to the attitudes and feelings of the stakeholders based on theories of virtue, the relationship between healer and healed based on the ethics of "caring" or the theories of fundamental rights based on nature or reason [5] as seen throughout the course of our study.

– *Analyzing by establishing links between relevant facts and appropriate ethical reference points bearing the problematic situation in mind*: the ethical principles in question are those of autonomy, beneficence, non-maleficence and justice, as previously integrated within our ethical model. They must be explained based on the purpose of the healthcare sector and the problematic situations that these encounter. They imply a moral obligation for healthcare professionals.

– *Suggesting an ethically acceptable framework and discussing this with the parties concerned to reach consensus on a code of ethics to be instigated*: it is in this phase that the four fundamental ethical principles of our conceptual framework enter into play. This stage is aimed at avoiding that power games develop and that the code does not serve any interest other than that of the patient's well-being.

– *Implementing the code of ethics*: this ethical reference document has the aim of advising healthcare professionals as well as the creator of the IS to integrate ethical behaviors into their daily work with the system. This code is therefore relevant to all the internal users as well as the professionals that are involved in the creation and implementation of the IS. For this reason, it is necessary to integrate these recommendations within the existing procedures.

– *Evaluating the intervention and documenting it in a report*: this final step addresses the assessment and drafting of a report that serves as the memory of the healthcare establishment using the code of ethics. Over time, this will come to make up the organization's own philosophy. Human resources–related mechanisms can be used for this purpose, as well as for supervision and assessment of the staff so as to ensure monitoring and assessment of individual contributions to teaching the IS. Supervising the implementation of an IS requires simultaneous implementation of a schedule designed to receive feedback on a daily basis such that all users can express any difficulties they face.

Furthermore, according to the "Clusif", the control and protection of information requires action such as:

– identifying vulnerabilities, both those relative to technology but also those relating to various human, organizational or physical factors used by the organization;

---

5 Theories that are based on human relationships, a sensitivity with regard to the feelings, attitudes and values of the recipients, suitable response to the perceived needs, which generates the duties and responsibilities.

– selecting which information requires protection;

– defining and assessing acceptable risk levels, bearing in mind their consequences as well as the costs and constraints resulting from reducing them;

– ensuring that all measures put into place are proportional to the value of the information in question, both in terms of acceptable costs but also such that communication possibilities are not endangered and without imposing disproportionate constraints on users;

– opting for a comprehensive and consistent approach;

– stopping classification rules of information and the terms ofdistribution, operating conditions, storage and destruction;

– not limiting oneself to protecting information exclusively within the organization but also any information that enters, exits or orbits it. [BAL 06]

Furthermore, the quality of the IT tool is a direct result of specifically adapted management combined with an established decision process. For this reason, we believe it is important for certain key reflective elements and techniques that contribute to improving the quality of an IS to be highlighted:

– supplier choices;

– role distribution;

– cost distribution;

– security and access rights monitoring;

– data integration;

– data backup;

– network monitoring;

– hardware monitoring;

– user assistance and ease of use;

– IT department's ensured technical competence;

– study, research and development implementation.

Finally, this new strategic and methodological focus contributes to increasing the dissemination of internal information while making it more relevant to the coordination of collective patient healthcare within a healthcare establishment.

For this reason, IS-related methods must evolve so as to include and return reliable and relevant medical information while tending toward greater interconnectivity of information, resulting in a decisive IT network and excellent collective performance.

Ultimately, the recommendations and suggested courses of action for this sector can be summarized as shown in Table 3.7.

20 Actions
– Establish an adapted management, accompanied by an established decision-making process
– Identify the ethical and medical challenges associated with patient rights in the IS
– List patient needs relating to the nature, quality and quantity of medical information shared by the IS
– Collect, identify and (statistically) analyze information of facts relevant to taking patients into care
– List the individuals affected by the IS, their missions, their goals and their levels of access to medical information
– Calculate the impact of the IS on the daily workload of healthcare professionals
– Enforce a rigorous and evolving security policy
– Identify the different possible options for the healthcare professional to act on the IS
– Ensure patient participation in the choice of the medical decision that will be taken
– Transmit as much concise and essential information as possible to the patient via the IS
– Establish links between relevant facts and the IS' ethical reference points that are applicable to the patient
– Suggest a reasonable ethical framework on the acquisition and accessibility criteria of medical information by the patient
– Implement a code of ethics on the handling of medical data around the patient
– Assess healthcare interventions and publically document them using reports
– Carry out a retrospective study on the evolution of the methods put into place compared to the initially envisaged objectives
– Create an information master plan of the IS based on the existing version
– Develop a comprehensive project methodology centered on the IS
– Create a steering committee for the IS
– Create a monitoring committee for the IS
– Use planning techniques (Pert, Gantt, History Network, MPM, dashboards, activity indicators and assessment criteria)

Table 3.7. *Recommendations for the strategic and methodological domain*

Here, it can be clearly seen that the challenges to IS are significant. Our passive IS require tending toward greater interoperability with the real world. It is for this reason that ICTs require greater involvement in organization and regulations in these conditions.

3.3.3. *From an organizational and regulatory perspective*

Organizations allow for individual behaviors to tend toward a common goal. They register their existence and activity within an environment undergoing continual change. ICTs cause organizational changes at the level of technological structures and human management methods. This refers to the socio-technical school of thought emerging from the research conducted by Eric Trist at the Tavistock Institute of London and by Einar Thorsrud in Norway.

It is based on the observation the group work depends on both technology and group behavior. An organization is at once a social and a technical system, which means that it is a socio-technical system. Creating an information system is a mutual transformation process wherein organization and technology are simultaneously transformed during the implementation process. This process is part of a greater strategy leading to the transformation of an organization. According to the socio-technological approach [BER 01], this is a mutual transformation process. The IS should contribute to the transformation of primary and secondary tasks.

In these conditions, a specific action plan must be put in place so that various stakeholders can work together to solve the issues raised by adjusting the organization to its environment.

Within healthcare establishments, the IS are on the whole created to exchange relevant information in order to prepare for various activities, such as providing the best possible patient care or publishing and distributing information to patients. They must contribute to organizational decisions, such as medical or long-term management decisions. In this way, information tools have the purpose of improving the consistency of the institution: their implementation implies a "precise analysis of the organization of different processes concurrent to the conducting of an imaging exam and the transmission of its results (workflows)" [BRU 07]. Henceforth, all of the computer application is organized around the workflow, that is to say, the professional work process: reception, examination, interpretation, report, distribution to clinicians, archiving, etc. [DEC 06].

According to Abbad [ABB 01], "driving change only makes sense in the search of a new organization that places mankind at the center of its concerns". The keys to this change rely on organization and management. This organization allows for unsuitable life or work attitudes to be corrected and refined as well as to manage costs. It is studied from the point of view of different parameters that it covers: its borders, structure, specialization, distribution of power, coordination methods, mission, identity, culture, etc.

Moreover, all activities of an organization are just a chain of interactions and communications processes: they are the oil that allows for the organizational cogs to function. Generally speaking, the science of organization represents an interaction between four forces: technology, activities, individuals and structure (see Figure 3.3).

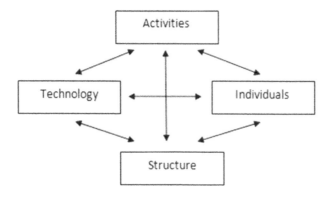

Figure 3.3. *Forces that characterize organization*

Architecture of an IS must be relevant to the organization of the healthcare structure already in place. To accomplish this, we deem it necessary to cover the various aspects of an IS organization:

– *Functional*: the IS comprises software applications considered to be "vertical", which is to say that they serve to respond to overall requirements, and of professionals, who add technical value.

– *Integrational*: this is the driver of communication. The aim here is to have all interfaces converge in a single point. These interfaces make up the foundation of the IS. This also includes integration of PACSs or other medical storage systems within the existing IS, whether at departmental level or for the whole establishment.

An IS is a setup that evolves across time and whose interfaces are not always defined by standards. When choosing a product (notably a PACS), it is extremely important to be vigilant and choose the product that conforms the most to current standards (such as DICOM and HL-7 in medicine). It is essential to choose a developer that is able to integrate the setup with the IS.

– *Consolidation*: the creator of the IS must identify the source of reference information.

– *Distribution*: this can be illustrated by an intranet. This transmission of information is characterized by:

- standardization of the user interface;

- technical flexibility;

- a system unaffected by the number of accessed servers and the number of applications used;

- adaptability;

- a system unaffected by the physical location of servers;

- an array of services allowing for messaging, discussion forums, database access, image/video visualization, audio transfer, etc. to be combined.

– *Coordination*: this is resource management. Beyond the vertical division of services within the healthcare establishment and the transversal division by general use tools (such as the Internet messaging or the Internet access), there is space for tools that partially cross both axes, which are known as "virtual communities".

Coordination refers to a setup of fluid virtual structures based on relational and expertise-based networks, and on intelligent use of human and technical resources. A database server can be considered to be an active member of a study group.

– *Cooperation*: this has the aim of:

- obtaining better project organization and management;

- possessing as much available knowledge as possible;

- harmonizing decisions (coordination and synchronization);

- contributing to the integration and control of many trades involved in the project (reciprocal learning).

The collective action of an organization requires to be based around task specialization [PED 04] in which each individual does that which he or she is best at. This model can work only if a function, that of coordination and interrelational communication, is constantly active.

According to the *Comité Consultatif National d'Ethique* or National Ethics Consultation Committee (CCNE), the spirit of cooperation is a key measure of success of a new approach. The users of an IS must feel involved and integrate as much in the creation of protocols as in the coordination of working groups.

– *Federative level*: This corresponds to an opening onto the world and expansion toward it.

Furthermore, all large human organizations require numerous individuals in different categories work together coherently while following any applicable rules or laws. This is all the more true for a healthcare establishment in which the terms "multiplicity" and "multi-professionalism" are key words. According to Fessler and Grémy [FES 01], the collective characteristics involve defining and respecting common goals, rules of life, duties and rights.

In this sense, ethics leads to many definitions. In these conditions, the creation and use of an IS must answer to three "keys" at the organizational level of a healthcare establishment:

– *The first key* corresponds to the shared belief that an IS,above everythingelse,is a tool for social coherence within the institution.

– *The second key* constitutes a veritable democratic debate between all the stakeholders involved. Such a debate is democratic both due to the transparency of its content and due to the reliable manner in which it is led. It involves multi-professional reflection and a process that defines, accepts and puts the collective goals into action. It therefore requires common semantics, a timetable of the specific goals that have to be carried out successively, the rights and duties to access treatment results, and appropriate regulations.

Such agreements and procedures cannot be obtained without mutual respect between the different stakeholders directly or indirectly involved with the IS. They cannot, therefore, be arrived at without frank and honest discussions theoretically leading to mutual trust.

– *The third key* represents the belief that all have a common obligation that transcends their individual professional ambitions: to construct a structure and system centered on the patient, within which healthcare quality, respect for others and consideration of patient desires and wishes are permanent and simultaneously considered by all stakeholders.

Clearly, the collective preoccupations of a healthcare establishment have a significant impact on the creation, setup and use of an IS. Certain tools and specific methods can be useful for the execution of these "keys", such as

– auditing systems;

– referral centers for good information practices;

– specific ethical charter issuance;

– ethical information committees for resolving specific cases;

– organization of intranet forums;

– models allowing for future issues to be anticipated;

– multidisciplinary teams to develop the guidelines, procedures and policies to be implemented;

– a liaison position to support the management and transmission of knowledge and use of the IS;

– a scope statement considering the current setup of the healthcare establishment, allowing it to evolve in such a way that it mirrors the IS[6];

– a training plan for the project management and the project owner to have a common language and develop a project method, conducting interviews or meetings, etc.;

– a well-identified project manager who is supported by the management offices. It must be an individual convinced that the project will succeed and who believes that the IS will be beneficial. They will motivate the organization and their enthusiasm shall win the support of even the most reluctant. From this point of view, supporting the hierarchy is a kind of legitimacy guarantee;

– services associated with the delivery of the IT product (connecting to the existing network, training, operation).

In the context of an ethical reflection on the organization, collective action cannot be removed from the concept of subsidiarity that designates the same social reality but oriented toward the principle of justice. This notion is therefore based on the values of liberty and responsibility of each individual relative to society. As was highlighted by Patrick Pirazzoli in 1995[7] during a university/industry dialogue on the theme of *the spread of new technology and the analysis of consequences*, "ethics cannot be the business of the structure. It is the responsibility of every individual" [HER 96].

---

6 As highlighted by Le Hen and Lefevre [LEH 04], "no computer system has ever introduced organization or cooperation where they did not exist before".

7 Marketing director of 3M – Medical Imagery.

The importance of personal imitative is therefore highlighted, thus overturning the common concept of authority within the division of labor. The association of the principle of subsidiarity applied to collective action shows that the latter is as much a question of justice as of performance. The purpose of hierarchical authority is to contribute to the common well-being by allowing the individuals concerned to state their skills, abilities and talents, and to reveal their sense of initiative.

However, the improvement of an organization has the aim of creating a convergence of different interests and to orient itself toward the personal fulfillment of individuals. It is therefore responsible for intrinsic elements. According to Hertzberg's theory, when all these intrinsic factors are positive, they have the ability to motivate individuals. The efficiency of organization results from rigorous management and regulation, among other things. This hospital management must be applied to information security with the apparition and institutionalization of healthcare data, measure of how optimized the healthcare quality is.

An organization is the harmonious and optimal implementation of means (installations and equipment) and resources (human and financial) so as to carry out a mission and permanently offer services that conform to needs. Its role is to produce goods and expected services for the best price, at the right time.

Ultimately, the success of organization within a healthcare establishment partly relies on the convergence of several factors, such as the assertion of participatory management, service and technology quality, the professionalism of the social body and the management style of human resources. According to the *Comité National de l'Organisation Française* or National Committee of French Organization [8], "the introduction of new techniques will only be successful if it is accompanied by a change deep within management styles, both at the level of the organization of the company and at the level of management methods and the involvement of men at work".

It would be ideal to create a culture said to be "rational and organic", in which a company is split into several result centers each having its own aims and abilities to assess the efficiency of managers. Responsibilities are decentralized from a project manager who takes the expectations and recommendations of the user base into account.

The organizational chart, which defines entities and their superiors, is the centerpiece of an organization. It must be sufficiently stable over time such that commitments and results can be confronted. Hierarchical control is based on past events and responds to malfunctions by adapting processes.

8 Integration of new technologies (April 1998).

Responsibility is decentralized to the project manager and those undertaking the implementation. The staff are molded by working. The qualities expected of them are adaptability (being able to activate many processes), common sense (making decisions in specific cases) and the spirit of responsibility (taking responsibility for decisions without worry).

Ultimately, the recommendations for this sector can be summarized as shown in Table 3.8.

20 Actions
– Create the architecture of the IS following the existing organization of healthcare
– Create a liaison position with the exterior to support the management and transmission of knowledge and use of the IS
– Create a scope statement that takes into account the methods used for distributing medical information via the IS
– Establish a training program allowing for the project management and the project owner to have a common language around the IS
– Apply data storage and hosting rules as instituted by the CNIL
– Apply medical information distribution rules as instituted by the CNIL
– Control the processes put into place for the IS hierarchically
– Deploy specific management techniques and means, accessible to all tiers of the organization and adapted to the decision-making level so as to focus on overall performance
– Establish 24/7 maintenance (maintenance contract)
– Bring preliminary information on the progress of patient healthcare via the IS
– Define the aims of the IS based on the analysis of user needs and the characteristics of the problems faced;
– Integrate the IS in the communications setup so as to become one of the partners and participate in resolving actions (doctor–patient–IS triangulation)
– Install the intranet within the healthcare structure
– Develop an interface for exchanging and sharing information that refers to the IS between the doctor and the patient
– Identify and conceal any personal information that is not required for the patient's care in the IS
– Identify and choose exchanged data to favor inter-service communications
– Carry out structural and organizational changes (organizational charts, superiors, etc.) to accompany the implementation of the IS
– Identify the legal, social, deontological, institutional and governmental norms and constraints
– Apply the legal, social, deontological, institutional and governmental norms and constraints that concern information access

Table 3.8. *Recommendations for the organizational and legislative domain*

Finally, the successful implementation of an IS does not rely only on organizational and legislative characteristics. Relational elements must also be considered in order to develop a true human–IS culture. Thus, the success of an IS fundamentally depends on the quality of the individuals concerned and their management of the tool.

3.3.4. *From a relational and cultural perspective*

The computerization of a healthcare establishment can be seen not only through technical modifications but also by a perturbation of the entirety of human relationships insofar as IT impacts on the main influential factor, that is, information. The technical setup cannot substitute for human relationships, which remain essential for an optimal medical organization. The relationship between technology and behavior when using the system is unpredictable.

According to Oumar Bagayoko et al. [OUM 08], "an individual, being a physical person, is at the heart of issues surrounding information systems".

Any IS can be a source of conflict and disorder between individuals. For this reason, such a process cannot be developed without the consent and approval of senior management and future users of the tool [BER 01]. In fact, all the choices established within a collective IS depend on the views that the creators have of the types of relationships that exist between users, both among them and the managers. These social, ideological and cultural choices have strong ethical connotations: the division of labor and rights between members of staff, conforming to the general aims of the organization.

When an IS is built for a specific category of professionals, considerable risk would be involved in believing that it can be built for them while ignoring the aims and interests of others. This is particularly important in the case of medical information systems, but even more so in management information systems.

Thus, medical specialization is reflective of the omnipresence of the therapeutic act for which human relationship techniques should not be added. It is this approach that we develop throughout this section. The concept of simplicity via relationships goes against the technical belief that complexity is born from the processes within systems.

Communication is ambivalent. It is not perfect, as parts of individual experience cannot be communicated. However, it is the richest element without which life in organized societies, which rely on exchanges, would be inconceivable. Relational communication is a key activity of the life of an organization that we have seen previously. It must continuously guarantee the correct communication of an organizational project with the strategy of human resources and the action plans put into place.

It therefore becomes a fundamental and operational tool for overseeing change, incentivizing social dialogue. This instrument puts at least three parameters into play: its form, its content and its users (producer and consumers).

On the basis of this characteristic, the psychology of communication must articulate three levels, that of

– the subject: its motivations and cognitive and emotional functions;

– interaction and its relational dynamics;

– the social context: its norms, rituals and roles.

This communication is involved in the search for a relational equilibrium favoring cooperation and individual development. It also becomes one of the solutions for breaking the extremely hierarchical partitioning of the structure put into question so as to ensure better patient care.

In these conditions of equilibrium and relational harmony, individual morals are associated with collective reason so as to better resolve medical ethics issues. In the current case, reason is therefore not in opposition to morals, it merely facilitates their expression [MIC 07]. According to Abbad [ABB 01], this social communication is essential for the growth, development and affirmation of each organization. It contributes to nourishing a corporate culture characterized by a system of values, norms and concepts. According to him, the structure of a social dialogue contributes to

– organizing reflection and defining projects;

– enriching and reinforcing inter-professional relations;

– encouraging staff adhesion;

– developing social dialogue.

To interpret the behavior of communicating individuals, we must seek to understand the meaning that they are giving to their actions. This meaning is the product of an interaction between the act of communication and all the other elements that form this context. It results in various parameters such as the physical and sensory environment, spatial organization, temporal data, norms, positioning processes of individuals and the expression of identity, fundamental to "relational quality". Through this complex combination of process criteria, a system is thus formed, which the individual will give meaning to their way of communicating and behaving.

For this reason, the first challenge is the "creation of shared meaning" and organization is an integral part in this situation.

Thus, it is essential to rely on as many multidisciplinary working groups as possible. These allow for a stronger dynamic to be created around the computerization project and facilitate the adherence of a vast user base by involving them in the implementation process.

Moreover, culture is one of the results of a learning process that an individual uses to understand, assimilate and respond to the world around him or her. It is social in nature and is a key process for developing the capacities of individuals and organizations. The IS usually reflect the values of the healthcare establishment. This cultural vision is not only based on knowledge but also involves ideas, skills, values, beliefs, habits, attitudes, wisdom, feelings, self-consciousness and common concepts.

It corresponds to a development process that simultaneously combines ethical reflection and medical practice. Culture gives a specific purpose to the use of technical knowledge by always being specific to a given context. The successful integration and use of an IS must pass by organizational learning perfectly integrated within organizational culture. In effect, this will result in encouraging, rewarding, valuing and using what its members have learnt, both individually and collectively.

Moreover, health facilities still operate by hierarchy. It is therefore essential to convince those at the top (heads of departments, hospital doctors) of the utility of the IS. The adherence of these medical "decision-makers" will have a much greater impact than that of the administration on other users. It is also important to win the trust of the doctors that use the IS on a daily basis by showing them that technical obstacles are reduced. To do this, the organizers must identify their skills, availability and roles; answer their fears, especially in terms of training them to use the IS; and convince them of the usefulness of the IT setup and its potential integration into their daily practices.

From these results, it seems essential to develop mechanisms aiming to institute a collective culture in response to the result and use of the IS. The challenges are, therefore:

– to establish trusting relationships and reinforce interpersonal relationships;

– to create a position of coordinator–host essential for maintaining a cohesive and credible system, especially if it is accessibly by many users;

– to set up mentoring and support systems;

– to create a clear organizational vision of the way in which organizational learning can contribute to capacity, efficiency and durability of the IS within an organization;

– to recognize the importance of cultural dimensions of the use of an IS when developing skills, processes, methods, protocols and tools for patient healthcare;

– to raise staff awareness as to correct ITC use while preserving individual liberty;

– to make individuals handling sensitive information accountable so that they ensure its security [BAL 06];

– to create consensus between the different stakeholders of the structure.

Ultimately, the recommendations for this sector can be illustrated as given in Table 3.9.

20 Actions
– Develop a social communication essential to the growth, development and affirmation of each organization
– Rely as heavily as possible on multidisciplinary work groups (federative and adhesive element)
– Establish a working method accompanied by a counselor and efficient framework around the individuals involved
– Create an IS satisfaction questionnaire to be given to patients

– Put reactive collective learning mechanisms dealing with the errors and risk management linked with the IS in place

– Conduct a patient satisfaction survey on the choice and quality of shared information

– Establish training action groups (initial/continuous), lessons, workshops and practicing communities dedicated to the correct use of the IS

– Carry out learning assessments of the healthcare professionals on individual use of the IS

– Make patients aware of their responsibilities and roles within the healthcare system

– Ensure the patient's participation in the making of medical decisions by allowing the better access to and explanation of the information delivered by the IS

– Set up a technical, medical, organizational and economic expertise unit to accompany the installation and operation of the IS

– Create a coordinator/host position essential for maintaining cohesion and credibility of the entire setup

– Set up mentoring and support systems

– Make patients aware of the information transmitted by the IS and help them understand it

– Convince those in charge (heads of departments, hospital doctors) of the utility of the IS

– Explain how personal medical data are used to patients

– Explain in what formats personal medical data are created, distributed and stored to patients

– Develop training and awareness programs so as to ensure the best use and understanding of the system– Explain personal medical data rights to patients

– Hold awareness days

Table 3.9. *Recommendations for the relational and cultural domain*

On the basis of these recommendations and the ethical issues surrounding the environment of an IS, we can establish a code of ethics on the implementation and use of a healthcare IS.

3.4. Creating an ethical charter on the "ideal" computational tool for a healthcare establishment

Health facilities can no longer ignore the constant changes made by ICT in individual behaviors, in labor relations and in medicinal practices. In these conditions, we deemed it essential to establish a code of ethics that covers all issues in this context in perpetual evolution.

Thus, "the quality of the capture, storage and use of medical data in healthcare establishments, on one hand, and the quality of tools provided by the industry to meet these quality aims, on the other hand, should be an explicit requirement established in an ethical charter on the subject" [OUM 08].

The aim of this chapter is, therefore, to develop perspectives on the "ideal" IS whose purpose is care management in cancer and meeting ethical concerns that industry would have to build in the near future.

We therefore announce the birth of an ethical charter on the creation and use of a "human-faced" IS, which aims to apply and adapt the rights and fundamental principles to the context of healthcare establishments, by placing the patient and the healthcare professional at the center of the IT setup. This charter must therefore address the moral side of individual behaviors as compared to oneself and those around one in a professional context. From this perspective, the used semantic concept will be that of the morals applied to this professional and medical environment surrounding the IS.

3.4.1. Missions and areas of action

This charter aims to give all of the stakeholders involved with the IS an ethical and legal foundation as well as tools that are useful or necessary for the creation, implementation and correct use of the system. It serves as a reference and a behavioral guide for individual decisions taken in good faith. It allows for the pitfalls of extended and enlarged regulations created when faced with the introduction of ICT in healthcare, by primarily calling on the professional conscience and knowledge of each individual, and protecting the individual liberties of all internal and external users of the healthcare establishment.

This charter intervenes in two main ways:

– as a reminder of the principles that must usually regulate the correct performance of a profession such as to avoid imprudent actions, any lack of oversight or negligence;

– as a reference to be referred to so as to clarify professional challenges and duties.

For these reasons, this charter must be mastered, understood, integrated and applied (as much as is realistically possible) by all staff. The ethical, legal and technical foundations therefore reinforce the mission of healthcare establishments by developing the best professional practices that respect the rights and liberties of all individuals.

Before presenting and explaining this ethical charter, it is useful for the following to be explained:

– The definition of rights, values and principles implies that the citizens and healthcare actors take the responsibilities that fall to them. The social and human notions are not without responsibilities and duties.

– The charter is applicable to the creators and managers of the IS, to healthcare policies and to the users of such systems.

– The charter has the intention to decide on the ethical issues that the technical aspects of the IS create.

– The charter defines rights, values and principles that are currently valid in the French healthcare system. It will therefore have to be reviewed and modified to be adapted for any evolutions or developments of scientific and technological knowledge on the subject.

– The ethical principles are integrated within social and human values and, as such, must be independently recognized and respected from financial or economic constraints.

– The respect of these ethical principles implies the fulfillment of technical, logistic and organizational as well as professional behavioral requirements. The social values associated with these principles thus demand a comprehensive reform of the mode of operation and use of IS in healthcare with the implementation of standards applied to their creation.

– Each article of the charter contains non-exhaustive definitions and specifications.

– The charter is partly experimental because it is led to evolve over time depending on the development of technologies that will vary and modify ethical issues. It is therefore not a fixed reference and must be adapted based on the events faced by the stakeholders.

In addition, this document is original in that it gives equal importance to events, whether scientific, technical or contextual, and to the ethical benchmarks and standards from the relevant guidelines, principles and theories. From this point of view, disciplinary knowledge is essential to the process as it provides the expertise necessary to assess the healthcare issue in question, the definition of possible interventions and methods developed by the healthcare establishment for its IS. As designed here, this charter is built on partnership in developing solutions that will meet consensus when faced with the goals, achievements and resources concerning healthcare IS, all the while respecting the ethical principles and standards depending on the healthcare situation and context in question. Over the years, it will become an integral part of the philosophy of the healthcare establishment, which will strengthen ties and respect between medical, technical and administrative disciplines. Finally, "the integration of the ethical dimension for use via the procedural framework presented here should be able to prevent a number of ethical issues, dilemmas and conflicts in practice and create what authors in infirmary science call an ethical environment" [STO 04].

3.4.2. *Contents*

We built our ethical charter by relying especially on the statistical study of the perception of cancer care establishments for the major objectives of an ISand the means put in place.

Specifically, we validate and integrate a goal in this charter when it gets a score that is higher than or equal to 2 with all the interviewed stakeholders so as to obtain a global consensus. From this process, we have created the following code of ethics, which consists of 33 ethical recommendations (see Table 3.10).

Among these items, nine are respectively associated with the principles of autonomy, beneficence and non-maleficence; and six relate to the principle of justice.

We can also categorize these by the nature of their associated social values:

− 10 belong to "preserving social links";

− 6 belong to "efficiency";

− 5 belong to "care for persons";

− 5 belong to "precaution";

− 4 belong to "universality";

− 2 belong to "responsibility";

− 1 belongs to "social justice".

1: Aiding medical decision-making as described by the healthcare professional

2: Promoting quality, organization, management and planning of patient healthcare

3: Working for the good of the patient

4: Sharing transparent and accessible information between the patient and the healthcare professional

5: Ensuring the quality and choice of the information transmitted to the patient

6: Improving continued healthcare

7: Sustaining the monitoring of all healthcare activities

8: Establishing legitimacy of rights and data management with the patient

9: Establishing an obligation for the security, integrity, traceability and protection of medical data

10: Evaluating performance and locating areas where action is required by investigating existing faults

11: Efficiently directing the healthcare establishment by managing costs

12: Allowing for epidemiological or statistical analyses

13: Improving and encouraging interactions with actors outside the healthcare establishment

14: Respecting equal access and distribution of information rules regardless of the profile or status of the patient: conceptofsocial justice

15: Sharing the same information and assistance to medical decision-making among all healthcare professionals involved in the patient care

16: Putting the patient back at the center of the decision by giving him or her more comprehensive and rapid medical information: better patient autonomy

17: Ensuring the consent and compliance of the patient

18: Respecting private life and the right to medical secrecy and confidentiality

19: Respecting the right to prior information, rectification and opposition as described in the "Information Technology and Freedom" law

20: Reinforcing the transversality of services within the structure

21: Establishing individual and/or collective use of medical information

22: Equating use of medical information with the organization of the healthcare establishment

23: Adapting technology to the knowledge and know-how of the healthcare professional

24: Institution of a management and guidance policy on the use of medical information

25: Following legislative regulations concerning medical data

26: Respecting storage, hosting and distribution rules as established by the NCIL

27: Maximizing the ethical quality of decisions and the concern for efficiency and organizational effectiveness of the use of medical information

28: Developing an organization oriented toward collective performance

29: Minimizing or eliminating harm caused to patients due to misinformation

30: Possessing certainty that used methods must not exceed that which is necessary to attain desired objectives

31: Reducing useless or poorly calculated risks

32: Ensuring the reliability and continuity of medical data collection

33: Ensuring the technical utility and human merits of the tool

Table 3.10. *Ethical charter on the aims surrounding the creation, implementation and use of a healthcare information system*

In general, the evolution of IT causes considerable repercussions at all levels: it transforms society as a whole and also affects organizations and institutions. It also modifies all social and human interactions. New challenges, and also conflicts, have emerged. They influence its users, condition them and change their worldview. An IS is mainly useful for the relationships it creates: information is the symbol, the key and the requirement of human interaction because it facilitates exchange. However, information can be a nuisance if it represents a desire to dominate and becomes an obstacle to transparency. The challenge is, therefore, to create conditions that are likely to lead to healthy interactions between the legal, political and moral standards, industrial strategies and the protection of patients against possible deviations from the use of their own medical information via new technologies.

The proper use of ICT demands maturity and good upbringing in contrast to the fragility of some neophytes. The culture of use must therefore accompany the implementation of these tools. Too often the rules of common sense are ignored in healthcare ethics in favor of the technical nature of the IS. Therefore, these two opposing worlds – ethics and computing – must learn to coexist together.

Consequently, healthcare establishments must use specific management methods and means, accessible to all layers of the organization, adapted to the decision-making level so as to focus on overall performance. This allows for the IS to be implemented and operated optimally, as the foundation of the structure and the reflections and dialogue of the decision-makers at all levels of the structure. It is from this reflection on environmental parameters of healthcare IS that a driving ethical approach to future changes must be applied to maintain a place for privacy and above all confidence in the doctor–patient relationship. For without medical confidentiality, there can be no medicine. Does Hippocratic medicine not risk losing its essence if inter-human relationships are disrupted? What roles will the patient have in this setup? Will the dematerialization of the doctor–patient relationship not weaken human relationships? These are some of many questions that the ethics applied to ICT will have to answer in the near future.

4

Ethics-Oriented Personalized Medicine

In light of the complexity of many medical situations, the uncertainties into which they lead us and the possibility and, indeed, the requirement of ever-better performances, it is becoming increasingly important to support health professionals in practicing their faculty of discernment. Doctors are also becoming aware of those scenarios that they do not know but can only guess. With their growing knowledge, they are forced to constantly ask themselves: What are the consequences of this new knowledge, and how should we act on it? Do doctors have the moral obligation to satisfy all demands that they are technically able to satisfy?

Experience shows us that in order to resolve these situations, which are difficult for both the patients and those around them, doctors need frameworks to help structure the analysis of the situation and to better understand the issues. The quest for discernment is one of the crucial aims of a dialogue-based approach: a demanding approach whose application is more complicated than simply writing a prescription. Perhaps one of the fundamental goals of ethics is that everyone, every day, should be able to create his/her own way of becoming more human [MAL 00].

In this ethical approach, doctors themselves play a privileged role, witnessing and indeed aiding the progress of science simply by doing their jobs every day. It is up to them to determine their own human values as a frame of reference and to define their own ethical behavior so as to achieve true practical wisdom in their therapeutic activities.

4.1. The evolution of society toward an ethical ideal based on information

The detailed description, given earlier, of the path that leads from data to knowledge and thus to practical wisdom seems crucial in developing a complete understanding of how should the theoretical and practical implications of the information gleaned from NICT in society be evaluated. In view of this observation, we can construct a diagram illustrating the relationship between data, information, knowledge and practical wisdom (Figure 4.1). This illustration shows the evolution of society toward an ethical ideal built around information.

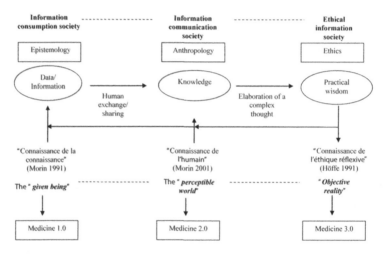

Figure 4.1. *Evolution of an information society using NICT*

Today's society is an information consumption society, in which focus is given to the epistemological aspect, in which data and information as such predominate. In the medium term, this society is likely to transform into an information communication society, centering on human exchange and sharing. In other words, it should be based on links rather than the information "goods" held by people. This anthropological outlook is crucial for the conversion of information into knowledge. In order to remain faithful to the Hippocratic spirit, we need to learn to better understand and know human beings in the digital environment. Indeed, ICT should serve the concrete needs of both carers and patients, whether in a medical, medico-social or human dimension. However, it is possible for knowledge to be incorrectly handled. For this reason, the achievement of "complex thought" leading to a philosophy of solidarity and non-coercion seems crucial in progressing to the third and final stage – a so-called ethical information society. In and of itself, complex thought feeds into reflexive ethics[1], the purpose of which is to lend "legitimacy" to every practice and every standard. The challenge in today's world, therefore, is to rehabilitate the "relational person", by structured networks for cumulative, non-exclusive knowledge exchange. With this goal in mind, we need to develop a controlled ethical framework and new local links based on NICT to create a new art of "living together".

This thought process is guided by ethical values, which serve as both normative and critical markers. By weaving together pieces of knowledge, it weighs in favor of reliance between humans and turns the knowledge into *"practical wisdom"* [RIC 90], which is crucial in making an optimal decision. With practical wisdom, duty itself needs to stand the test of prudent, sensible decision-making, in view of each specific situation. According to Edgar Morin [MOR 04], "the principle of non-separation lends itself to solidarity. Thus, complex thought leads to an ethics of responsibility (relatively autonomous subject-recognition) and solidarity (cogent thought). It leads to an ethics of understanding, which is an ethics of pacification of human relations. It shows that the greater the social complexity, the greater are the freedoms and the greater the need for solidarity to ensure the social link".

In addition, it is noteworthy that this evolution of society also includes the classic three levels of modeling from antiquity, which we can turn into contemporary medical events, namely

– the *"given being"*, represented by the epistemological aspect. It is everything that makes up the world to which humans have indirect or partial access through our senses. This can be denoted as Medicine 1.0, of the past, corresponding to a passive attitude;

– the *"perceptible world"*, illustrated by the anthropological domain centered on human relations. It represents the world of sensations, and measuring is the only data source that can be used to obtain information about the real world or the given being. It can be illustrated as being Medicine 2.0, of today, with a collaborative approach whereby everybody can produce their own expression on the Internet. This constitutes today's society, involving an exchange between people – notably via forums and social networks;

---

1 Hence, ethics is eternally bound *"to remain vigilant in its quest for legitimization, and led to mobilize its reflexive capacity in reference to values"* [HÖF 91].

– the *"objective reality"*, characterized by philosophical thoughts. It corresponds to a space entirely designed by the human mind. It consists of constructing explanatory models expressing the data gleaned from the perceptible world. This last phase can represent Medicine 3.0, of the future, which involves significant ethical dominance. Primarily, it consists of respecting a deontology and human values so that the virtual can integrate harmoniously with the real. This form of medicine must be independent and respectful of the doctor–patient relationship so as to become the guide for our concerns [ETI 12]. This situation is illustrated by our doctor–patient–IS triangulation (as seen previously), in which the machine becomes intelligent, with the capability to manage and perceive meaningful data. Medicine 3.0, designed with ethics and intelligence, opens the way to the improvement of the caregiving relationship, a return to semiology and the establishment of real-time epidemiology based on dialogue between the doctor and the patient.

In addition, on the basis of our neo-Platonic systemic ethical model, we can establish a new representation of knowledge, integrating different levels of modeling depending on the fields of study. Each field of study corresponds to an area of Medicine (see Figure 4.2).

This pyramidal representation tends toward personalized ethical medicine, assisted by NICT, with the following features:

– it increases the sense of taking charge of care;

– it decreases the entropy (degree of disorder) of a healthcare organization.

Our model has shown the final stage of knowledge processing – namely artificial intelligence (AI), where machines can evolve on their own initiative, without human intervention. This step corresponds to the level of the model known as "evolutive virtuality", in which cybernetics[2] is based on ethics in the computosphere[3], tending toward Medicine 4.0 (see Table 4.1).

Here, we again see the concept of the Internet of Things that Joël de Rosnay called 4.0, which pertains to the capacity of intelligent machines to communicate between themselves, independently of human volition. Now

---

2 Science of self-regulating systems, where the focus is not so much on the components themselves as on the ways in which they interact, and above all, their overall behavior is considered. It is a model of the relationship between the elements of a system, by studying information and the principles of interaction.
3 A set of digitized data constituting an information universe and a communication medium, pertaining to the interconnection of computers. It constitutes the support for the informational interconnection between machines.

we are entering into the universe of Isaac Asimov[4], the science-fiction author, who sought to offer a rational view of robots, where one of the fundamental laws is that a machine cannot turn against humans and is merely a possession of its human masters. All the problems caused by robots in Asimov's universe are actually caused by their creators.

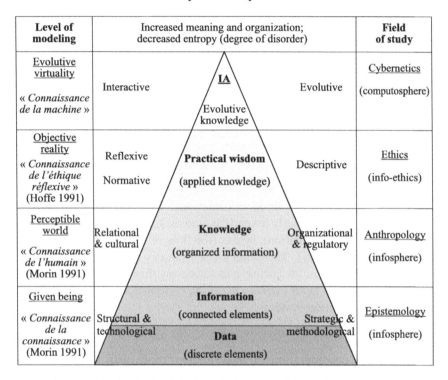

Level of modeling	Increased meaning and organization; decreased entropy (degree of disorder)			Field of study
Evolutive virtuality

« *Connaissance de la machine* » | Interactive | **IA** Evolutive knowledge | Evolutive | Cybernetics

(computosphere) |
| Objective reality

« *Connaissance de l'éthique réflexive* » (Hoffe 1991) | Reflexive

Normative | **Practical wisdom**

(applied knowledge) | Descriptive | Ethics

(info-ethics) |
| Perceptible world

« *Connaissance de l'humain* » (Morin 1991) | Relational & cultural | **Knowledge**

(organized information) | Organizational & regulatory | Anthropology

(infosphere) |
| Given being

« *Connaissance de la connaissance* » (Morin 1991) | Structural & technological | **Information**

(connected elements)

Data

(discrete elements) | Strategic & methodological | Epistemology

(infosphere) |

Figure 4.2. *Analysis of the knowledge pyramid via ethical modeling*

The idea of the computosphere is an interesting idea, because while a numerical solution organizes and always maintains a link with its designers, a computer, on its part, performs computations without the need to report to its designers, because it computes its own evolution.

---

4 "I, Robot" is a compilation of nine science-fiction short stories written by Isaac Asimov, first published by Gnome Press in 1950.

	Environment			
	Infosphere		**Info-ethics**	**Computosphere**
Field of study	Epistemology	Anthropology	Ethics	Cybernetics
Level of modeling	Given being	Perceptible world	Objective reality	Evolutive virtuality
Nature of the knowledge elements	Data/information	Knowledge	Practical wisdom	Artificial intelligence (AI)
Type of Medicine	Medicine 1.0	Medicine 2.0	Medicine 3.0	Medicine 4.0
Time period	Past	Present	Near future	Medium-term future
Nature of the relationship	Man–machine	Man–machine	Inter-human	Inter-machine
Purpose of care management	To do it right	To do it right	To do good	To drive forward its evolution

Table 4.1. *Components characterizing the environment surrounding knowledge*

The computosphere has three informational characteristics, components of technical IS – particularly expert diagnosis-support systems: semantics (the meaning of the information), syntax (the flow of information) and lexicons (the store of information). The semanticist François Rastier [RAS 01], after recapping the positions of Turing and Grice on this subject, proposed six "precepts" conditioning an evolved dialogue system, specifying that they are already used by existing systems:

– objectivity (use of a knowledge base by the system);

– textuality (consideration of interventions more than one sentence in length, whether originating from the system or from the user);

– learning (at least temporary integration of information gleaned from the user's statements);

– questioning (request for further details by the system);

– rectification (suggestion of solutions to the issue posed, when necessary);

– explanation (explanation, by the system, of a response that it has previously given)

Rastier also suggests that the system must be able to independently create a representation of the user it is dealing with, in order to adapt to that user. For their part, users tend to adapt to the system as soon as they understand the fact that they are dealing with a machine. For the designer, this presents the pragmatic advantage of simplifying certain aspects of the dialogue. With regard to cybernetics, it comprises the set of theories on the control and communication processes and the way in which they are regulated in living creatures, in machines and in sociological and economic systems. Its primary object is the study of the interactions between "governing systems" (or control systems) and "governed systems" (or operational systems), under the aegis of feedback processes. This explains the origin of the term "cybernetics": it comes from the Greek word *kubernesis*, which means the action of directing, of governing, in the figurative sense. The organization is active and self-structured, and is dependent and in solidarity with the environment. The organization also reacts on the basis of the information. Information is a stable configuration of symbols, which is both sign and signified. It enables the organization to adapt its behavior at any time by regulation, to transform and to redress a balance so as to preserve an osmotic relationship with the environmental parameters of the infosphere, info-ethics and the computosphere (see Appendix 6).

Thus, the information gives rise to a process of constant adjustment of the organization by channels (the system adapts by accommodation) and codes (the system adapts by assimilation) for communication in relation to a project. In order to represent the organization, Rastier proposes a model comprising a decision-making system, an IS and an operating system.

In addition, this pyramid-shaped illustration involves control filters for each degree of maturation of Medicine and field of study (see Table 4.2):

– visualization/perception filter and design/establishment filter in epistemology (Medicine 1.0);

– cartography and use filters in anthropology (Medicine 2.0);

– effectuation, regulation and legitimization filters in ethics (Medicine 3.0);

– evolution filter in cybernetics (Medicine 4.0).

On the basis of this view of the evolution of our information society, we have constructed our model of ethical analysis applied to NICT. Note that the idea of using mathematics to describe the "perceptible world" appears to have originated with Pythagoras or his disciples [DIX 03].

Level of knowledge	Nature	Content	Function	Filter
Data: discrete elements	Epistemology	Numbers	Categorize	Visualization and perception (What?)
		Codes	Calculate	
		Tables	Collect	
		Databases	Measure	
			Compile	
Information: connected elements	Epistemology	Sentences	Contextualize	Design and establishment (How?)
		Paragraphs	Compare	
		Equations	Organize	
		Concepts	Converse	
		Ideas	Filter	
		Questions	Frame	
		Simple statements	Rank	
Knowledge: organized information	Anthropology	Chapters	Structure	Cartography and usage (Why?)
		Theories	Understand	
		Axioms	Interpret	
		Conceptual frameworks	Evaluate	
		Complex statements	Demolish	
Practical wisdom: applied knowledge	Ethics	Books	Protect	Effectuation, regulation and legitimization (What is best?)
		Paradigms	Incarnate	
		Systems	Adapt	
		Religions/ Beliefs	Synthesize	
		Philosophies	Apply	
		Traditions		
		Principles		
		Truths		
		Schools of thought		
Artificial intelligence (AI): evolutive knowledge	Cybernetics	Black box	Changing	Evolution (How can things be made to change?)
		Analysis software	Expressing	
		Feedback process	Explaining	
		Processing algorithm		

Table 4.2. *Structure of knowledge pyramid*

In summary, a complex thought links epistemology and anthropology in a loop. Epistemology enables us to design anthropology – an essential condition for a philosophical thought, which is integrated into a loop where each step is necessary for the others, culminating in the creation of ethics. Finally, cybernetics relies on info-ethics in developing AI – the evolutive knowledge of expert diagnosis-support systems. In other words, these four macroscopic stages of society can be illustrated by a microscopic approach to an IS, comprising its design, development, usage and evolution.

Finally, if we apply this model to the economy, we see that, for a long time, we have been in stage 3.0: individuals, society and machine exchange intelligent data (the data are intelligent because they are intelligible). Hence, the markets and certain economic and financial mechanisms are already operating in stage 4.0^5, and humans have become the pawns of the system.

This should alert us to the fact that if Medicine 3.0 is not centered on the ethics of inter-human relations, which surround NICT and big data in healthcare, then humans will become dependent on Medicine 4.0, where our existences and our fate will be at the mercy of rational medical decisions made by machines. Thus, we need to call on deontology and human behavior to ensure the confidentiality and protection of personal data. With this in mind, we need an ethical charter that covers design, implementation and usage of the personal data. In our view, proper balancing of these medical big data inevitably requires an ethical reflection about the procedures of control and structuring of these metadata to preserve the primacy of confidentiality and trust toward actors in the field of healthcare, and thus help, to a certain extent, to manage the risks and their deviation. This being the case, it is crucial that the processing of these metadata be governed by an ethical charter covering the sharing of personal data in healthcare. Such an ethical framework would help to strengthen public–private partnerships with a view to investing in predictive healthcare, while preserving the security of personal data in trusted networks.

Finally, the use of big data, alongside the medical advances made, marks the passage from traditional curative medicine to preventive medicine tailored to each individual, on the basis of behavioral data. In order to be fully appreciated, this change of medical paradigm needs to be integrated into medical training, to encourage the analysis of these metadata and interdisciplinary exchanges in this domain. This necessitates the raising of the ethical awareness of the scientific community regarding the study, development and use of big data in the field of healthcare.

---

5 The course taken by oil tankers depends on the trend of the price of crude oil, which is, in part, determined by projections made by computer programs about the cost per barrel.

4.2. The doctor–patient–IS triangulation

Above all, the relationship between a patient and his or her doctor is a human relationship (i.e., intimate) and protected by doctor–patient confidentiality. The patient expresses a need to the doctor, who draws on his or her expertise to establish a diagnosis likely to lead to the resolution of the problem identified. When caring for a patient, the healthcare professionals must take a series of decisions, which finally lead to the therapeutic act. They follow a reasoning process that necessarily involves the notions of knowledge, uncertainty, risk and experience.

In summary, the doctor's intervention is characterized by two procedures: first "heuristic or investigation-based" approaches, which are intended to uncover an objective truth, and second, the so-called "decisional" approaches, which involve comparing the various possible courses of actions and acting on the choice of the best of those options.

For a long time, it has been claimed that diagnostic investigation by medical imaging tears open a breach in the doctor–patient relationship. In the eyes of some people, it contributes to the "mechanical assimilation of the human body, which ignores the three-dimensionality of that body" [BRE 99]. Its use by practitioners leads to a reductionist, dualist and mechanical view, in keeping with the Cartesian tradition. Today, man–machine communication is an important technological, industrial and social challenge. We use the term "machine"[6] to denote any device built to serve specific objectives. A machine may be autonomous or may be controlled by an operator. In order to work, it requires an energy source (electricity, fuel, human energy supplied by a crank handle, etc.) [CHA 11]. The patient, for his or her part, may simultaneously be the subject and the object of the medical practice.

The ethical issues surrounding this dual position cannot be dissociated from the realities that accompany the therapeutic act. Thus, the patient is a "subject who navigates between the individual and the social" [MEY 10]. The difficulty is no longer just one of further improving these performances but also of improving the information exchanges with the human user, adapting to the users' expectations and skills.

---

6 Here, we use the term "machine" in the broadest sense.

In addition, the Internet now forms part of the medical arsenal. Professionals consider this telecommunication tool as an ample and easily accessible reference library. More than half of healthcare professionals use the Internet on a daily basis for their clinical practice, finding a piece of information that they deem generally relevant [LUP 10]. NICT is becoming a complementary tool to the doctor–patient relationship and is likely to become the means of a transformation of that relationship [MÉA 10]. This situation necessitates the growth of a dialogue and human observation between the practitioner and the patient.

Now, linguistics, ethics, cognitive psychology, and social psychology need to be integrated into the computer models, as does computer culture. No longer is the IS merely a set of technological elements; now it represents a way of life, a relational web with personnel who understand and exploit it.

4.2.1. Man–machine interface

Technology is becoming an intermediary that interposes between humans and our environment. In a social and natural context, human relations are being restructured to include technology. The technological world is far from being a counterpoint outside of ourselves but drives us to make progress in our activities, structures our desires and plans, and transforms our relations. We use the term "man–machine interface" to denote the perimeter encapsulating all aspects of the IS that influence the participation of internal and external users in the computerized projects.

It represents all the software and hardware devices that enable a user to communicate with an interactive system. This can be represented by medical decision-support systems (MDSSs)[7], which are integral parts of this technology. The functional architecture of this IS, therefore, comprises a knowledge base, an inference engine or an execution engine and interfaces to facilitate communication between the IS and the user, the patient's file, the prescription support system, etc.

To develop this computer tool, which simulates reasoning and the medical approach, it is necessary to create models of medical practice [BEC 01].

---

7 MDSSs are "computer applications whose purpose is to provide clinicians, at the appropriate place and time, with the information describing a patient's clinical situation, as well as any knowledge appropriate to the situation, correctly filtered and presented, in order to improve the quality of care and patients' health" [LOB 07].

MDSSs must be of immediate assistance to doctors, offering them an overview of each case in their daily practice [CLÉ 02]. Hence, that interface includes the design, implementation and evaluation elements of interactive computer systems. The purpose is to encourage understanding between the people and the other elements of a technological system. By nature, the interface deals both with the machine and the human, as it is on the boundary between them. Hence, the study of an IS must be accompanied by a holistic approach integrating the cognitive, social, organization, structural and environmental parameters.

Aristotle said: "the *raison d'être* of all things lies in their function", meaning that a thing's function and purpose justify its existence.

On the basis of this observation, we are led to wonder about the place of the IS in the doctor–patient relationship. In order to answer this question, there are two possible approaches:

On the one hand, we have the techno-centered approach, in which the machine and its possibilities are the focus of all attention. The user thus needs to adapt to the technological tool. This helps us to consider the technology as a simple diagnosis support for health management.

On the other hand, we have the anthropo-centered approach, which places human and their needs at the center. In this case, the machine has to adapt to the users. With this perspective, the technical tool is a shared decision-support tool taking consideration of the requirements and expectations both of the healthcare professional and of the patient.

The advantage of the latter approach is that it serves users' communicational needs and ways of thinking by uniting with them. This interface must reflect all the human components – even the least rational – that motivate and involve the user in the task at hand. It plays a structuring role for the user, offering comparisons and cultural resistances.

On the basis of our definition and description of the man–machine interface, we feel it is more consistent to speak of it as a mediator between humans who are communicating with one another, an "impedance adaptor" with a machine. The IS is integrated into the actual communication device, becoming one of the partners and participating in the resolution of an action or a problem. It has an entirely separate place in the socialized dialogue between the practitioner and his or her patient.

Contemporary medicine is subject to a new model: "that which involves becoming familiar with large numbers of starting points for the care relationship", as NICT, and digital and medical imaging technologies are becoming part of medical practice. This anthromorphic approach to the identity of the technological tool lends itself to the idea of "triangulation" of the doctor–patient–IS relationship (see Figure 4.3).

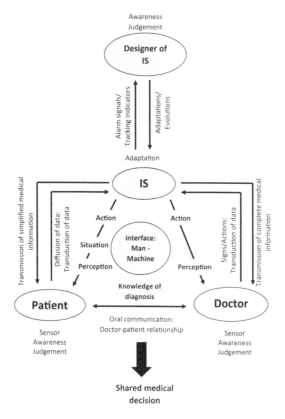

Figure 4.3. *Triangulation of the doctor–patient–IS relationship*

This new arrangement in the carer–patient relationship is somewhat reminiscent of Hippocrates' "three Ms rule", whereby the *Malade*, the *Médecin* and the *Maladie* (the patient, the doctor and the disease) are considered as three non-dissociable entities, no one of which can be discounted. In our triangulation, the disease, which is a part of the overall environment, a background noise in care management, is replaced by the IS. This triangular circulation of medical information, and particular of the digital image, is becoming characteristic of the relationship defining care in radiology [CLÈ 96].

This three-way doctor–patient–IS relationship can be described as follows:

The patient sends data to the IS. Having examined the situation and perceived the patient's ailments, the computer system displays simplified medical information to the patient. On their part, doctors operate the IS by giving it commands, expressed as signs and actions. In turn, the technical tool sends them complete medical information after analyzing the situation and determining what is required. It is noteworthy that the passage of data from the human mind (that of the patient and that of the doctor) to a transcription in digital form for the IS involves a compression of those data[8]. This phenomenon simply means that the actors have reduced the overall quantity of data into a signal, so as to preserve the usefulness of the transmitted data[9].

This natural tendency takes place via notes and codes, and by a dropdown menu listing the possible choices that will be taken into account by the IS. This stage is comparable, in analog terms, to a transduction – that is, when a device converts one physical property (energy or a signal) into another [SCO 10]. This being the case, the patient and the doctor can be characterized as being transducers. Consider the example of a loudspeaker, which transforms an electrical signal into sound.

4.2.2. *Data compression*

This triangulation shows lossy data compression or perceptual encoding, when that loss of fidelity is acceptable. It is guided by research into the way in which individuals perceive the data in question. Thus, we see that this degradation and reduction of the information is at the heart of an ethical

---

8 In computer science and information theory, data compression, source coding or reduction of the bitrate is the process of encrypting the information using fewer bits than are used in the original representation. The design of data compression systems involves finding a balance between different factors, including the compression rate, the distortion caused (if we are dealing with a lossy compression system), and the computational resources needed to compress and decompress the data. We use the term "lossless" to speak of compression algorithms that use statistical redundancy to represent the sender's data more concisely, without any errors.

9 The theoretical context of lossy compression is given by the bitrate-distortion theory. These fields of study were essentially founded by Claude Shannon. The theory of encryption is also linked. The idea of data compression is very strongly linked to statistical inference.

dilemma. Do we or do we not need to voluntarily lose information in order to regulate the doctor–patient–IS triangulation and make it work?

In an attempt to answer this question, we have taken Willard Gibbs' thermodynamic equation, which was repeated in similar terms by Claude Shannon in his information theory: $G = \Delta H \square T\Delta S$.

The Gibbs free energy (G) becomes negative when the entropy (S) is high – that is, when there is a high degree of disorder, disinformation, inexactness or loss associated with the transmission of the data to the IS. On the other hand, if we consider James Clerk Maxwell's model, which uses Gibbs' figures to establish a three-dimensional model of the thermodynamic surface, with the energy (Z), entropy (X) and volume (Y), the energy decreases if the volume or entropy increases (see Figure 4.4).

On this basis, we can put forward the idea that the Gibbs free energy (G) will be high when the entropy is negative and the volume is small. In other words, in our view, this means that a precise process of transduction (characterized by an effective reduction of the data, filtering only those data that are essential and useful) will contribute to the creation of an ordered system with negative entropy.

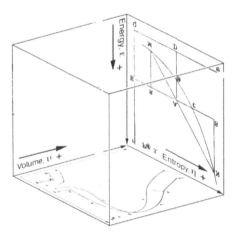

Figure 4.4. *Maxwell's three-dimensional model*

It is noteworthy that this data compression can be considered as a special case of "data differencing", which consists of producing a difference between the data of the source and target. In this case, data compression can be represented by the entropy and "data differencing" by the relative entropy.

4.2.3. *Flexibility and technical adaptation to the users*

In correlation, the doctor and patient are also sensors before and after their data are sent to the IS. Indeed, they gather raw data and transmit them to the IS which, in turn, sends them coded, digitized data. Thus, because of the appropriate intervention of the IS, the oral communication between the healthcare professional and the patient leads to better knowledge of the diagnosis and therefore a shared medical decision arrived at on the basis of human judgments. This last stage is very important in the doctor–patient relationship. It constitutes the moment when the information is of the highest quality in relation to the IS. The information exchanged therefore must lead to a decision that is shared, desired, wanted and based on mutual respect. It requires the presence of two main actors in the therapeutic relationship: first, the doctor, who knows more about treatments and medications, and second, the patient, who is in charge of his or her priorities: only the patient can say what is most important from his or her point of view – particularly in terms of the qualitative and quantitative aspects of life.

In these conditions, we can envisage the presence of alarm signals addressed to the designer of the IS. On the basis of these tracking indicators, the computer scientists can alter the functions of the technological tool in order to adjust the technical actions to the situation at hand. The software designer must, as far as possible, leave the ethical choice to the IS users and, when it is not possible, the ethical hypotheses underlying the algorithms making up those software programs should be made transparent and easy to identify [KRA 11]. With this in mind, the designer must develop an algorithm that is flexible and applicable to the users' ethical requirements. This may lead to new procedures to go along with the IS. It would be appropriate for doctors using the IS to be given training before using the software, receiving information about the situations in which the algorithm was developed by the designer (choice of transparency) and how the software should be used.

We can look at the example of a type of algorithm used in medical imaging technologies, to precisely represent human and biological structures on a computer in order to improve the prospects of diagnosis or treatment of illnesses. One of the numerous ethical issues raised by these algorithms is the risk of producing false-positive[10] and false-negative results[11]. Hence, these algorithms include an essential element of judgment of values and therefore an ethical code. Its designer, therefore, needs to find a compromise between minimizing false-positive results or the number of false-negative results[12].

Inevitably, this compromise will be based on a judgment of values. Generally speaking, designers choose a reasonable value for the threshold or setting of the software. The user bases his or her decisions on the results output by the software, constructed using settings based on ethical hypotheses made by the software designer. Thus, it is important that these ethical hypotheses be similar to those that the user him or herself would make.

Hence, the design of an algorithm must enable the user to choose the settings corresponding most closely to his or her circumstances. It is therefore necessary for the designer of the IS to allow the user to specify the ethical parameters that are to be applied. The designer leaves it up to the user to define the default state of the program [STR 08].

Given these observations, we advocate the application of a "semi-active" means of intervention by the IS:

– the device is engaged automatically after settings have been put in place by the designer and once the doctor using the system has been validated. This is known as a "guard dog" system;

– the auto-callback device supervises the user's behavior and actions. This helps prevent prescription errors or redundant investigation and ensures that the protocols in place are respected;

– the alarm device draws attention to any change in the patient's situation. For example, it might alert users to abnormal biological values or unusual changes to a physiological parameter [SÉR 04].

---

10 The algorithm triggers a counting system (counting of cells, symptoms of a disease, etc.) in a digital environment that is not really there.

11 The algorithm is unable to identify a structure in the image that actually exists.

12 The algorithm designer has to deal with a decision-making process that, in many respects, is similar to that encountered by people who design other technological artifacts. This implies that the value judgments built into an algorithm are similar to those involved in the design processes.

In these conditions, four main functions regarding the IS appear crucial in ensuring the harmony of the doctor–patient–IS triangulation:

– obtaining data via a standardized interface with the environment[13];

– using knowledge (provided in the form of professional rules, computational algorithms) from its own knowledge base or from other databases;

– including an "execution engine" or "inference engine", capable of using a patient's data as input and applying rules expressing knowledge to produce interpretations, classifications, recommendations or information requests as output;

– being able to communicate the result of the application of the rules to the user in the form of alerts, recommendations and reminders, and to the applied environment (prescription system, computerized patient file)[14].

4.2.4. *Shared knowledge engineering*

The development of an IS must begin with the definition of its objectives, based on an analysis of the user requirements and the specifics of the problems at hand. These objectives depend on the users, their actions and their knowledge. The degree of decision support and the functions required also need to be defined. This IS enables us to gain a complete understanding of the patient's status with regard to diagnostic or prognostic decision-making. The aim here is to reduce uncertainty as to the patient's situation. The ultimate goal is to be able to develop a better strategy for taking care of the patient.

In this context, the man–machine interface is a sort of crossroads between the rationality of the IS' technical actions (illustrated by objective reports transcribed in coded form) and the emotional awareness of the doctor and patient (represented by their impressions and judgments, which are rather subjective)[15]. We see a high level of involvement of the patients in

13 Entered by the user, or harvesting of information from a patient file or another application, or information provided directly by the external application invoking the IS.
14 Ideally, the user needs to be able to go on to use the output to advise on a suitable course of action or enter the required data without having to change the working environment.
15 We see a trio with the IS designer when adjustments and evolutions need to be applied to the computer device.

regard to elements of the diagnosis, whether that be written reports, additional examinations undergone or medical records.

Because of patients' deep-seated ambivalence regarding their desire for knowledge, we know that accessing diagnostic elements without accompaniment and support may be problematic for them. Therefore, it seems essential to carry out a prior evaluation of the patients' knowledge and expectations before stating the information. The ability to adapt one's discourse on the basis of patients' emotional expressions also seems to be of fundamental importance [DUT 08]. The increasing appropriation of diagnostic elements by the patients means that the healthcare professional is needed to walk them through everything. On the basis of these considerations, the stressful effects of a technical examination need to be taken into account. It is not enough to merely understand the technical side of things: doctors also need the capacity to establish an attentive relationship with the patient. For instance, radiologists cannot hide behind the highly technical nature of their field of specialty [CLÈ 06]. This need is often touched upon in the existing body of literature, with emphasis being placed identifying a patient's intellectual level or that of those around him or her, rather than falling into the trap of technical discourse whereby all emotion is buried under excessive rationalization [BOI 06]. Only the practitioner can weave together the diagnostic elements with the specific symptoms of the patient's condition. In actual fact, it would be counterproductive from the patients' point of the view to "capitalize" a mass of information about the disease without being able to bring together, organize and single out these elements in connection with the peculiarities of their particular ailment.

Ultimately, this triangulation leads to true engineering of the shared knowledge. It is characterized by a view based on cognitive psychology, the modeling of information-processing devices and the representation of symbolic knowledge with a view to improving medical decision-making. Thus, the IS constitutes a node and a complex relational link between the healthcare actors with emotions, perception and cognition. It represents the "connecting line" in the doctor–patient relationship.

It is therefore on the basis of this new form of organization of healthcare management that the therapeutic action is devised. This interface guides communication on the action and increases the possibility for perception of and action upon the caregiving relationship. It integrates these possibilities and becomes a participant, a partner, in the action. For this reason, for the IS to be pertinent and coherent, it is essential to adapt the evolutionary knowledge and dialogue strategies to the healthcare situation and to the particular users.

Consequently, the ability to understand and visualize the inside of the patient's body from a technical point of view must be accompanied by an exchange and understanding of the perception, the emotional feelings and the individual identity of the person under care. In our view, the harmony and balance of this three-way relationship necessarily involve this exchange and compromise between the rationalizing technique and the human conscience.

4.3. Ethical use of an information system in healthcare

Both the complexity of an organization's IS and the organization's dependence on that system have led to an increase in the number of regulations, good practice guides, protocols and control of that system. Paradoxically, as pointed out by Gérard Ponçon [PON 09][16], the use contexts of ICT in hospitals are very numerous, varied and, often, complex. Thus, it becomes impossible to regulate everything by procedures and control systems, which would quickly become unworkable. For this reason, it is preferable, and more effective, to make the fundamental resources available to each person who is responsible for carrying out their own duties; they can thus adopt the appropriate behavior and make the correct decision in all working situations that they encounter. These resources actually weaken the system that they are supposed to protect. Thus, it is important to give users the responsibility for making correct use of the system and possibly use active or passive protection devices.

In addition, the ethical policy concerning the use of an IS, as determined by an organization, needs to be specific to that organization, shared by all within it and consistent with the morality and deontology of the disciplines practiced in the hospital. It is a response to the complexity of the IS and to the healthcare establishment's dependence upon it. Such an ethical code will lend greater importance and consistency to the healthcare professional's taking responsibility. Medical decision-making, therefore, is part of a multifaceted relational process involving human values and ethical principles. In so-called "simple", therapeutic situations, it does not seem

16 Sector head at the *Direction Informatique et Réseau* (Computer and Networking Directorate) – AP-HM (Public Hospital Service in Marseilles, France).

necessary to consult ethics: deontology, experience and empathy are sufficient, most of the time. Ethics becomes indispensable when the practitioner is faced with conflicting or contrary obligations, when the therapeutic act and the medical decision are not clear-cut, when multiple values and choices are at play simultaneously and when there is confrontation and division. According to Pierre Le Coz [COZ 07], ethics refers to the reflection that arises from the conflict between those values. Following an in-depth study of international literature on bioethics, we can distinguish four universal ethical principles [BEA 01], which are constant from country to country: autonomy, beneficence, non-malfeasance and fairness.

When we apply these four fundamental principles in the doctor–patient–IS triangulation, we see that:

– in keeping with the principle of autonomy, the healthcare professional must be capable of understanding, reasoning, making independent choices and involving the patient in the taking of the medical decision;

– in keeping with the principle of beneficence, the doctor and the IS must contribute to producing good for the care receiver. With this in mind, it is necessary to put in place training and awareness-raising programs to ensure the best possible use is made of the system and to adopt the best *savoir-faire* in relation to the doctor;

– in keeping with the principle of non-malfeasance, the user of the IS must focus fully on his or her tasks to avoid any risks of causing harm to the patient. This essentially involves avoiding unnecessary harm or suffering for the patient;

– in keeping with the principle of fairness, the hospital practitioner must carry out the same actions with the same level of attention, determination and concentration, whoever the patient is. The objective is to share equivalent available resources (time, energy, attention, money, etc.) between all the patients.

Thus, the ethics of using the IS must be shared between all the actors within the structure and must conform to the deontology and professional moral code in force in that establishment. That code of ethics brings consistency to the level of responsibility borne by the healthcare professionals, who can no longer hide behind the checks and formal protocols enacted by the system. They must be able to exercise responsibility in order to do their job as freely as possible, and make reports *a posteriori* without apprehension. This being the case, the design and use of an IS must conform to three "levels of organizational requirements" in a healthcare establishment:

– the *first* corresponds to the shared conviction that an IS, above all, is a social cohesion tool associated with shared concerns among all the actors within the healthcare structure;

– the *second* constitutes a true democratic debate, based on the transparency of its content, trust and mutual respect between all the actors involved;

– the *third* represents the conviction that everyone has a shared obligation – which transcends their respective professional ambitions – to build a structure and a patient-centered system in which quality of care, respect for others and consideration for the patients' needs and wishes are constantly present.

With this in mind, the framework needs to be founded on the four universal ethical principles, which are closely associated with a person's professional conscience, whether that person is a user of information or is in charge of its evolution. The objective is to ensure the quality of the healthcare received by the patient. Finally, the shared medical decision must take account not only of the patients' motivations (emotional, financial, etc.) but also of a certain balance between the well-being of the patient and the good of the society.

In a social and natural context, human relations are being restructured, with the inclusion of technology. The technological world is far from being a counterpoint outside of ourselves but drives us to make progress in our activities, structures our desires and plans, and transforms our relations. Thus, ICT is becoming an intermediary that interposes between humans and our environment. It is therefore from the basis of this new healthcare organization, centered on a doctor–patient–IS triangular partnership, that the therapeutic action is devised. This interface guides communication on the action and increases the possibility for perception of and action on the caregiving relationship. It integrates these possibilities and becomes a participant, a partner, in the action. For this reason, for the IS to be pertinent and coherent, it is essential to adapt the evolutionary knowledge and dialogue strategies to the healthcare situation and to the particular users. Thus, the ethics attached to human emotions constitutes one of the major issues in the shared medical decision. The ability to understand and visualize the inside of the patient's body from a technical point of view must be accompanied by an exchange and understanding of the perception, the emotional feelings and the individual identity of the person under care. In our view, the harmony and balance of this three-way relationship necessarily involve this exchange and compromise between the rationalizing technique and the human conscience.

In addition, the use of the IS has repercussions for all of the actors involved in hospital life: the staff, the patient, the families and the publishers of the IS. This means that the designers of the IS must reflect on multisectorial issues, such as standards, norms, rules and procedures, good practice guides, protocols, the significant judicial implications[17] and the interrelations between the day-to-day use of the IS, in the various working contexts and management thereof.

In conclusion, to develop an IS, it is essential to involve multidisciplinary groups, functioning as an "ad hoc-racy" – that is, an organizational configuration that, in the context of unstable and complex environments, involves pluridisciplinary, specialist and cross-cutting skills, to perform specific tasks [MIN 89]. Therefore, the crucial step is to identify the ethical objectives and the place of the IS in relation to the doctor and the patient within the healthcare organization.

Thus, the ethics of use of an IS is a response to the complexity of the IS and to the dependence of the healthcare establishment on it. That code of ethics brings greater importance and consistency to the level of responsibility borne by the healthcare professional. The ethical policy needs to be specific to that healthcare structure, shared by all within it and consistent with the morality and deontology of the disciplines practiced in the hospital. According to Jacques Lucas, the main objective of setting up an IS within a healthcare structure must be not only to serve the patient, by taking account of his or her concerns but also to "facilitate equality of professional practices by integrating the needs of the healthcare professionals" [LUC 13], whose involvement is fundamentally crucial to the operation of the system. The users cannot hide behind the checks and formal protocols enacted by the system. They must be able to exercise responsibility in order to do their job as freely as possible and make reports *a posteriori* without apprehension. The practitioner realizes that the use of the IS brings with it a responsibility to other people and thinks about the ethical purpose

---

17 Data conservation, hosting, authentication, identification, etc.

of the decisions and actions taken using this tool. With this in mind, the framework needs to be founded upon a number of universal ethical principles, which are closely associated with a person's professional conscience, whether that person is a user of information or is in charge of its evolution.

Healthcare professionals who, in order to discharge their duties to the fullest extent possible, enter the data from patient files into the computer system themselves (rather than delegating the task), therefore, expect excellent user-friendliness from the system[18], an easily grasped user interface (i.e., which does not require any prior training), the ability to access a patient's data quickly and reliably (in emergencies or tense situations), and completely transparent management of the data and of the users (secure messaging) [HER 07]. Such a framework of use necessitates the definition of the conditions of perennity and development of the IS, the inventorying of the risks, issues and dangers with which the tool may have to deal, the construction of a system of values specific to the IS and its users, and the deduction of norms and rules of behavior for the use of the system. Given this observation, it become crucially important for the healthcare professionals:

– not to hide behind the checks and formal protocols enacted by the system;

– to be able to exercise responsibility and do their job properly without reservation;

– to be able to give reports after the fact, without any problems;

– draw on their professional conscience, which is based on the four fundamental ethical principles:

  - autonomy: the user must be capable of comprehension; the patients must be able to be involved in their own care,

  - beneficence: it is important to provide functionally operative services; to develop the best *savoir-faire* and take measures that are beneficial for the quality of the care,

---

18 Cohesion of the order of data entry with the carrying out of medical examination: the writing of initial specifications for the application proves to be a necessary and helpful exercise.

- non-malfeasance: presence of an emergency access device; negligent use may cause harm to the patients,

- fairness: the healthcare structure must be fair toward the healthcare professional to whom it entrusts an activity[19]; the user must operate with the same degree of determination irrespective of who the patient is (here we see the concept of equity).

Ultimately, an IS is designed to be used whenever it may serve the users' needs. The definition of such systems is based on a precise knowledge of what they do and of the diversity of the situations in which they exist.

4.4. Ethics-oriented personalized medicine

Any medical action must be based on a clear, precise goal that determines the patients' moral and social needs in relation to their situation and to the context. This goal gives rise to a strategy and recommendations to serve these healthcare requirements. It evolves, depending on the appropriate strategy. Only by very closely re-examining the human condition, our expectations, choices and fate can we effectively support medical practice and ensure that the patient's dignity is respected, offering fair healthcare. The purpose of a medical action is the "why" – the meaning – as opposed to the "how" – the mechanisms or functions that the action involves. It is taken as a piece of evidence when we resolve to do something or to obtain a result. This evidence enables us to interpret someone else's observed action as "finished:" what does that person want to do? What is the meaning behind his or her act? We can observe purpose not only in the actions of a person but also in the behavior or structure of an organism – even the organism that is believed to be insentient – if we see a certain adaptation of means to an end. Where do our ethical concerns come from? How are we to make the distinction between right and wrong in a medical decision? Such questions help us to examine purpose. Goals do not only govern human activities, they are also the basis for orders, recruiting human efforts to achieve those goals. Therefore, they also define states, duties attached to these states and the qualities or virtues required to successfully fulfill those duties. Questions such as these lead us to re-think medical practice, considering that the performance of a medical action must be based on ethics-oriented personalized medicine, which is founded on modeling, appropriate management and self-evaluation of medical practice.

---

19 The "right to be wrong", depending on his or her skills and abilities.

4.4.1. *Value of management*

The French healthcare system and the professionals who keep it running all day are embroiled in a "maelstrom" of reforms, which is profoundly altering their ways of working, their beliefs and, perhaps, their guiding values. It might even be said that change is the norm, and stability is the exception. In this context, executives' discomfort (real or imagined) is little spoken of and is almost never expressed formally. In the view of the management, evolution is about looking at not only the new ways of organizing the workload but also the relationship that everyone has with the work.

What role is played by evolution in organizations in the full throes of new governance and based on much-maligned managerial models? Does conventional participative management still make sense in healthcare structures? What is the true goal of the medical activities? Questions like these often remain unanswered, for lack of well-founded institutional reflections on the subject of management [COU 06].

Our bibliographical studies on the subject have shown that the establishment of a strategy based on a working method cannot work without the involvement of an advisor and effective framing to guide the people involved in the process. The consultant constructs "a relationship which requires trust on both sides" [PED 04]. The position of this ethical management is as a sort of intermediary – a "halfway:" between the individual and the action, between the person's interaction and the implementation of the action, and between professional life and personal life. Its action is, therefore, significantly important for the actors in the doctor–patient relationship, because it is primarily oriented toward the aim and meaning of a medical action. This inevitably involves a good command and sharing of the information that is circulating.

Hence, the consultant helps optimize the hospital practitioner's predisposition for change, individual performance and organization [PED 04]. The aim of this human supervision is not to look for the "why" of things but rather to optimize the consequences and effects of the actions. However, the ethics lies primarily in the intention behind the acts – the goal they serve.

Therefore, healthcare structures need to use management methods and concrete resources, which are accessible at all levels of the organization, appropriate at the decision level to achieve overall performance. This enables us to construct and optimally operate the information system, based on structure, reflections and dialogue between the decision-makers at the different levels of control. These healthcare organizations need to implement reactive mechanisms of collective learning from their own mistakes and proactive mechanisms of risk control. This inevitably involves a good command and sharing of the information that is circulating. Healthcare establishments thus need, day by day, to weave multiple connections, interactions, interrelations, synergies, affluences, confluences, innumerable and varied influences, guided by a managerial strategy hinging on collective performance, giving meaning and purpose (see Table 4.3).

Types of measures	Methods	Questions
Vision	–	What does the organization want to become?
Mission		What is the legitimacy of the organization?
Values		What are the organization's principles of behavior and decision?
Medium-term strategic avenues	Balanced scorecard	What are the medium-term strategic approaches and are they consistent?
Main strategic priorities		What are the strategic priorities that must be borne in mind by everyone?
Process objectives	Hoshin	What are the annual performance- and progress-related objectives of the processes?
Team objectives	Objective conventions	What are the collective objectives and targets, mainly determined by the leadership?
Individual objectives	Yearly interview	What are the singular objectives or the contribution of each individual to the objectives of the teams?

Table 4.3. *Strategic deployment: giving meaning and goals*

We can take the example of the implementation of an IS in a healthcare structure where, according to Avis 91 of the CCNE[20], its success depends on what is put into it, in terms of human resources and the security of the application, which is proportional to the number of qualified people. Hence, it appears crucial that users should have sufficient training time. Users "internal" to the healthcare establishment must be guided by the IS designers and managers involved in the implementation of the chosen system, so as to properly understand the way it works and how it should be used. Thus, if computer scientists are available to help the healthcare workers who need to

---

20 Avis 91 of the *Conseil Consultatif National d'Ethique* (CCNE – National Ethical Consultation Council): note on the ethical problems posed by the computerization of hospital prescriptions and patient files.

train the other members of staff at the healthcare establishment, it would help to adjust mentalities in favor of the most efficient IS tools. The surest way of encouraging healthcare professionals to trust these new technologies would be to allow them to undergo progressive training. This would help users to anticipate the ways to deal with technical anomalies and understand the complexity of the circuit.

This necessitates the creation of:

– training/action groups (initial/continuous), classes, workshops and practice groups devoted to the proper use of the IS;

– learning reviews.

4.4.2. *Ethical management*

Medical communication should contribute to the finding of a relational balance favoring teamwork and staff training to improve the patients' care. In these conditions of relational balance and harmony, individual morality goes hand in hand with collective reasoning in an attempt to solve ethical questions in medicine. In the view of Jean Abbad [ABB 01], social communication is crucially important for the prosperity, development and affirmation of every medical organization marked by a system of values, standards and achievements. For this reason, in order to interpret people's behavior in a communication situation, we need to try and understand the meaning that those people attach to their action. This meaning is the product of an interaction between the fact of communicating and all of the elements that make up the medical context. Various parameters are involved, including the physical and sensory environment, the spatial organization, the temporal data, the standards, processes of positioning of individuals and of identity expression, and the need for "relational quality". Thus, through this complex combination of these procedural criteria making up a system, the doctor and patient give meaning to their way of communicating and acting with one another. Increasingly, medical decision-making raises difficult ethical issues. It is a field of research that is expanding rapidly, drawing on not only ethics and fundamental knowledge but also practice and experience [LLO 04].

Generally, the majority of medical decisions does not require pronounced ethical reflection but is based more on *savoir-faire*, respect for the deontological code, the concretization of protocols and best-professional-practices recommendations, as well as the practitioner's technological skill.

Ethical decision-making is highly complex and requires prudence and experience. Ethics comes into play when the healthcare professionals are faced with choices where their values or socially accepted values come into conflict with one another. In other words, ethics is the reflection that arises from friction between our values. Medical decision-making, therefore, is part of a multifaceted relational device. Medical action is based on the practitioners' capacity for reasoning and their ability to make decisions in spite of the fact that the medical data may be tainted with uncertainty – particularly when NICT is used. This uncertainty may arise from multiple sources: there is the possibility for error in the data entry or ambiguity of the representation of the existing knowledge and so on.

NICT alters the distribution circuit, the responsibilities and the value chain in the medical domain [SIL 09]. Despite the fact that this new technology helps reach the correct diagnosis, we see a dehumanization of the healthcare relationship, which is already rather cold and unnerving for those who are not used to it. Could it be that everything is reduced to the provision of "processes" – that is, procedures – to the detriment of professional conscience, creativity, instinct and occasional inventiveness to make better use of the existing resources? Does technology fog or replace the doctor–patient relationship? All these questions lead us to wonder whether, in fact, the very idea of progress undermines the philosophy of healthcare which, since the days of Hippocrates, has been based on face-to-face meeting – the one-on-one conference between the patient and the doctor?

In these conditions, uncertainty becomes the ethical driving force behind the medical decision, with an absolute necessity of moral vigilance. Ethics as a discipline must remain rational, open and accessible to all the actors in the human and medical sciences and users in the field of healthcare. This leads us to ask the question: which ethical values could be accepted by everyone?

Finally, we can make the recommendation to base an organization's approach on the establishment of a cell of technical, medical, organizational and economic experts to oversee the installation and operation of the IS. This "functioning cell" [CHA 06] can include users and staff involved in the more general management of activities between the different departments services. The missions of this team might be as follows:

– assessment of the initial needs;

– management of the objectives of the adopted strategy;

– definition of the technical specifications;

– installation of the tool and user training;

– monitoring and evaluation of activity on the IS;

– provision of encouragement within the IS;

– provision of decision analysis support;

– provision of consensus- and discussion-based conflict resolution;

– provision of participation in the quality approach and responsibility promotion;

– consideration of the viewpoint of the various actors;

– establishment of an activity indicator and evaluation criteria;

– development of a collective culture and team cohesion with shared values.

In our view, one of the solutions inevitably requires an effort toward awareness-raising and educating the healthcare professionals and users.

4.5. Tool for the establishment and constant improvement of information systems for ethical practice in hospitals

In order to facilitate the work and the homogeneity of internal management for ethical performance in hospitals for the IS, we offer this guide to the creation of a "dashboard" system tailored to the requirements of healthcare establishments for the establishment and continuous improvement of the IS. This guide proposes an approach and provides tools that can be put into practice directly. This "starter kit" shows that there is plenty of opportunity to improve hospitals' ethical performance for IS. It could constitute an avenue to be pursued in the future as a continuous improvement tool. This tool is sufficiently flexible to be easily adapted to the specific needs of each situation.

The objectives of the dashboard system are to:

– monitor the policy of a hospital's ethical performance for the IS;

– monitor the quality of the IS between the different departments within the hospital;

– analyze the shortfalls and causes of breakdowns;

– raise any necessary alarms to prevent malfunctions;

– facilitate the reviewing of the actions under way, at a glance;

– provide a support tool to the IS' ethical assurance and management system.

This starter kit comprises two main parts:

– first, a discussion of the construction of the dashboards *stricto sensu*, which will inform the content of the coming presentation of the dashboard tool;

– second, a presentation of the methodology by which to implement and use these evolutionary management dashboards.

4.5.1. *Construction of the dashboards*

On the basis of foreign initiatives and our extensive conceptual research, we propose a model of the construction of dashboards to better visualize the ethical situation of the IS in a healthcare establishment. On the basis of the research seen earlier, we see a plan of action for this hospital management based on an approach of interlocking three mutually complementary dashboards linking the different hierarchical levels of the healthcare establishment:

– *the so-called "strategic" (visualization) dashboard (DB1)*, to deal with the issues of the IS' ethical performance. DB1 is fed by *ethical process indicators* (namely, the 40 items on questionnaire Q1 in the study);

– *the "tactical" (intervention) dashboard (DB2)*, to establish concrete actions on the ethical performance of the IS. DB 2 is fed by *ethical guidance indicators* (the 80 actions/recommendations listed in the study);

– *the "operational" (control) dashboard (DB3)*, to monitor whether or not the prescribed actions for the IS are put into practice. DB 3 works by the integration of the *ethical reporting indicators* (the 80 items on questionnaire Q2 in the study) (see Table 4.4)

Dashboard	"Strategic" – visualization (DB1)	"Tactical" – intervention (DB2)	"Operational" – control (DB3)
Indicator	Ethical "process"	Ethical "piloting"	Ethical "reporting"

Ethical principle	Ethical purpose	Regulatory action	Action checklist
B1	Supporting medical decision-making by the healthcare professional	Integrating good-practice protocols into the computer system	Are the professional good-practice protocols integrated into your establishment's computer system?
		Establishing an appropriate management protocol, accompanied by an established decision-making process	Has the number of medical mistakes been decreasing since your IS was installed?
B2	Promoting quality, organization, management and planning of the patient's care	Using management methods and concrete resources, which are accessible at all levels of the organization, appropriate at the decision level to achieve overall performance	Does your IS help improve the qualitative performance of your patient care?
		Establishing a detailed project methodology around the IS	Since your IS was installed, have you noticed an improvement in the internal means of quality management of the medical information given to the patient?
B3	Working for the good of the patient	Creating a patient-satisfaction questionnaire concerning your IS	Have you often received compliments from your patients or from patients' associations regarding the quality of your IS?
		Defining the objectives of the IS on the basis of an analysis of the users' needs and of the characteristics of the problems posed	After quality of care, are cost management and productivity among the main aims of your IS?
B4	Sharing common, transparent and accessible information	Developing an interface for the exchange and sharing of information between doctor and patient, hinging on the IS	Does your IS have a sharing platform where patients can access medical information pertaining to themselves?
		Listing the patients' needs in terms of the nature,	Is the sharing and pooling of medical information

Dashboard	"Strategic" – visualization (DB1)	"Tactical" – intervention (DB2)	"Operational" – control (DB3)
Indicator	Ethical "process"	Ethical "piloting"	Ethical "reporting"

Ethical principle	Ethical purpose	Regulatory action	Action checklist
		quality and quantity of medical information shared by the IS	about the patient the main purpose of your IS?
B5	Ensuring quality and choice of the information transmitted	Carrying out a patient-satisfaction survey about the choice and quality of the information shared	Have you carried out a patient-satisfaction survey about the choice and quality of the information distributed?
		Establishing a 24/7 on-call system	Does your IS include a monitoring device to check that the information it is transferring is not erroneous or deteriorated by usage
B6	Improving the continuity of the care given	Being able to communicate the result of the application of rules (to the patient's data) to the user, in the form of alerts, recommendations, reminders, etc. and to the application environment (prescription system, computerized patient file, etc.)	Is your IS capable of keeping patients informed (within a fairly short timeframe) of their medical results, via their doctor?
		Covering a larger range of action than that which is delimited by the premises of the organization	Does your IS facilitate exchanges and communication between doctors and other healthcare providers?
B7	Supporting the monitoring of all the healthcare activities	Installing the Intranet within the healthcare structure	Within your healthcare structure, is the medical information easily transferable from one department to another via your internal connection or network?
		Designating and choosing the data exchanged to aid inter-departmental exchanges	Does your system have good transversality between the different healthcare activities?

Dashboard	"Strategic" – visualization (DB1)	"Tactical" – intervention (DB2)	"Operational" – control (DB3)
Indicator	Ethical "process"	Ethical "piloting"	Ethical "reporting"

Ethical principle	Ethical purpose	Regulatory action	Action checklist
B8	Helping the Health Ministry to serve healthcare users' expectations and cancer treatment	Installing a system to export activity data to the State or its subsidiaries (regional health authorities)	Does your IS send the State and the Ministry the necessary information to determine the political objectives and the strategy to be implemented to serve the needs of all the healthcare actors?
		Installing a system for exporting epidemiological data and public health data, for use by the State or its subsidiaries (regional health authorities)	Does your IS send the medical information to the State or its subsidiaries so that they can plan changes to the national healthcare system?
B9	Providing legal legitimacy and information processing	Identifying the ethical and medical issues involved in the IS in relation with the patients' rights	In your view, does your IS confer legitimacy of the right to information for the patient?
		Enforcing the "ethical charter" regarding the handling of patients' medical information	In your view, does your IS confer legitimacy of the information processing for the patient?
B10	Establishing a duty of security, integrity, traceability and protection of medical data	Identifying and understanding the potential hacking threats	Have you properly identified all the stakes and the risks relating to the security of the data sent via your IS (e.g., deterioration, loss, theft, identity theft)?
		Having a rigorous, evolving security policy	Have you fully applied all the available methods and tools to secure data exchanges, such as identification, authentication, encryption, electronic signature, certification, technical specifications of the computer system and the backup systems?

Dashboard	"Strategic" – visualization (DB1)	"Tactical" – intervention (DB2)	"Operational" – control (DB3)
Indicator	Ethical "process"	Ethical "piloting"	Ethical "reporting"

Ethical principle	Ethical purpose	Regulatory action	Action checklist
J1	Evaluating performances and identifying those areas where action is required, listing the points of weakness	Making structural and organizational changes to go along with the implementation of the IS	Have you made structural changes or new actions within your structure, after analyzing data provided by the IS?
		Installing an automated tool that has an alarm function in case of the malfunction of the IS	Does your IS have a standby device that alerts the manager when an abnormal situation or activity occurs?
J2	Running the healthcare structure efficiently while keeping costs under control	Being aware of all the equipment installed for the IS so as to be able to develop a management strategy centered around it	Have you applied a management policy for your establishment on the basis of your existing IS?
		Controlling the processes implemented for the IS from a hierarchical point of view	Does your IS exert a significant impact on the "decisional" departments for the direction of your establishment?
J3	Facilitating epidemiological or statistical analysis (*SAE* – annual healthcare establishment review in France)	Gathering, identifying and (statistically) analyzing the information about facts that are relevant for healthcare	Are the medical data that feed into your IS used for statistical studies?
		Evaluating healthcare intervention and publishing the results of that evaluation in a public health report	Have the medical data that feed into your IS been used for epidemiological studies?
J4	Improving and strengthening interactivity with the actors outside the healthcare structure	Appointing an external liaison officer to support the management and transmission of knowledge and usage of the IS	Has your IS saved you time in your contact or exchanges with a healthcare actor outside the establishment?
		Setting up awareness-raising days	Since your IS has been operating, have you had more regular contact with the other healthcare actors on a daily basis?

Dashboard	"Strategic" – visualization (DB1)	"Tactical" – intervention (DB2)	"Operational" – control (DB3)
Indicator	Ethical "process"	Ethical "piloting"	Ethical "reporting"
Ethical principle	Ethical purpose	Regulatory action	Action checklist
J5	Making healthcare actors more available	Integrating the IS into the actual communication device so that it becomes one of the partners and participates in the resolution of an action (doctor–patient–IS triangulation)	Has your computer system enabled the healthcare professionals to have more frequent and more regular contact with their patients?
		Developing social communication, which is crucially important for the prosperity, development and affirmation of every medical organization	Do you believe your IS has helped improve the availability of the healthcare actors in your structure?
J6	Facilitating access to medical information for all users: reduction of social inequality	Finding out the legal, social, deontological, institutional and governmental standards and constraints	Does your IS contribute to correction of the social inequalities in terms of access to medical information among your patients?
		Applying the legal, social, deontological, institutional and governmental standards and constraints	Does your IS have precise regulations about the nature of professional status among your staff and the possibility of accessing certain medical information?
J7	Respecting the same rule of access to and distribution of information regardless of the patient's profile or status	Constructing a set of technical specifications, including the way in which medical information is to be distributed via the IS	Does your IS have precise regulations about the way in which medical information is distributed?
		Putting forward an ethically acceptable framework based on the criteria of acquisition and accessibility of medical information for the patient	Have you received comments from healthcare users regarding unfairness in the acquisition of medical information?
J8	Distributing the advantages and disadvantages of	Establishing a computer system that is appropriate for, and	Have you distributed the workload of the healthcare personnel on

Dashboard	"Strategic" – visualization (DB1)	"Tactical" – intervention (DB2)	"Operational" – control (DB3)
Indicator	Ethical "process"	Ethical "piloting"	Ethical "reporting"
Ethical principle	Ethical purpose	Regulatory action	Action checklist
	such a tool equitably in the healthcare professional's workload	coherence with, the organization of healthcare	the basis of their IS user profiles?
		Identifying the impact of the IS on the healthcare professionals' daily workload	Have you drawn up a breakdown of the advantages and disadvantages of using the IS in terms of their daily workload?
J9	Sharing the same information and the same medical decision support for all the healthcare professionals involved in the patient's healthcare circuit within the structure	Listing the people affected by the IS, their duties, their objectives and the degree of their access to medical information	Does your IS transmit the same information to all the healthcare professionals involved in the patient's healthcare circuit within your structure?
		Identifying the different possible options in terms of interventions on the IS for the healthcare professional	Does your IS represent the same decision-support tool for all the healthcare professionals involved in the patient's healthcare circuit within your structure?
J10	Developing and sharing information that is precise and is appropriate for everyone	Constructing a technical solution for the IS that is comprehensible, useful and usable from the point of view of the user	Is the information output by your IS clearly understood by your patients?
		Raising the patient's awareness and explaining the information transmitted by the IS to him or her	Do your patients complain about the inaccuracy of the information divulged by your IS?

Dashboard	"Strategic" – visualization (DB1)	"Tactical" – intervention (DB2)	"Operational" – control (DB3)
Indicator	Ethical "process"	Ethical "piloting"	Ethical "reporting"
Ethical principle	Ethical purpose	Regulatory action	Action checklist
A1	Putting the patient back at the center of the decision-making process by providing him or her with more complete medical information, more quickly	Involving the patient in the medical decision-making process	Since your IS has been operating, have your patients had more of an influence on the medical decisions that affect them?
		Using the IS to transmit the maximum amount of concise information that is essential for the patient	In your view, does your IS provide patients with fuller and more reactive information?
A2	Ensuring the patient consents and sticks to the plan	Explaining to the patients the nature of the use that is made of their personal medical data	Are your patients aware of the nature of the use that is made of their medical data?
		Explaining to the patient the form in which his or her medical data will be constructed, distributed and stored	Do your patients know the form in which their medical data will be constructed, distributed and stored?

Dashboard	"Strategic" – visualization (DB1)	"Tactical" – intervention (DB2)	"Operational" – control (DB3)
Indicator	Ethical "process"	Ethical "piloting"	Ethical "reporting"
Ethical principle	Ethical purpose	Regulatory action	Action checklist
A3	Respecting private life, the right to medical secrecy and confidentiality	Inserting settings into the IS that are able to conceal the patient's identity	Does your IS have settings to mask the patient's identity for which the medical information is associated?
		Identifying and masking the personal information relating to the patient integrated into the IS, which is not absolutely crucial for adequate healthcare	Does your IS handle information relating to your patients' private life that you deem indispensable in order for that system to work?
A4	Respecting the right to prior information, rectification and opposition	Inserting settings into the IS, which enable the patient to rectify and/or challenge the medical data that have been posted	Is your IS fully compliant with the law on "ICT and Freedom"?
		Providing prior information to the patient about the way in which the system is used in healthcare	Does your IS respect your patients' right to prior information?
A5	Reducing the asymmetry of information between the doctor and the patient: establishing a better balance in the doctor–patient relationship	Explaining to patients their rights concerning access to their personal medical information	Does your healthcare establishment clearly explain to the patients the rules concerning access to data pertaining to their health (see France's law of 4 August 2002; patient information; direct access to the medical file; shared medical information)?
		Obtaining data via a standard interface, adapted to suit its user (doctor or patient)	Do you think your IS helps reduce the informational imbalance between the doctor and the patient?
A6	Increasing transversality of services within the healthcare structure	Establishing a training plan that allows the management team and supervisors to constructing a common language surrounding the IS	Does your IS have good computer integration and functional interoperability?
		Employing a coordinator/organizer, who is indispensable in preserving cohesion and overall credibility of the system	In your view, does an IS enhance cooperation with the other applications and computerized devices used in the different departments?

Dashboard	"Strategic" – visualization (DB1)	"Tactical" – intervention (DB2)	"Operational" – control (DB3)
Indicator	Ethical "process"	Ethical "piloting"	Ethical "reporting"

Ethical principle	Ethical purpose	Regulatory action	Action checklist
A7	Establishing an individual and/or collective use of the medical information	Conducting learning reviews as regard the individual usage of the IS by the healthcare professionals	Is your IS subject to individual usage?
		Using multidisciplinary working groups for support (such groups help bring team members together and promote adhesion) as far as possible	Is your IS subject to collective usage?
A8	Adapting the use of the medical information to suit the organization of the healthcare structure	Setting up training programs and awareness-raising programs to ensure the best possible use of the system and to promote the adoption of the best *savoir-faire*	Has your establishment agreed to devote a financial and/or human effort in the evolution of the IS?
		Establishing a cell of experts in the technical, medical, organizational and economic fields to oversee the installation and operation of the IS	Does your IS have good flexibility of implementation within your structure?
A9	Adapting a technology to the knowledge and *savoir-faire* of the healthcare professional	Establishing training/action groups (initial/continuous), classes, workshops and practice groups dedicated to the proper use of the IS	Have you received requests for training from your staff to better grasp and understand the tool?
		Putting in place reactive mechanisms of collective learning about errors and management of the risk of errors linked to the IS	Within your structure, have you noticed mistakes in the way your staff use the IS?
A10	Establishing a management/piloting policy concerning the use of medical information	Drawing up an informational guideline to the IS, based on the existing document	Has your organization undertaken the writing of guidelines for the use of the IS?
		Establishing a working methodology accompanied by an advisor and effective management for the people involved	When your IS was installed, was there a real policy of monitoring the change in order to adapt your establishment to the new modes of information management?

Dashboard	"Strategic" – visualization (DB1)	"Tactical" – intervention (DB2)	"Operational" – control (DB3)
Indicator	Ethical "process"	Ethical "piloting"	Ethical "reporting"

Ethical principle	Ethical purpose	Regulatory action	Action checklist
NM1	Obeying the legislative regulation of medical data	Integrating homogeneous technological solutions with references respecting all regulations in force (DICOM, HL7, etc.)	Does your IS obey all the regulations in force (DICOM and HL7) regarding medical data?
		Creating an IS that is flexible, adaptable and evolves over time	Does your IS have the ability to evolve on the basis of the adjustments imposed by the legislation in force?
NM2	Respecting the rules concerning storage, hosting and distribution established by the CNIL (France's National Commission on ICT and Freedom) or similar authorities	Applying the rules on storage and hosting established by the CNIL	Does your IS obey the rules concerning storage and hosting as enacted by the CNIL?
		Applying the rules on the dissemination of medical information established by the CNIL	Does your IS obey the rules concerning the distribution of medical information as enacted by the CNIL?
NM3	Maximizing the use of medical information: ethical quality of medical decision	Convincing the relevant authorities (heads of department, hospital practitioners) of the usefulness of the IS in order to achieve a dynamic	Does your IS contribute to the advancement of organizational efficiency in the use of the medical information?
		Setting up patronage and oversight systems in relation to the use of the IS	Have you adapted the organization of your structure to improve the use of the medical information?
NM4	Developing an organization oriented toward collective performance	Establishing a supervisory board for the IS	In your view, does your IS support the strategic objectives defined in the overall ambition of your structure?
		Installing the IS at the heart of the space making up the departments involved in the particular branch of healthcare in question	Has your IS contributed to the development of actions involving all of the staff at your structure?

Dashboard	"Strategic" – visualization (DB1)	"Tactical" – intervention (DB2)	"Operational" – control (DB3)
Indicator	Ethical "process"	Ethical "piloting"	Ethical "reporting"

Ethical principle	Ethical purpose	Regulatory action	Action checklist
NM5	Minimizing or eliminating harm done to patients because of incorrect information	Using reliable knowledge (professional rules, computational algorithms) drawn from the organization's own knowledge base or any of a large number of other known databases	Have you been the subject of a lawsuit brought by a healthcare user because of erroneous medical information given to him or her?
		Putting supervision and monitoring tools in place	Has your IS helped you to avoid or reduce harm done to your patients because of improper distribution of the medical information?
NM6	Ensuring that the resources used do not exceed what is necessary to achieve the desired objectives	Using planning techniques (Pert, Gantt, Precedence Diagram Method, MPM, etc.)	In your view, are the resources used appropriate for the desired objectives for your IS?
		Carrying out a retrospective study regarding the evolution of the resources put in place in relation to the objectives initially envisaged	Have you carried out a retrospective study regarding the evolution of the resources mobilized in relation to the objectives initially envisaged?
NM7	Reducing unnecessary or misjudged risks	Identifying and ranking all the issues and risks associated with the IS	Does your establishment have an analysis of the issues and ranked risks for the IS?
		Setting up an oversight committee for the IS	Has your establishment developed a policy of prevention and precaution regarding to the possible consequences of the operation of your IS?
NM8	Ensuring the reliability of the medical data collection and its permanence	Having internal resource people present to regularly monitor the IS	Does your IS have a system to check the quality of the stored medical data?
		Having a backup system and a continuity plan for the IS	Does your IS have a maintenance system that keeps it operational 24/7?

Dashboard	"Strategic" – visualization (DB1)	"Tactical" – intervention (DB2)	"Operational" – control (DB3)
Indicator	Ethical "process"	Ethical "piloting"	Ethical "reporting"

Ethical principle	Ethical purpose	Regulatory action	Action checklist
NM9	Ensuring the technical relevance and human appropriateness of the IS	Performing an analysis by establishing links between the relevant facts and the ethical frameworks linked to the IS and oriented toward the patient	Are the main objectives of your IS primarily oriented toward the patient's interest?
		Mirroring the architecture of the IS with the organization of the healthcare put in place	Is the computer system consistent in its construction and technical assembly?
NM10	Making the whole collective responsible for the conduct of the healthcare user	Making patients aware of their responsibility and their role in the healthcare system	Do you believe that your IS gives the healthcare user more responsibility toward the collective?
		Having the patient take part in the medical decision-making process by way of better access and explanation of the information provided by the IS	In your view, is one of the aims of your IS to increase the patients' own responsibility by offering them greater independence in the making of the medical decision?

Table 4.4. *Structure and composition of the three dashboards*

4.5.1.1. *Strategic dashboard (visualization)*

The strategic dashboard (visualization) enables us to obtain a precise idea of the situation in time and space of the IS' ethical performance. It comprises:

– 4 ethical dimensions corresponding to the 4 ethical principles: beneficence, autonomy, non-malfeasance and fairness;

– 40 ethical process indicators, represented by the 40 ethical justifications.

4.5.1.1.1. Representation

– For an ethical principle:

Strategic dashboard n°...				Department ...			... at end ...	month M and year Y	
Program									
Strategies	**Ethical process indicator**		**Objectives**	**Targets**	**External influences**	**Observations**	**Tendencies**	**Comments**	
	1.	A1							
	2.	A2							
	3.	A3							
	4.	A4							
	5.								
	6.								
	7.								
	8.								
	9.								
	10.								
Read on ...					**Signature of Head of Department: ...**				
Read on ...					**Signature of the Doctor Resp. for the MID: ...**				

Format: *A4 sheet*
Color coding
We draw up the same table for the other 3 principles

Table 4.5. *Representation of the strategic dashboard – visualization. For a color version of the table, see www.iste.co.uk/beranger/ethics.com*

4.5.1.1.2. Operation

The tables are reviewed every month or every trimester[21]. If the observation and the tendency are coded "orange" or "red" for a given indicator, then we need to fill in the integral "tactical" dashboard governing intervention for that indicator.

NB: Green = score of 3/3; orange = score 2/3; red = score 1/3 or 0/3

4.5.1.1.3. Explanations of color coding

The criteria are characterized by four indissociable elements for general visualization of the ethical situation of the IS:

– *The observation:* indicates the current measured value of the indicator in relation to the set objective.

Color coding – Green: The set objectives have been achieved.

The situation is consistent with the prediction and expectations.

---

21 Depending on the total duration of the strategic process, the nature of the indicator, the need for reactivity, feasibility and the internal organization of the plan of action.

Orange: The objectives have only partly been achieved.

The difficulties have been identified and are in the process of being resolved.

The situation needs to be discussed at a meeting.

Red: The objectives have not been achieved.

The negative points need to be dealt with at a meeting.

– The tendency: shows the indicator's short- and medium-term evolution.

Color coding – Green: The predictable evolution is favorable/satisfactory.

Orange: The predictable evolution is uncertain.

The difficulties need to be projected.

This needs to be discussed at a meeting.

Red: The predictable evolution is unfavorable.

The indicator's measured value is seriously lowered.

This needs to be dealt with at a meeting.

– The comment: it takes the form of a written evaluation. It analyzes the seriousness/urgency (or lack thereof) of the actions taken and/or to be taken to achieve the objectives.

Color coding – Red: When the observation is "orange" or "red"?

When the tendency is "orange" or "red"?

This needs to be dealt with at a meeting.

It is interesting to construct a graphic representation such as a radar plot or a spider web graph of this dashboard.

4.5.1.2. *Tactical dashboard (intervention)*

The "tactical" dashboard (intervention) enables us to establish a plan of action based on piloting indicators of the real-world environmental parameters (REPs) in order to put strategies in place that are specific to the shortfalling sector. It comprises:

– 2 ethical "piloting" indicators, associated with 1 ethical "process" indicator;

– 80 ethical "piloting" indicators, representing 80 actions from our recommendations.

4.5.1.2.1. Representation

– For an ethical "process" indicator:

Tactical dashboard n° ...	Department at ... at end ... month M and year Y			
	Real-world environmental parameters (REPs)			
	Political and strategic level		Organizational and technological level	
	Strategy and Methodology (SM)	Relation and Culture (RC)	Organization and Regulation (OR)	Structure and Technology (ST)
Ethical piloting indicator 1				
Ethical piloting indicator 2				

Format: *A4 sheet*   **Color coding**

Table 4.6. *Representation of the "tactical" dashboard – intervention. For a color version of the table, see www.iste.co.uk/beranger/ethics.com*

4.5.1.2.2. Operation

We create as many "tactical" dashboards as there are ethical "process" indicators with an alarm signal ("orange" or "red") for the observation and tendency. These dashboards are reviewed monthly.

The ethical piloting indicators are strategic indicators that can be used to monitor the proper implementation of the strategy.

NB: Green = score of 3/3; orange = score 2/3; red = score 1/3 or 0/3

4.5.1.2.3. Explanations of color coding

Color coding – Green: The strategy has been properly implemented.

Orange: The strategy has not yet been totally implemented.

Red: There are major problems with the implementation of the strategy.

4.5.1.3. *"Operational" dashboard (control)*

The "operational" dashboard (control) enables us to monitor the proper implementation and the impact of these various strategies for daily life at the hospital. The aim is to send back information to the Directorate General so that they can follow the evolution of the situation and make the right decisions. It comprises:

– as many ethical "reporting" indicators as there are ethical "piloting" indicators;

– 80 ethical "reporting" indicators representing the result of checks representative of the strategy;

– indicators that are necessary to visualize the impact of the strategy and the evolution of the IS after the implementation of the REP strategies.

Note that if the 40 process indicators have an "orange" or "red" signal, then we would have 40 "tactical" dashboards and 40 "operational" dashboards associated therewith.

4.5.1.3.1. Representation

– For an ethical process indicator:

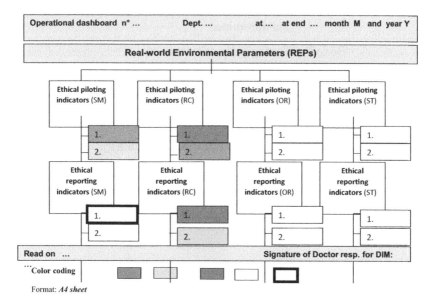

Table 4.7. *Representation of operational dashboard – control. For a color version of the table, see www.iste.co.uk/beranger/ethics.com*

4.5.1.3.2. Operation

We construct as many "operational" dashboards as there are "tactical" dashboards per ethical "process" indicator with an alert signal in the observation and tendency categories: "orange" or "red". These dashboards are read monthly.

NB: Green = score of 3/3; orange = score 2/3; red = score 1/3 or 0/3

4.5.1.3.3. Explanations of color coding

Color coding – Green: The target has been fully achieved.

Orange: The target has not yet been totally achieved.

Red: The target has not been achieved.

The strategy does not produce the predicted effect.

Reflect on how the strategy in question should be modified.

This must be dealt with at a meeting.

White: The data for these indicators have not yet been linked and transmitted.

Boxed: Strategically criticable

4.5.2. *Methodology of implementation and use*

The method of implementation and use is divided into four successive steps, spread out over the course of a year (see Table 4.8).

This iterative approach means we can ensure that the dashboards are consistent with the strategic objectives and the evolutions for the IS within the hospital.

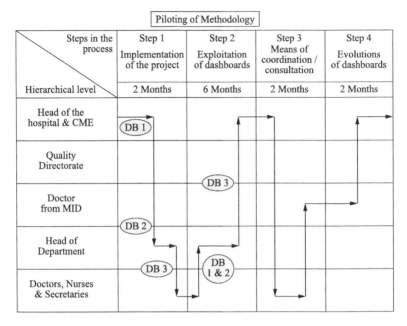

	Piloting of Methodology			
Steps in the process	Step 1 Implementation of the project	Step 2 Exploitation of dashboards	Step 3 Means of coordination / consultation	Step 4 Evolutions of dashboards
Hierarchical level	2 Months	6 Months	2 Months	2 Months
Head of the hospital & CME	DB 1			
Quality Directorate		DB 3		
Doctor from MID	DB 2			
Head of Department	DB 3	DB 1 & 2		
Doctors, Nurses & Secretaries				

Table 4.8. *Intrahospital coordination and strategic planning*

4.5.2.1. *Step 1: Implementation of the project "Hospital Dashboard"*

Implementation consists of identifying and mobilizing the actors to make up working groups:

– a "usage" group, defining the need for dashboards on the basis of the functional needs identified;

– a "technical" group, validating the feasibility of the dashboards and their relevance in relation to the technical realities of the IS;

– a "piloting" group, handling the costs and recurrent expenses associated with the dashboards in the production phase;

– an "operating" group, ensuring that the dashboards and procedures can be operated easily both in terms of their constitution and of their use.

It is crucial to analyze and describe the cycles or phases of prediction and planning, if they are present, because this sets the pace for the unit's activity, within the organization. This analysis is important because, in part, it conditions the design of the dashboards from the following three angles:

– *Anticipation:* The dashboards may contain information and indicators that, when the time comes, can illuminate the choices, orientations and compromises, which are necessarily involved in all processes of prediction and planning of the IS.

– *Schedule:* The prediction and planning procedures are a succession of steps, after each of which, specific tasks need to be performed or specific documents need to be drawn up. The procedures can be assimilated to projects and can be managed as such.

– *Monitoring and control:* The function of prediction and planning leads us to specify objectives over time and allocate the available resources. By analyzing these cycles of prediction and planning, we shall be able to more precisely what needs to be monitored and when it is best to perform these checks on the IS.

4.5.2.1.1. Recommendations

– Bring together all the actors in the healthcare establishments around the same program.

– Make all the hospital actors share a vision of the strategic objectives of management.

– Establish a connection between the strategy and the piloting system, with strategic alignment of the indicators, and adaptation to the new orientations or new projects.

– Assign responsibilities to everyone – in other words, determine who is to review the data and who is to take action.

– Involve the executives, managers and medical staff more directly in the quality management and in the program, bringing them in for the data collection process and the use of the dashboard.

– Use the most appropriate means of communication and awareness-raising.

– Provide training to the hospital staff regarding the collection, analysis and usage of the data used in the dashboard.

– Demonstrate the performance of the dashboard and share it at all levels of the organization: information dissemination.

The learning of the performance is "collective" and takes place over an extended period of time.

For these two reasons, the "socio-organizational" piloting practices play an essential role in the effectiveness of the system.

– The organizational development is more useful in "educational" arrangements to facilitate practices when the functioning of a team is more important than ever.

– The piloting system must be carefully linked with human resource management – in particular, with the evaluation of individual performances and the organization's incentive system (remunerations, career management, recognition of merits with a financial bonus).

– On average, this stage typically lasts approximately 2 months.

4.5.2.2. *Step 2: Usage of the hospital dashboards*

This step consists of publishing and exploiting the dashboards in accordance with the projected review periods. Thus, it entails:

– gathering the constitutive data:

  - collation,

  - processing,

  - calculation of the indicators;

– using the dashboards in the decision-making process.

4.5.2.2.1. Recommendations

– Maintain a constant view and monitor the evolution of the indicators.

– Provide raw data (unadjusted) so that clinicians and managers can conduct an analysis for their own ends.

– Be sure of the integrity of the data, and therefore, be extremely rigorous regarding the quality of the data used.

– Use familiar mechanisms for the display of terminology and data.

– Respect the periodicity of reading of each dashboard.

– Provide a report card for the organization each month.

– On average, this stage typically lasts approximately 6 months.

4.5.2.3. *Step 3: Modes of coordination and working in concert*

The life of the unit is punctuated by a certain number of meetings where points are raised, and we examine the problems that have arisen, the advancement of the projects, any new facts, etc. Usually, these meetings are teamwork sessions at which the situations are discussed and evaluated, and in general, decisions tend to be made. In order to be effective, these meetings require preparation. There again, the piloting system and the dashboards are appropriate instruments. The production of the dashboards can be finalized on the meeting schedules. Thus, it is essential to take stock and to analyze the scheduled meetings in which the actors participate. This reflection highlights two aspects:

– the information and key data necessary for each type of team meeting and coordination meeting (content of dashboards);

– the frequency and schedule for construction of the dashboards.

4.5.2.3.1. Recommendations

– Establish management of the study before, during and after the execution.

– Consider having the head of each dashboard clearly date and sign the document when it has been read, so as to preserve the traceability of the viewing by level.

– Do not include, on a weekly dashboard, any indicators or information pertaining to objectives or functions that are only checked and monitored on a monthly basis.

– Publish the dashboards in the departments concerned.

– Communicate them to the units or collaborators of level L-1.

– Collect the dashboards from the collaborators.

– Discuss the impact of that tool on daily life at the hospital.

– Information is political: the hospitals must also carefully consider the potential consequences of disseminating the information and be prepared to react in case of inappropriate use.

– First allow the healthcare establishment and its staff to familiarize themselves with the dashboard before publishing their data.

– On average, this stage typically lasts approximately 2 months.

4.5.2.4. *Step 4: Evolution of hospital dashboards*

By monitoring the dashboards, we are able to see whether they need to be altered, on the basis of the following situations:

– poor quality of the indicators (ergonomics, consistency, relevance, etc.);

– evolution of the hospital context for the IS;

– evolution of the objectives of the hospital ethical performance for the IS;

– inappropriacy of the indicators in relation to the strategic objectives;

– change of the addressees depending on the hospital department in question.

4.5.2.4.1. Recommendations

– The visual representation of the indicators needs to be simple and communicative.

For that information to be truly meaningful, it is desirable to simultaneously present:

- the initial value of the objective,

- the result attained and the gap between that result and the objective,

- the evolution of the results over time.

– Check that the parameters both internal and external to the hospital have not changed since the dashboard was set up.

– Develop reflection and self-evaluation regarding the process put in place.

– On average, this stage typically lasts approximately 2 months.

4.5.2.5. *Reflection of the hospital organogram*

The hospital's policy is handed down from the top to the bottom. Meanwhile, the indicators are communicated from the bottom upward. In these conditions, the medical information about the ethics of the IS represented by the dashboards (DBs) must be transmitted in such a way as to fully respect the hierarchy within the hospital. Thus, we see that DBs 1 and 2 are filled in by the doctors, nurses and secretaries in each department. They send back the information to the head of each medical department, who sends the summary of the results of DBs 1 and 2, using the "reporting" DB 3, to the doctor from the medical information department (MID) (see Figure 4.5).

The path of events is as follows:

– When the ethical process indicator (DB1) is orange or red, the person in charge of picking up the alert signals must mention that indicator in a meeting with the managing decision-making team so that they can make the appropriate decisions to remedy the situation by establishing a piloting plan of action.

– When the ethical piloting indicator (DB2) for a particular sector is orange or red, the head of department must conduct a meeting with the staff in that department to reflect together on the implementation and resolving of that deficient strategy.

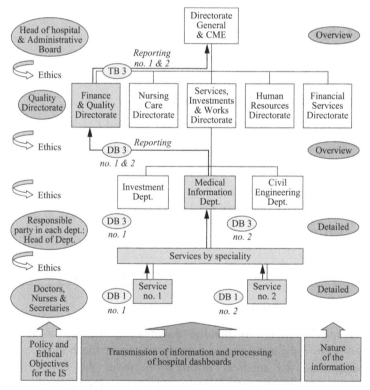

Figure 4.5. *Use of dashboards in the hospital organogram*

– When the ethical reporting indicator (DB3) for such a strategy is red (i.e., when the target is less than 95% of the way to being achieved), the staff in that department must mention that indicator in a meeting with the head of the department and the doctor from the MID, who will feed back the information to the managing decision-making team, so that they can decide on a change of strategy.

– After compilation of all the reports of DB3, the quality directorate will feed back the information to the administrative board or directly to the head of the hospital.

4.5.2.5.1. Recommendations

– The plan of action and the ethical objectives for the IS obey a top–down vertical movement in terms of the hierarchy.

– The implementation of the indicators in a hospital department first requires a decision from the head of department, followed by an action of awareness-raising and training of the hospital team.

– The indicators must allow for information widely distributed to those people whom it affects. It must be communicated to those people in an accessible form.

– A diagnostic of the IS' existing situation is necessary to establish the initial objectives.

– The hospital's internal communication must be based on a strong policy of displaying the ethical quality indicators devoted to the IS Therefore, those indicators must periodically be distributed using simple tools such as graphs, plots and tables, which are easily interpretable for any reader.

– Learning must be oriented toward action and collective performance.

– The socio-organizational piloting practices play an essential role in the effectiveness of the internal management of such a program.

– The process must function in such a way that individual learning comes together and coagulates into collective learning – organizational learning, so to speak.

– This feeding back of information from the dashboards to the board of directors rises through the ranks of the hierarchy from the bottom up.

– The management receives concise and precise reports on the ethics of the IS.

Conclusions

Generally speaking, the evolution of information technologies is giving rise to considerable repercussions on all levels: it is not only transforming society as a whole, but also organizations and institutions. It is also modifying all forms of social interaction, and even individuals. New challenges and conflicts have emerged.

According to technological determinism, NICT and Big Data are not neutral. They have an influence on their users; they condition them and modify their view of the world. An IS is mainly useful because of the relations that it creates: information is the symbol, the key and the condition of human interaction because it facilitate sex changes. Nevertheless, information can be a nuisance if it represents a vector of will to domination and becomes an obstacle to transparency. Technology and human in genuity always have a certain role in advance of legislation and human thinking. The gaps between NICT, legislation and ethics are growing ever larger. For this reason, information distributors must conform to certain ethical principles, values and virtues such as honesty, sincerity, veracity, reliability, equality and fairness, which requires equal distribution of informational resources for all citizens. In this context, data, information and knowledge necessitate an epistemological and ethical framework to produce decisive "practical wisdom" [RYA 07]. Thus, the challenge is to create conditions propitious for healthy interaction between moral, political and judicial standards, industrial strategies and protection of the healthcare users from potential deviations from the use of their own medical information by new technologies.

Computer technology in itself is not the problem. It is merely the automation of an existing, underlying process. It crystallizes and amplifies an existing problem like a revelation test. Its success heavily depends on the way in which it corresponds to clinical workflows, the way in which the technology is introduced into an organization, the quality of the information pertaining to training and support, and the motivation of the users and their use of the system [BER 99, POL 01]. Hence, it is important to clearly define the processes and establish a roadmap considering the possible deviances and detours in its use.

Proper use of NICT and big data requires a certain amount of maturity and *savoir-vivre*, which is contrary to the febrile anxiousness of certain neophytes. The culture of usages must accompany the implementation of these tools. This usage requires modesty, good sense, perseverant energy and a great deal of courage – because it is important to dare to take certain personal risks in order to advance the technology. Here, we see the classic precepts of the humanists in the Renaissance, namely taking time to reflect, sort and prune information; taking a step back to keep his or her own activity; and constructing overviews and techniques carefully. Frequently, these rules of simple good sense in the service of ethics of healthcare are swept aside in favor of the technicality of the IS. For this reason, these two totally opposing worlds – ethics and information technology – must learn to coexist.

The modeling of ethical behavior based on medical information represents a fundamental link between the digitization of the real world and the practical aspect of medicine. This "digitization"of ethics though does not mean that the techno-scientific system encompasses everything, including human freedom of thought, which would engender major problems of morality. Indeed, one of the major goals of our model is to provide a thought-support tool. This mathematical framework thus constitutes dynamic and changeable conditions conducive to free ethical reflection about medical information through the medium of NICT. As stressed by Galileo [GAL 00], "philosophy, written in the great book of the universe, is formulated in the language of mathematics. Without that language, it is humanly impossible to understand anything at all, and we can only stumble around in a darkened maze". Therefore, our research offers readers a number of avenues for reflections designed to conceive, think, commission and use the IS from an ethical standpoint while considering the issues and fluctuations (political, strategic, technical, organizational, regulatory, relational or cultural) that such a system could cause. These avenues enable us to organize our ethical reflections about an IS from the time of its creation to its usage, via an ethical model based on the four universal ethical principles and on the "accepted contingence".

Hence, this ethical model constitutes a tool for evaluating information systems in healthcare, which is based on a scoring device enabling us to translate and weight the technological requirements into ethical requirements and vice versa. The purpose here is to fit into a dynamic of evolution of the healthcare actors toward a socio-environmental quality of continuous improvements concerning these IS and medical Big Data.

In addition, in this book, we have laid the foundations of an ethical charter for the construction and implementation of an IS. The purpose of this is to facilitate medical informationin oncology. Beyond the simple satisfaction of technical or financial success, ethical questioning in IS projects can help evaluate the human and environmental success. This reflection was developed to ensure ethical practice and to defend the rights of patients in their relations with healthcare professionals in terms of all issues pertaining to medical information. Indeed, the actors who have access to that medical information will be likely to better know and apprehend the rules that govern that information and relate to the patients' rights. The healthcare consumer and, more broadly, society in general, will become the final beneficiaries of the ethical practices and principles thus applied.

The main objective is to improve in terms of quality and efficiency the patients' care. With this in mind, it is important to remove a series of barriers – structural, technological, and cultural – in order to fully make use of the potential offered by ICT.

In addition, the ethics of an IS, and more generally of a healthcare organization, may help it not only to have meaning but also to ensure longer-term survival. Thus, ethical practice is a tool of humanization that is used at all times and ultimately leads us to evaluate the transcendence and uniqueness of the doctor–patient–IS relationship. This ethical reflection is shared, and the values can be displayed and experienced differently from person to person. Certain goals may be common to several actors, and it allows men and women to work together in an organization with strong values. Hence, this reflection contributes to structure.

However, in the face of the requirement for ethics created by the vagaries of a new world, which are conditioned by NICT and, mainly, Big Data, we cannot avoid wondering about the counterweights, the corrections and regulations needing to be put in place. *A priori*, it seems absolutely crucial to have a set of rules in place. Such rules do not only pertain to a relational ethical problem but also to a technical necessity, which is essential so that a patient can form an opinion about the different possible options. As medicineis constantly evolving, we felt it important to revisit not only Hippocrates' texts but also those of his successors, his translators and his commentators, from antiquity right up to the present day, in order to feel "the force of a train of thought resistant to facility and compromise, which is just as stringent in its restrictions as it is creative of ideas, knowledge, standards and behaviors" [SIC 11]. A model in itself! Ethics as a questioning process drives changes forward, enabling people and organizations to take the steps necessary for their own respective evolutions. Ideally based on efficiency and transparency, an IS must contribute to the germination of intelligence, in the contextof pronounced human freedom. Is it not possible that this drive for transparency, in which the least confidentiality is rejected, will, in the long term, unwittingly turn against the patients' interests, giving rise to a cold and dehumanized society in which the warmth and subtlety of human relations are no longer valued? We hope that our ethical reflection on the subject has contributed to preserving a place for confidentiality, and in particular, for trust – both of which are fundamental (particularly in the doctor–patient relationship). Without medical confidentiality, there can be no medicine. Such a remark leads us to wonder whether, under the auspices of defending patient intimacy, medical secrecy might not actually be the figure head for a terrifying medical paternalism that could arise in a new form.

As we have observed throughout the work, in addition to its individual dimension, medical decision-making has taken on an unavoidable collective aspect, and the ethical requirements have therefore become more complex. The ethical rules involved in "*savoir-être*" become more stringent in light of the technical pressure exerted by "*savoir-faire*" [GOM 01]. Therefore, it seems to be a matter of urgency to reintroduce the ethical aspects into initial medical and care training undergone by the users of such an IS, at the cost of uncomfortable questioning of the usefulness of techniques already developed and socially adopted as "norms". By better mutual understanding of their respective disciplines, ethicists, jurists, sociologists, healthcare professionals and ICT experts can ensure that the IS of tomorrow will truly be respectful of, and will serve, the person in question. In the medium term, we are confident that our model will serve for the construction of an analysis table to help with the ethical labeling of IS in the field of healthcare.

Finally, the patient is at the crossroads between all these actors involved with the IS and Big Data. By nature, there is no collective responsibility; only individual responsibility. On the basis of this observation, we have the right to wonder whether it would not be better to give a greater degree of responsibility to the healthcare user himself or herself, by providing him or her with greater means, control and therefore power over the management of his or her own health? This will inevitably involve awareness-raising and education in the long term.

Appendix 1

Classification of the Justifications in terms
of the Different Real-world Environmental
Parameters and Fundamental Ethical
Principles pertaining to the Major
Objectives of an IS in Healthcare

Justifications of the purposes of the major objectives of an IS in healthcare	Real-world environmental parameters	Fundamental ethical principles
– Supporting medical decision-making by the healthcare professional	Strategic and methodological	Beneficence
– Promoting quality, organization, management and planning of the patient's care	Organizational and regulatory	
– Working for the good of the patient	Relational and cultural	
– Sharing common, transparent and accessible information	Strategic and methodological	
– Ensuring quality and choice of the information transmitted	Structural and technological	
– Improving continuity of care	Strategic and methodological	
– Supporting the monitoring of all healthcare activities	Strategic and methodological	
– Helping the Health Ministry to serve the expectations and treatment of cancer for the healthcare user	Relational and cultural	
– Establishing legitimacy of the law and of information processing	Organizational and regulatory	
– Establishing a duty of security, integrity, traceability and medical data protection	Structural and technological	
– Evaluating performance and defining the domains where action is required, listing the points of dysfunction	Strategic and methodological	Fairness
– Steering the healthcare structure efficiently while keeping costs under control	Relational and cultural	
– Improving and strengthening interactivity with the actors outside the healthcare structure	Relational and cultural	
– Increasing the availability of the healthcare actors	Organizational and regulatory	
– Facilitating access to medical information for all users: reducing social inequality	Structural and technological	
– Respecting the same rule of access to and distribution of the information irrespective of the patient's profile or status: idea of social fairness	Organizational and regulatory	
– Distributing the advantages and disadvantages of such a tool equitably in the workload of the healthcare staff	Strategic and methodological	
– Sharing the same information and the same medical decision-support tool with all the healthcare professionals in the structure involved in the patient's healthcare circuit	Strategic and methodological	
– Developing and sharing information that is precise and appropriate for everyone	Strategic and methodological	
– Facilitating epidemiological or statistical analysis (SAE)	Structural and technological	

Table A1.1. *Justifications of the purposes of the major objectives of an IS in healthcare in terms of the real-world environmental parameters*

Justifications of the limitations of the major objectives of an IS in healthcare	Real-world environmental parameters	Fundamental ethical principles
– Putting the patient back at the center of the decision-making process by providing him or her with more complete medical information, more quickly: better patient autonomy	Structural and technological	Autonomy
– Ensuring the patient consents and sticks to the plan	Relational and cultural	
– Respecting private life, and the right to medical secrecy and confidentiality	Relational and cultural	
– Respecting the right to prior information, rectification and opposition described in the "ICT and Freedom" law	Organizational and regulatory	
– Establishing individual and/or collective use of medical information	Structural and technological	
– Reducing the asymmetry of information between the doctor and the patient: establishing a better balance in the doctor–patient relationship	Relational and cultural	
– Adapting the way in which the IS works to suit the organization of the healthcare structure	Organizational and regulatory	
– Establishing a management/piloting policy concerning the use of medical information	Strategic and methodological	
– Increasing transversality of services within the healthcare structure	Organizational and regulatory	
– Adapting a technology to the knowledge and *savoir-faire* of the healthcare professional	Structural and technological	
– Making the whole collective responsible for the conduct of the healthcare user	Relational and cultural	Non-malfeasance
– Developing an organization oriented toward collective performance	Organizational and regulatory	
– Obeying the legislative regulation of medical data	Organizational and regulatory	
– Respecting the rules concerning storage, hosting and distribution established by the CNIL or similar authorities	Organizational and regulatory	
– Maximizing the ethical quality of the decision, the aim of efficiency and organizational efficacy in the usage of the medical information	Organizational and regulatory	
– Minimizing or eliminating harm done to patients because of incorrect information	Relational and cultural	
– Ensuring the reliability of the medical data collection and its permanence	Structural and technological	
– Ensuring that the resources employed do not exceed what is necessary to achieve the desired objectives	Strategic and methodological	
– Reducing unnecessary or misjudged risks	Strategic and methodological	
– Ensuring the technical relevance and human appropriateness of the IS	Structural and technological	

Table A1.2. *Justifications of the limitations of the major objectives of an IS in healthcare in terms of the real-world environmental parameters*

Appendix 2

Questionnaire 1: Designed to Analyze the Perception of Actors in Oncology about the Primary Objectives of an IS in Healthcare

In your view, the information systems of a healthcare structure should have the major objectives of	*Tick the box that corresponds to your answer*			
	YES, absolutely	YES, partly	NO, not really	NO, not at all
1. supporting medical decision-making by the healthcare professional				
2. promoting quality, organization, management and planning of the patient's care				
3. working for the good of the patient				
4. sharing common, transparent and accessible information				
5. ensuring quality and choice of the information transmitted				
6. improving continuity of care				
7. supporting the monitoring of all healthcare activities				
8. evaluating performances and defining the domains where action is required, listing the points of dysfunction				
9. steering the healthcare structure efficiently, while keeping costs under control				
10. helping the Health Ministry to serve the expectations and treatment of cancer for the healthcare user				

	Tick the box that corresponds to your answer			
In your view, the information systems of a healthcare structure should have the major objectives of	**YES, absolutely**	**YES, partly**	**NO, not really**	**NO, not at all**
11. establishing legitimacy of the law and of information processing				
12. establishing a duty of security, integrity, traceability and medical data protection				
13. improving and strengthening interactivity with the actors outside the healthcare structure				
14. increasing the availability of the healthcare actors				
15. facilitating access to medical information for all users: reducing social inequality				
16. respecting the same rule of access to and distribution of information irrespective of the patient's profile or status				
17. distributing the advantages and disadvantages of such a tool equitably in the workload of the healthcare professionals				
18. sharing the same information and the same medical decision-support tool with all of the healthcare professionals in the structure involved in the patient's healthcare circuit				
19. developing and sharing information that is precise and appropriate for everyone				
20. facilitating epidemiological or statistical analysis (SAE)				
21. making the whole collective responsible for the conduct of the healthcare user				
22. developing an organization oriented toward collective performance				
23. minimizing or eliminating harm done to patients because of incorrect information				
24. putting the patient back at the center of the decision-making process by providing him or her with more complete medical information, more quickly				
25. ensuring the patient consents and sticks to the plan				
26. respecting private life, and the right to medical secrecy and confidentiality				
27. respecting the right to prior information, rectification and opposition described in the "ICT and Freedom" law				

In your view, the information systems of a healthcare structure should have the major objectives of	Tick the box that corresponds to your answer			
	YES, absolutely	YES, partly	NO, not really	NO, not at all
28. ensuring the reliability of the medical data collection and its permanence				
29. establishing individual and/or collective use of medical information				
30. reducing the asymmetry of information between the doctor and the patient: better balance in the doctor–patient relationship				
31. obeying the legislative regulation of medical data				
32. respecting the rules concerning storage, hosting and distribution established by the CNIL or similar authorities				
33. optimizing the usage of the medical information: ethical quality of medical decision-making				
34. adapting the use of the medical information to suit the organization of the healthcare structure				
35. establishing a management/piloting policy concerning the use of medical information				
36. improving transversality of services within the healthcare structure				
37. adapting a technology to the knowledge and *savoir-faire* of the healthcare professional				
38. ensuring that the resources employed do not exceed what is necessary to achieve the desired objectives				
39. reducing unnecessary or misjudged risks				
40. ensuring the technical relevance and human appropriateness of the IS				

Table A2.1. *Questionnaire 1, designed to analyze the perception of actors in oncology about the primary objectives of an IS in healthcare*

Appendix 3

Questionnaire 1′: Designed to Analyze Healthcare Users' Perceptions of the Main Objectives of an IS in Healthcare

In your view, the information systems designed to handle healthcare in oncology in an establishment should have the major objectives of	Tick the box that corresponds to your answer			
	YES, absolutely	YES, partly	NO, not really	NO, not at all
– assisting medical decision-making – working for the good of the patient – improving the continuity of healthcare – evaluating the patient's care – guiding the healthcare structure effectively while keeping costs under control – establishing a duty of security and protection of the medical data – improving the healthcare professionals' availability – facilitating access to medical information for all users – sharing precise information, suited for the whole population – facilitating a statistical analysis – making the healthcare user aware of his or her responsibility to the collective				

	Tick the box that corresponds to your answer			
In your view, the information systems designed to handle healthcare in oncology in an establishment should have the major objectives of	YES, absolutely	YES, partly	NO, not really	NO, not at all
– making the healthcare user aware of his or her responsibility to the collective – reducing harm done to the patients because of incorrect information – providing more complete and quick medical information for the patient – ensuring the patient's consent and adhesion – respecting patients' private lives, and their right to medical secrecy and confidentiality – obeying the legislative regulation governing medical data – establishing a policy to make better use of medical information – strengthening communication within the healthcare services – being easily usable for the staff in the healthcare establishment – reducing unnecessary or poorly calculated risks				

Table A3.1. *Questionnaire 1', designed to analyze healthcare users' perceptions of the main objectives of an IS in healthcare*

Questionnaire 2: Designed to Study the Realization and Characteristics of the IS Tool, to be used by the Designer of the IS and to the "Internal" Users

	Tick the box that corresponds to your answer			
Regarding the information systems used by your structure	**YES, absolutely**	**YES, partly**	**NO, not really**	**NO, not at all**
1-1. Are good professional practice protocols integrated into the establishment's computer system?				
1-2. Has the number of medical errors decreased since the installation of your IS?				
2-1. Does your IS help to improve the qualitative performance of your patient care?				
2-2. Since the implementation of your IS, have you noticed an improvement in the means of internal quality management of the medical information given to the patient?				
3-1. Have you often received compliments from your patients or from patients' associations about the quality of your IS?				

	Tick the box that corresponds to your answer			
Regarding the information systems used by your structure	**YES, absolutely**	**YES, partly**	**NO, not really**	**NO, not at all**
3-2. After quality of care, are cost management and productivity among the primary objectives of your IS?				
4-1. Does your IS have a sharing platform where the patient can access medical information relevant to him or her?				
4-2. Is the sharing and pooling of medical information with the patient on the primary objectives of your IS?				
5-1. Have you surveyed your patients regarding their satisfaction with the quality and choice of the information disseminated?				
5-2. Does your IS have a monitoring device to check that the information it is transmitting is not erroneous or deteriorated by usage?				
6-1. Does your IS enable the patient to be kept informed (within a relatively short period) of medical results pertaining to him or her, via the doctor?				
6-2. Does your IS facilitate exchanges and communication between the doctors and the other providers of healthcare services?				
7-1. Within your healthcare structure, is medical information easily transferrable from one department to another via your internal connection or network?				
7-2. Does your computer system show good transversality between the different healthcare activities?				
8-1. Have you enacted structural changes or new actions within your organization after analyzing data collected by the IS?				
8-2. Does your IS have a monitoring device to alert the manager when a situation or activity is abnormal?				

Regarding the information systems used by your structure	Tick the box that corresponds to your answer			
	YES, absolutely	YES, partly	NO, not really	NO, not at all
9-1. Have you applied a piloting policy for your establishment on the basis of your existing IS?				
9-2. Does your IS have a significant impact on the "decisional" departments for the management of your establishment?				
10-1. Does your IS feed back to the State and the Ministry the information necessary to determine the political objectives, the strategy to be implemented in order to cater for the expectations of all actors involved in the healthcare chain?				
10-2. Does your IS transmit medical information to the State or its subsidiaries so that they can plan any changes to the national healthcare system?				
11-1. Does your IS establish legitimacy of the patients' right to information?				
11-2. Does your IS establish legitimacy of the information processing for the patient?				
12-1. Have you clearly identified all the issues and risks linked to data security via your IS (deterioration, loss, theft, identity fraud, etc.)?				
12-2. Have you properly applied all methods and tools to secure data exchanges, such as identification, authentication, encryption, electronic signatures, certification, technical specifications for the computer system and the backup systems?				
13-1. Has your IS helped you to gain time in your contacts or exchanges with a healthcare actor outside your establishment?				

	Tick the box that corresponds to your answer			
Regarding the information systems used by your structure	YES, absolutely	YES, partly	NO, not really	NO, not at all
13-2. Since the installation of your IS, have you had more regular contacts with other healthcare actors day to day?				
14-1. Has your computer system enabled the healthcare professionals to have more frequent and regular contact with patients?				
14-2. Do you believe your IS has helped improve the availability of the healthcare actors in your structure?				
15-1. Does your IS help correct the social imbalances in terms of accessibility to medical information for your patients?				
15-2. Does your IS have specific regulations concerning the nature of professional status among your staff and the possibility of access to a certain piece of medical information?				
16-1. Does your IS have specific regulations as to the way in which medical information is distributed?				
16-2. Have you received comments from healthcare users regarding unfairness in the acquisition of medical information?				
17-1. Have you adjusted the workload of the healthcare staff, on the basis of their user profiles on the IS?				
17-2. Have you drawn up a breakdown of the advantages and disadvantages of using the IS in terms of their daily workload?				
18-1. Does your IS transmit the same information to all the healthcare professionals involved in the patient's healthcare circuit within your structure?				

Regarding the information systems used by your structure	*Tick the box that corresponds to your answer*			
	YES, absolutely	YES, partly	NO, not really	NO, not at all
18-2. Does your IS represent the same decision-support tool for all the healthcare professionals involved in the patient's healthcare circuit within your structure?				
19-1. Is the information output by your IS clearly understood by your patients?				
19-2. Do your patients complain about the inaccuracy of the information divulged by your IS?				
20-1. Are the medical data that feed into your IS used for statistical studies?				
20-2. Have the medical data that feed into your IS been used for epidemiological studies?				
21-1. Do you believe that your IS gives the healthcare user more responsibility toward the collective?				
21-2. Is increasing the patients' own responsibility by offering them greater independence in the making of the medical decision one of the aims of your IS?				
22-1. Does your IS support the strategic objectives defined in the overall ambition of your structure?				
22-2. Has your IS contributed to the development of actions involving all the staff at your structure?				
23-1. Have you been the subject of a lawsuit brought by a healthcare user because of erroneous medical information given to him or her?				
23-2. Has your IS helped you to avoid or reduce harm done to your patients because of improper distribution of the medical information?				
24-1. Since your IS has been operating, have your patients had more of an influence on the medical decisions that affect them?				

	Tick the box that corresponds to your answer			
Regarding the information systems used by your structure	YES, absolutely	YES, partly	NO, not really	NO, not at all
24-2. Does your IS provide patients with fuller and more reactive information?				
25-1. Are your patients aware of the nature of the use that is made of their medical data?				
25-2. Do your patients know the form in which their medical data will be constructed, distributed and stored?				
26-1. Does your IS have settings to anonymize patients for which the medical information is associated?				
26-2. Does your IS handle information relating to your patients' private life that you deem indispensable in order for that system to work?				
27-1. Is your IS fully compliant with the law on "ICT and Freedom"?				
27-2. Does your IS respect your patients' right to prior information?				
28-1. Does your IS have a system to check the quality of the stored medical data?				
28-2. Does your IS have a maintenance system that keeps it operational 24/7?				
29-1. Is your IS subject to individual usage?				
29-2. Is your IS subject to collective usage?				
30-1. Does your healthcare establishment clearly explain to the patients the rules concerning access to data pertaining to their health (see France's law of August 4, 2002; patient information; direct access to the medical file; shared medical information)?				
30-2. Does your IS help reduce the informational imbalance between the doctor and the patient?				
31-1. Does your IS obey all the regulations in force (DICOM and HL7) regarding medical data?				

Regarding the information systems used by your structure	Tick the box that corresponds to your answer			
	YES, absolutely	YES, partly	NO, not really	NO, not at all
31-2. Does your IS have the ability to evolve on the basis of the adjustments imposed by the legislation in force?				
32-1. Does your IS obey the rules concerning storage and hosting as enacted by the CNIL?				
32-2. Does your IS obey the rules concerning the distribution of medical information as enacted by the CNIL?				
33-1. Does your IS contribute to the advancement of organizational efficiency in the use of the medical information?				
33-2. Have you adapted the organization of your structure to improve the use of the medical information?				
34-1. Has your establishment agreed to devote a financial and/or human effort in the evolution of the IS?				
34-2. Does your IS have good flexibility of implementation within your structure?				
35-1. Has your organization undertaken the writing of guidelines for the use of the IS?				
35-2. When your IS was installed, was there a real policy of monitoring the change in order to adapt your establishment to the new modes of information management?				
36-1. Does your IS have good computer integration and functional interoperability?				
36-2. Does an IS enhance cooperation with the other applications and computerized devices used in the different departments?				
37-1. Have you received requests for training from your staff to better grasp and understand the tool?				

	Tick the box that corresponds to your answer			
Regarding the information systems used by your structure	**YES, absolutely**	**YES, partly**	**NO, not really**	**NO, not at all**
37-2. Within your structure, have you noticed mistakes in the way your staff use the IS?				
38-1. Are the resources used appropriate for the desired objectives for your IS?				
38-2. Have you carried out a retrospective study regarding the evolution of the resources mobilized in relation to the objectives initially envisaged?				
39-1. Does your establishment have an analysis of the issues and ranked risks for the IS?				
39-2. Has your establishment developed a policy of prevention and precaution regarding the possible consequences of the operation of your IS?				
40-1. Are the main objectives of your IS primarily oriented toward the patient's interest?				
40-2. Is the computer system consistent in its construction and technical assembly?				

Table A4.1. *Questionnaire 2, designed to study the realization and characteristics of the IS tool, to be used by the designer of the IS and the "internal" users*

Questionnaire 3: Designed to Analyze the Methods and Tools Put in Place to Enable the IS to Work

Regarding the information systems used by the healthcare structure	Tick the box that corresponds to your answer		
	YES, absolutely	YES, partly	NO, not at all
– When developing your IS, did you have to draw up an Information Guideline Diagram?			
– Was the implementation of your IS guided by a detailed project methodology?			
– Does your healthcare structure have a management policy that governs the operation of your IS?			
– Has your healthcare establishment undergone structural and organizational changes along with the installation of your IS?			
– What resources have been put in place to ensure the reliability and robustness of your IS:			
- integration of homogeneous reference technological solutions			
- signing of a maintenance contract			
- realization of a concordance text on the computer devices			
- instauration of a backup plan			
- establishment of a 24/7 on-call service			
- implementation of monitoring and surveillance tools			
– What monitoring activities are in place for your IS:			

Regarding the information systems used by the healthcare structure	*Tick the box that corresponds to your answer*		
	YES, absolutely	**YES, partly**	**NO, not at all**
- installation of an automated tool with an alarm signal in case of a malfunction of the IS			
- establishment of a data export control system			
- presence of internal personnel charged with regularly checking the IS			
– What strategies have been used to support the piloting of your IS:			
- creation of a governing committee			
- creation of a monitoring committee			
- use of planning techniques (Pert, Gantt, Precedence Diagram Method, MPM, etc.)			
- use of dashboards			
– What means have been used to accompany the use of your IS:			
- creation of awareness-raising days			
- establishment of internal training sessions for the IS tool			
- instauration of practical workshops on the use of the IS			
– Has the amount of money spent on the creation and operation of your IS been in line with the initial budget set aside for this purpose?			

Table A5.1. *Questionnaire 3, designed to analyze the methods and tools put in place to enable the IS to work*

Appendix 6

Environmental Parameters of the Knowledge Pyramid

Field of study	Info-ethics		
	Descriptive ethics (practical)	Normative ethics (deontological)	Reflexive ethics (questioning)
Ethics:	Means	Norms	Principle of autonomy
	Devices	Codes	Principle of beneficence
	Ways	Rules	Principle of non-malfeasance
Practical wisdom	Procedures	Limits	Principle of fairness
	Application and effectuation	Regulation and adaptation	Legitimization

Table A6.1. *Environmental parameters of info-ethics*

Field of study	Computosphere	
	Interactive	Evolutive
Cybernetics:	Objectivity	Learning
	Textuality	Questioning
Artificial intelligence (AI)	Explanation	Correcting

Table A6.2. *Environmental parameters of the computosphere*

Bibliography

[ABB 01] ABBAD J., *Organisation et Management Hospitalier*, Berger-Levrault, Paris, vol. 25, p. 103, May 2001.

[AUB 09] AUBERT F., France 2025 Diagnostic Stratégique, Technologies et vie quotidienne, Report, March 2009.

[ALA 01] ALAVI M., LEIDNER D., "Knowledge management and knowledge management systems", *MIS Quarterly*, vol. 25, no. 1, pp. 107-136, 2001.

[ALP 86] ALPEROVITCH A., "De la théorie à la pratique de la décision médicale", *The Geneva Papers on Risk and Insurance*, vol. 11, no. 40, pp. 230-234, July 1986.

[AMA 07] AMANN J.P., GAILLE M., "Approche par les principes, approche par les cas: les limites philosophiques d'une opposition", *Ethique et Santé*, vol. 4, pp. 195-199, 2007.

[ASI 09] ASIP S., Cadre d'interopérabilité des SIS: document chapeau, Paris, vol. 1, p. 16, 24 February 2009.

[BAL 06] BALANÇA E., KERROUANTON B., LACROIX J., *et al.*, Maîtrise et protection de l'information, *Clusif*, pp. 1-24, June 2006.

[BAR 70] BARTHES R., "L'ancienne rhétorique – aide-mémoire", *Recherches rhétoriques, Communications*, Seuil, no. 16, pp. 172-229, December 1970.

[BEA 01] BEAUCHAMP T.L., CHILDRESS J., *Principles of Biomedical Ethics*, 5th ed., Oxford University Press, New York/Oxford, 2001.

[BEC 01] BECK J.R., "Médical decision making: 20 years of advancing the field", *Medical Decision Making*, vol. 21, no. 1, pp. 73, 75, 2001.

[BEL 08] BELKADI F., "Démarche de modélisation d'une situation de conception collaborative", *Document numérique*, vol. 8, pp. 93-106, 2008.

[BEL 09] BELLANOVA R., DE HERT P., "Protection des données personnelles et mesures de sécurité: vers une perspective transatlantique", *Cultures & Conflicts*, vol. 74, pp. 63-80, 2009.

[BEN 13] BENHAMOU B, "Les mutations économiques, social, et politiques de l'internet des objets", *Cahier français*, no. 372, January-February 2013.

[BER 99] BERG M., "Patient care information systems and healthcare work: a sociotechnical approach", *International Journal of Medical Informatics*, vol. 55, pp. 87-101, 1999.

[BER 01] BERG M., "Implementation information systems in healthcare organizations: myths and challenges", *International Journal of Medical Informatics*, vol. 64, pp. 143-156, 2001.

[BIC 10] BICLET P., "Hébergement et échange des données de santé", *Médecine & Droit*, vol. 118, pp. 159-160, 2010.

[BLO 93] BLONDEL M., *L'Action: essai d'une critique de la vie et d'une science de la pratique*, Alcan and PUF, Paris, 1893.

[BLO 13] BLONDEL V., "Nous étudions de nouveaux objects scientifiques", *La Recherche*, no. 482, p. 30, December 2013.

[BOI 08] BOISOT M., CANALS A., "Data, information and knowledge: have we got it right?" in BOISOT M., MACMILLAN I., HAN K.S. (eds), *Explorations in Information Space*, pp. 15-47. Oxford University Press, Oxford, UK, 2008.

[BOI 06] BOISSIÈRE-LACROIX M., "Le dispositif d'annonce du cancer du sein: quelle place pour le radiologue?" *Journal of Radiology*, Edition française de radiologie, Paris, vol. 87, pp. 105-108, 2006.

[BOL 91] BOLTANSKI L., THÉVENOT L., *De la justification. Les économies de la grandeur*, Gallimard, Paris, 1991.

[BON 07] BONHOMME D., PINAUDEAU D., "Imagerie Médicale: Des innovations au service de l'optimisation et de l'efficience", *Etat de l'art en imagerie*, 20124, IRBM News 2008, 2007.

[BOU 01] BOUGNOUX D., *Introduction aux sciences de la communication*, La Découverte, Paris, 2001.

[BOU 03] BOUILLON J.-L., "Pour une approche communicationnelle des processus de rationalisation cognitive des organisations: contours, enjeux et perspectives", *Xème colloque bilatéral franco-roumain*, CIFSIC Université de Bucarest, p. 17, 28 June-3 July 2003.

[BOU 07] BOUILLON J.-L., BOURDIN S., LONEUX C., "De la communication d'entreprise aux Approches Communicationnelles des Organisations: penser communication des organisations. Les sciences de l'information et de la communication: affirmation et pluralité", *XVIème congrès de la SFSIC*, Compiègne, 11-13 June 2007.

[BRA 13] BRASSEUR C., *Enjeux et usages du big data. Technologies, méthodes et mises en oeuvre*, Hermes Lavoisier, Paris, 2013.

[BRE 02] BRETON P., PROULX S., *L'explosion de la communication, à l'aube du XXI ème siècle*, La Découverte, Paris, 2002.

[BRU 07] BRUEL J.M., GALLIX B., AULAS P., "Impact d'un PACS/RIS sur la fluidité hospitalière. Expérience de Montpellier", *JFR*, 21 October 2007.

[CAR 12] CARAYOL V., GRAMACCIA G., "Modèles et modélisations, pour quels usages?", *Communication et organisation*, vol. 38, p. 30, 2012.

[CAR 00] CARLEY K.M., "Organizational change and the digital economy: a computational organization science perspective", in BRYNJOLFSSON E., KAHIN B. (eds), *Understanding the Digital Economy: Data Tools*, MIT Press, Cambridge, MA, pp. 325-351, 2000.

[CHA 06] CHARBONNEAU B., *Ecologie et liberté*, Edition Parangon, 2006.

[CHA 11] CHAPOUTHIER G., KAPLAN F., *L'Homme, l'Animal et la Machine*, CNRS, Paris, p. 7, 2011.

[CHA 98] CHANGEUX J.P., RICOEUR P., *Ce qui nous fait penser: la nature et la règle*, Editions Odile Jacob, Paris, 1998.

[CLA 11] CLASSEN C., *Les cahiers de Science et vie; Naissance de la Médecine*, no. 121, February – March, 2011.

[CLÉ 02] CLÉRET M., LE BREUX P., LE DUFF F., "Les systèmes d'aide à la décision médicale", *Les cahiers du numérique*, vol. 2, no. 125, p. 154, 2002.

[CNO 08] CNOM, L'information de la santé. Livre blanc de la télémédecine: Guide de bon usage, vol. 1, p. 20, May 2008.

[COE 10] COECKELBERGH M., "Health care, capabilities, and AI assistive technologies", *Ethical Theory and Moral Practice*, vol. 13, no. 2, pp. 181-190, 2010.

[COL 94] COLEY M.T., SAWADA D., *Mindscapes: L'épistémologie de Magoroh Maruyama*, Gordon & Breach Science, New York, 1994.

[COL 98] COLLINS H., KUSCH M., *The Shape of Actions: What Humans and Machines Can Do*, MIT Press, Cambridge, MA, 1998.

[COL 07] COLLINS H., "Bicycling on the moon: collective tacit knowledge and somatic-limit tacit knowledge", *Organization Studies*, vol. 28, no. 2, pp. 257-262, 2007.

[COM 69] COMTE A., *Système de politique positive. Traité de sociologie instituant la religion de l'humanité*, 3rd edition, PUF, Paris [1854], p. 212, 1969.

[COR 08] CORNU J.M., *ProspecTic, nouvelles technologies, nouvelles pensées*, FYP, vol. 20, p. 90, 2008.

[COR 09] CORNU D., *Journalisme et vérité: L'éthique de l'information au défi du changement médiatique*, Editions Labor et Fides, Genève, vol. 7, p. 118, 2009.

[COU 04] COUTÉ P., VASSEUR J.P., "Les pré-requis pour un SIR, SI et informatique Biomédicale", *ITBM – RBM News*, vol. 25, no. 4, 2004.

[COU 06] COUDRAY M.A., BARTHES R., *Le management hospitalier à la croisée des chemins*, Gestion hospitalière, pp. 18-19, January 2006.

[DÉT 09] DÉTRAIGNE Y., ESCOFFIER A-.M., La vie prirée à l'heure des mémoires numériques, Pour une Confiance renforcée entre citoyens et sociéte de l'information, Information Report no. 441, 27, May 2009.

[DEC 85] DECI E.L., RYAN R.M., *Intrinsic Motivation and Self-determination in Human Behavior*, Plenum, New York, 1985.

[DES 06] DECOUVELAERE M., WAHART G., "Technologies, toujours plus … d'efficience", *Journal of Radiology*, vol. 87, pp. 843-847, 2006.

[DES 04] DE SMEDT T., "Risques et communication: la communication dangereuse", *Recherche en communication*, vol. 22, p. 7, 2004.

[DEV 95] DEVÈZE J., "Information et communication: vers une éthique commune", *Communication & Organisation*, no. 8, 1995.

[DHE 07] DHERSE J.L., MINGUET H., *L'éthique ou le chaos?*, Presses de la Renaissance, vol. 1, p. 448, March 2007.

[DIX 03] DIXAUT M., BRANCACCI A., "Platon, Pythagore et les Pythagoriciens", in *Platon, Source des présocratiques. Histoire de la philosophie*, Vrin, Paris, p. 20, 2003.

[DRA 08] DRAY S., *Le secret médical: Du droit à l'éthique*, L'Harmattan, Paris, p. 23, 2008.

[DRE 99] DRETSKE F., *Knowledge and the Flow of Information*, CSCI Publications, Stanford, 1999.

[DUS 00] DUSSERRE L., "La commercialisation des informations médicales est-elle 'déontologiquement correcte?'" *Ordre National des Médecins, Conseil National de L'Ordre*, vol. 1, p. 7, 29-30 June 2000.

[DUT 08] DUTIER A., La place de l'imagerie médicale dans la relation soignant/soigné lors de l'annonce en cancérologie, Thesis, Université Paris V – Descartes, 10 December 2008.

[ETI 12] ETIENNE L., "Ethique dans les usages du numérique en santé", *Journée organisée par le Conseil National de l'Ordre des Médecins*, 14 November 2012.

[EVE 02] EVEILLARD P., *Ethique de l'Internet santé*, Ellipses, Paris, pp. 3-94, June 2002.

[FAI 06] FAINZANG S., *La relation médecin-malades: Information et mensonge*, Presses Universitaires de France, Paris, 2006.

[FES 01] FESSLER J.M., GRÉMY F., "Ethical problems in health information systems", *Methods of Information in Medicine*, vol. 40(4), pp. 359-361, 2001.

[FLO 98] FLORIDI L., *L'éthique télématique*, L'Agora, North-Hatley, Québec, vol. 5, no. 4, July 1998.

[FLO 02] FLORIDI L., *Ethique dans l'infosphère*, Blesok, no. 24, January-February 2002.

[FLO 04] FLORIDI L., "Information", in FLORIDI L. (ed.), *The Blackwell Guide to the Philosophy of Computing and Information*, Blackwell, Oxford, UK, pp. 40-46, 2004.

[FLO 05] FLORIDI L., "Is semantic information meaningful data?", *Philosophy and Phenomenological Research*, vol. 70, p. 2, 2005.

[FLO 07a] FLORIDI L., "Global information ethics: the importance of being environmentally earnest", *International Journal of Technology and Human Interaction*, vol. 3, no. 3, pp. 1-11, 2007.

[FLO 07b] FLORIDI L., "A look into the future impact of ICT on our lives", *The Information Society*, vol. 23, no. 1, pp. 59-64, 2007.

[FLO 10] FLORIDI L., *Information: A Very Short Introduction*, Oxford University Press, p. 152, 25 February 2010.

[FOU 08] FOURNIER T., "Ethique et cancérologie: Donner un sens au soin", *ONCORA*, p. 12, 29 January 2008.

[GAD 12] GADENNE E., *Le guide pratique du Quantified Self. Mieux gérer sa vie, sa santé, sa productivité*, FYP, Paris, 2012.

[GAL 00] GALILEO G., *Dialogue sur les deux grands systèmes du monde*, published in 1632, translated by René Fréneux and François de Gandt, Seuil, Point Sciences, Paris, 2000.

[GIB 05] GIBAUD B., CHABRIAIS J., "Systèmes de communication et d'archivage d'images et leur intégration dans les systèmes de gestion de dossiers patient", *Radiodiagnostic; Principes et techniques d'imagerie*, EMC, Elsevier SAS, Paris, pp. 35-125-A-10, 2005.

[GLA 79] GLANCY D.J., "The invention of the right to privacy", *Arizona Law Review*, vol. 21, p. 3, 1979.

[GOM 01] GOMAS J.M., "Démarche pour une décision éthique (DDE). Comment préparer en équipe la meilleure décision possible dans les situations de crises ou de fin de vie?", *La presse médicale*, vol. 30, no. 19, pp. 973-975, 26 May-2 June 2001.

[GRA 03] GRANGER G., *Philosophie, langage, science*, Les Ulis, EDP Sciences, Paris, 2003.

[GRU 93] GRUBER T., *Towards Principles for the Design of Ontologies Used for Knowledge Sharing in Formal Ontology in Conceptual Analysis and Knowledge Representation*, Kluwer Academic, 1993.

[GUT 96] GUTTMAN N., *Public Health Communication Interventions: Values and Ethical Dilemmas*, Sage, October 1996.

[HAB 87] HABERMAS J., *Théorie de l'agir communicationnel. Tome 1: Rationalité de l'agir et rationalisation de la société*, Fayard, Paris, 1987.

[HER 96] HERVÉ C., *Fondements d'une réflexion éthique managériale de santé*, L'Harmattan, Paris, vol. 111, p. 172, 1996.

[HER 97] HERVÉ C., *Ethique médicale ou Biomédicale? L'éthique en mouvement*, L'Harmattan, Paris, p. 160, 1997.

[HER 07] HERVÉ C., KNOPPERS B.M., MOLINORI P.A., *et al.*, *Systèmes de santé et circulation de l'information*, Encadrement éthique et juridique, Dalloz, vol. 79, p. 83, 2007.

[HÖF 91] HÖFFE O., *La justice politique: fondement d'une philosophie critique du droit et de l'Etat*, translated from the German by MERLE J.-C., PUF, Paris, vol. 38, p. 40, 1991.

[HOT 04] HOTTOIS G., *Philosophies des sciences, philosophies des techniques*, Collège de France, Odile Jacob, Paris, vol. 9, p. 201, October 2004.

[JEA 04] JEANNERET C., "Forme, pratique et pouvoir. Réflexion sur le cas de l'écriture", *Sciences de la société*, no. 63, SI organisationnels, pp. 41-55, October 2004.

[JOH 07] JOHNSTONE J., "Technology as empowerment: a capability approach to computer ethics", *Ethics and Information Technology*, vol. 9, pp. 73-87, 2007.

[KAN 93] KANT E., *Fondements de la métaphysique des mœurs (1785)*, Traduction nouvelle avec introduction et notes par Victor Delbos, Delagrave, Paris, 1993.

[KER 95] KERVEN G.Y., *Eléments fondamentaux des Cindyniques*, Economica, 1995.

[KRA 11] KRAEMER F., VAN OVERVELD K., PERTERSON M., "Is there an ethics of algorithms?", *Ethics in Technology*, vol. 13, pp. 251-260, 2011.

[LAC 06] LACHIÈZE-REY M., *L'espace physique entre mathématiques et philosophie*, EDP Sciences, Les Ulis, p. 205, 2006.

[LAG 00] LAGUARDIA, J.G., RYAN, R.M., "Buts personnels, besoins psychologiques fondamentaux et bien-être: théorie de l'autodétermination et applications", *Revue québécoise de psychologie*, vol. 21, no. 2, pp. 281-304, 2000.

[LAU 05] LAUDE A., "Information et santé: le droit à l'information du malade", *Les tribunes de la santé*, Presses de Science Politique, Sève, no. 9, pp. 43-51, winter 2005.

[LEB 99] LE BRETON D., *L'adieu au Corps*, Métaillé, Paris, p. 13, 1999.

[LEC 96] LECLÈRE J., OLLIVIER L., PASCAULT V. *et al.*, "La relation médecin-malade en échographie cancérologique", *Journal de Radiologie*, vol. 77, pp. 405-409, 1996.

[LEC 06] LECLÈRE J., OLLIVIER L., DOLBEAULT S. *et al.*, "Dialogue entre le radiologue et le patient atteint d'un cancer", *Journal de Radiologie*, vol. 87, pp. 99-104, 2006.

[LEC 07] LE COZ P., *Petit traité de la décision médicale*. Seuil, Paris, 2007.

[LEC 09a] LE COZ P., "Place de la réflexion philosophique dans la décision médicale", *Bulletin de l'Académie Nationale de Médecine*, Edition Académie de médecine, Paris, vol. 193, no. 2, pp. 499-510, 2009.

[LEC 09b] LE COZ P., "Les enjeux internationaux de la bio-éthique et le sommet mondial de Paris de 2008: Convergences et divergences en débats", *Annuaire français de relations internationales 2009*, vol.10, Bruylant, La Documentation française, Paris, pp. 1121-1131, 2009.

[LEG 85] LEGENDRE P., *L'inestimable objet de la transgression, étude sur le principe généalogique en Occident*, Fayard, Paris, p. 13, 1985.

[LEH 04] LE HEN A., LEFEVRE J.E., "PACS: Le pacs ne serait plus un problème s'il y avait pas toutes ces images!", *Journal of Radiology*, vol. 85, pp. 1046-1053, 2004.

[LEI 11] LEIGHTON T., "Internet: le patron d'Akamai craint un accident lié au 'cloud'", *Les Echos, High-Tech & Médias*, p. 28, 14 June 2011.

[LEM 90] LE MOIGNE J.-L., "Epistémologie constructive et science de l'organisation", *Economica*, Paris, 1990.

[LEM 98] LE MOIGNE J.L., "Théorie du système général, théorie de la modélisation", PUF, Paris, p. 22, p. 78, 1998.

[LEM 99] LE MOIGNE J.L., *La modélisation des systèmes complexes*, Dunod, Paris, 1999.

[LEM 07] LE MOIGNE J.L., *Les Epistémologies constructives. Que sais-je?*, PUF, 2007.

[LEN 95] LE NET M., Editorial, *Revue Entreprise Ethique*, no. 3, p. 4, October 1995.

[LER 04] LEROUX V., DARMONI S.J., *Choix d'un site, quels Critères ... de qualité de l'information de santé sur le Net*, ECP & CHU de Rouen, 2004.

[LES 13] LESAULNIER F., "Internet, santé et données personnelles", *Médecine & Droit*, pp. 1-2, 2013.

[LÉV 54] Lévi-Strauss C., "Les mathématiques de l'homme", *Bulletin International des Sciences Sociales*, vol. 6, no. 4, p. 644, October-December 1954.

[LLO 04]. Llorca G., *Guide pratique de la décision médicale, L'éthique en Clinique*, MED-LINE Editions, 2004.

[LOB 07] Lobach D.F., Kawamoto K., Anstrom K.J., *et al.*, "Development, deployment and usability of a point-of-care decision support system for chronic disease management using the recently – approved HL7 decision support service standard", *Studies in Health Technology and Informatics*, vol. 129, pp. 861-865, 2007.

[LOQ 95] Loquay P., "La communication au service de l'information", *Communication & Organisation*, vol. 8, 1995.

[LOV 08] Lovink G., "L'anonymat n'est pas qu'une notion nostalgique", Interview with Lechner M. in *Libération*, Paris, 13 January 2008.

[LUC 13] Lucas J., "Freins à lever pour structurer la médecine de premier recours avec la télémédecine", *Table ronde, 6e congrès européen de l'Association nationale de télémédecine (ANTEL): Le parcours de soins: rôle et place de la Télémédecine*, 16 November 2013.

[LUP 10] Lupianez-Villanueva F., Hardey M., Torrent J. *et al.*, "The integration of information and communication technology into medical practice", *International Journal of Medical Information*, vol. 79, no. 7, pp. 478-491, 2010.

[MAL 00] Malherbe J.-F., *Le nomade polyglotte*, Bellarmin, Montréal, p. 226, 2000.

[MAL 04] Malicier D., Feuglet P., Devèze F., *Le secret médical*, ESKA and Alexandre Lacassagne, Paris, 2004.

[MAL 13] Malle J.-P., "La triple rupture des Big Data", *ParisTech Review*, 2013.

[MAN 08] Mancini J., Information et participation de patients dans divers contextes de décision en cancérologie, Thèse réalisée à l'Université d'Aix-Marseille II – Faculté de médecine – Timone, 30 October 2008.

[MAN 06] Mantz J.-M., Wattel F., Importance de la Communication dans la relation soignant-soigné, Rapport de la Commission XV (Ethique et Responsabilité Professionnelle), Académie Nationale de Médecine, 20 June 2006.

[MAR 05] Maraninchi D., "Le médecin cancérologue et l'environnement du patient, Forum de l'Espace éthique Méditerranéen, *Le cancer Questions d'éthique*, no. 10, February 2005.

[MAR 01] Mariéthoz E., Bakonyi Moeschler M., "Nouvelles technologies de l'information comme outil d'empowerment en matière de santé: mythe, promesse ou réalité?" *Médecine et Hygiéne*, vol. 59, pp. 1858-1860, 2001.

[MAS 03] MASSE R., *Ethique et santé publique. Enjeux, valeur et normalité*, Presses de l'Université Laval, Québec, 2003.

[MAS 04] MASSIS T., "Santé, droit de la personnalité et liberté d'information", *La Gazette du Palais*, p. 3564, December 2004.

[MAT 05] MATTEI J.F., *De l'indignation*, La Table Ronde, Paris, 2005.

[MAY 13] MAYER-SCHÖNBERGER V., "Big Data: nouvelle étape de l'informatisation du monde", *Le Monde*, 24 May 2013.

[MEA 10] MÉADEL C., AKRICH M., "Internet, Tiers nébuleux de la relation patient-médecin", Presses de Science Politique, *Les tribunes de la santé*, no. 29, pp. 41-48, 2010.

[MEN 09] MENNERAT F., "Documents électroniques et soins de santé", *Document numérique*, vol. 12, pp. 9-21, 2009.

[MEY 10] MEYERS T., "Le patient comme catégorie de pensée", *Archives de philosophie*, Tome, vol. 73, pp. 687-701, 2010.

[MIC 07] MICHAUD J., *L'éthique à l'épreuve des techniques*, L'Harmattan, Paris, 2007.

[MIÈ 04] MIÈGE B., *L'information-communication, objet de connaissance*, De Boeck, Brussels, 2004.

[MIN 89] MINTZBERG H., *Structure et dynamique des organisations*, Editions d'organisation, Paris, 1989.

[MON 11] MONDOT J.-F., *Les cahiers de Science & Vie*, Naissance de la médecine, no. 121, p. 114, February-March 2011.

[MOO 05] MOORE, J., "Why we need better ethics for emerging technologies", *Ethics and Information Technology*, pp. 117-118, 2005.

[MOR 77] MORIN E., *La Méthode 1*. Seuil, 1977.

[MOR 01] MORIN E., *La Méthode 5: L'Humanité de l'humanité*, Seuil, 2001.

[MOR 04] MORIN E., *La Méthode 6: Ethique*, Seuil, November, 2004.

[MOR 05] MORIN E., *Complexité restreinte, complexité générale*, "Intelligence de la complexité: épistémologie et pragmatique" colloquium, Cerisy-La-Salle, 26 June 2005.

[MOR 06] MORIN E., "L'esprit de reliance active l'organisation de la connaissance", *Editorial Inter Lettre Chemin Faisant MCX-APC*, no. 35, November-December 2006.

[MOU 01] MOUNEYRAT M.H., *Ethique du secret et secret medical*, Pouvoirs, Paris, no. 97, pp. 47-61, April 2001.

[MUC 12] MUCCHIELLI A., "Deux modèles constructivistes pour le diagnostic des communications organisationnelles", *Communication & Organisation*, vol. 30, 2012.

[NEA 08] NEAME R., "Privacy and health information: health cards offer a workable solution", *Informatics in Primary Care*, vol. 16, pp. 263-270, Health Information Consulting Ltd., 2008.

[NEW 05] NEWTON I., *Principia: principes mathématiques de la philosophie naturelle 1686*, Dunod, Paris, 2005.

[NON 94] NONAKA I., "Dynamic theory organizational knowledge creation", *Organization Science*, vol. 5, no. 1, pp. 14-37, 1994.

[NON 06] NONAKA I., VON KROGH G., VOELPEL S. "Organizational knowledge creation theory: evolutionary paths and future advances", *Organization Studies*, vol. 27, no. 8, pp. 1179-1208, 2006.

[NON 11] NONAKA I., TAKEUCHI H. "The wise leader", *Harvard Business Review*, vol. 89, no. 5, May 2011.

[NOU 02] NOUVEL P., *Enquête sur le concept de Modèle*, PUF, Paris, p. 3, 2002.

[OGI 07] OGIEN R., *L'éthique aujourd'hui: Maximalistes et minimalistes*, Folio essais, Gallimard, 2007.

[OUM 08] OUMAR BAGAYOKO C., DUFOUR J.C., AXILLACH P. *et al.*, "Réflexions sur l'identification du patient dans les systèmes d'informations de santé", *IRBM*, vol. 29, pp. 302-309, 2008.

[PAL 03] PALAZZOLO J., *Informer le patient en psychiatrie: Rôle de chaque intervenant entre légitimité et obligation*, Masson, Paris, 2003.

[PED 04] PEDONE F. *et al. Le management éthique: La santé hors-limites*, no. 27, Liberté politique, Autonme, vol. 16, p. 60, 2004.

[POL 01] POLVIA S., SHARMA R., CONRATH D., "A sociotechnical framework for quality assessment of computer information systems", *Industrial Management and Data Systems*, vol. 101, no. 5, pp. 237-251, 2001.

[PON 09] PONÇON G., "Système d'information: Vers une éthique de l'usage?", *Revue hospitalière de France*, vol. 74, no. 531, p. 77, December 2009.

[PUE 06] PUECH P., *Téléradiologie: Etat de l'art, applications, perspectives et enjeux en*, CERIM, Lille, 7 November 2006.

[QUA 56] QUASTELR H., "A primer on information theory", in YOCKEY H.P. (ed.), *Symposium on Information Theory in Biology*, Gatlinbury, Tennessee, pp. 3-49, 29-31 October 1956.

[RAS 01] RASTIER F., *Sémantique et recherches cognitives*, 2nd edition, PUF, 2001.

[RAV 13] RAVIX V. Réflexions éthiques attachées à la dématérialisation des données de santé, Master's thesis, University of Aix-Marseille, p. 27, 2013.

[REI 00] REIGLE J., BOYLE R.J., "Ethical decision-making skills in Advanced Nursing Practice", in HARICK A.B., SPORSS J.A., HANSON C.M. (eds), *An Integrative Approach*, Saunders, Philadelphia, pp. 349-377, 2000.

[ROC 13] ROCHFELD J., MARTIAL-BRAZ N., GATTONE E., Quel avenir pour la protection des données à caractère personnel en Europe?, Dalloz, p. 2788, 2013.

[RIC 75] RICŒUR P., *La métaphore vive*, Seuil, Paris, 1975.

[RIC 90] RICŒUR P., *Soi-même comme un autre*, Seuil, Paris, p. 1990.

[RIC 91a] RICŒUR P., *Le Juste*, Seuil, Paris, 1991.

[RIC 91b] RICŒUR P., "Pour une éthique du compromise-e", *Revue Alternatives Non Violentes*, no. 80, October 1991.

[RIF 05] RIFKIN J., *L'âge de l'accès. La nouvelle culture du capitalisme,* La Découverte, Poche, Paris, 2005.

[RIG 03] RIGUIDEL M., "Une approche systémique de la sécurité: la sécurité des infosphères", *Les cahiers du numérique*, Lavoisier, vol. 4, pp. 13-49, 2003.

[ROD 08] RODRIGUES BOTELHO K., Fiche de lecture sur: La société de consommation de Jean Baudrillard (1970). Observatoire du Management Alternatif, Mastère Spécialisé Management du Développement Durable, HEC Paris, April 2008.

[RÜE 03] RÜEDI B., *Le secret médical est-il en danger?*, Bernard, Neuchâtel, 2003.

[RUL 99] RULE J., HUNTER L., *Towards Property Rights in Personal Data, in Visions of Privacy: Policy Choices for the Digital Age*, University of Toronto Press, Canada, p. 168, 1999.

[RUO 03] RUOTSALAINEN P., Interreg PACS. Attachment 8, Final Report, University of Helsinki, 2003.

[RUO 04a] RUOTSALAINEN P., "A cross-platform model for secure electronic health record communication", *International Journal of Medical Informatics*, vol. 73, 2004.

[RUO 04b] RUOTSALAINEN P., "Security requirements in EHR systems and archives", *Studies on Health Technology Informatics*, vol. 203, pp. 453-458, 2004.

[RUO 10] RUOTSALAINEN P., "Privacy and security in teleradiology", *European Journal of Radiology*, vol. 73, pp. 31-35, 2010.

[RYA 00] RYAN R.M, DECI E.L., "Self-determination theory and the facilitation of intrinsic motivation, social development, and well-being", *American Psychologist*, vol. 55, pp. 68-78, 2000.

[RYA 07] RYAN R.M., "Wisdom", *Stanford Encyclopedia of Philosophy*, 2007, 14 June 2010.

[RYA 97] RYAN R.M., FREDERICK C.M., "On energy, personality, and health: subjective vitality as a dynamic reflection of well-being", *Journal of Personality*, vol. 65, pp. 529-565, 1997.

[SAI 07] SAINT-ARNAUD J., "La démarche réflexive et interdisciplinaire en éthique de la santé: un outil d'intégration des savoirs et des pratiques", *Ethique et Santé*, vol. 4, pp. 200-206, 2007.

[SAR 04] SARGOS P., "Les principes d'immunité et de légitimité en matière de secret professionnel medical", *La semaine Juridique. Edition Générale*, no. 50 Paris, 2004.

[SCH 09] SCHERGER J., "Future vision: is family medicine ready for patient-directed care?", *Family Medicine*, vol. 41(4), pp. 285-288, 2009.

[SCO 10] SCOTT V., HAIG M.D., "Ethical choice in the medical applications of information theory", *Clinical Orthopedics and Related Research*, vol. 468, pp. 2672-2677, 2010.

[SEL 02] SELLES L., *Le secret professionnel à l'hôpital*, MB Edition, Paris, December 2002.

[SÉR 04] SÉROUSSI B., BOURAUD J., DRÉAU H. *et al.*, Modalités d'interaction avec des systèmes d'aide à la décision médicale par alerte ou à la demande pour délivrer des recommandations: une étude préléminaire dans le cadre de la prise en charge de l'hypertension, IC, vol. 1, p. 12, 2004.

[SHA 48] SHANNON C., "A mathematical theory of communication", *Bell System Technical Journal*, vol. 27, pp. 379-423, 623-656, July and October 1948.

[SIL 09] SILVESTRE A.L., SUE V.M., ALLEN J.L., "If you build it, will they come? The Kaiser Permanente model of online health care", *Health Affairs*, vol. 28, no. 2, pp. 334-344, 2009.

[SIM 71] SIMON H.A., NEWELL A., *Human problem solving*, Prentice Hall, 1971.

[SIM 07] SIMONNOT B. "Documentaliste", *Sciences de l'information*, vol. 44, no. 3, p. 215, 2007.

[SIN 99] SINACEUR H., "Modèle", in LECOURT D. (sous la direction de), *Dictionnaire d'histoire et philosophie des sciences*, PUF, Paris, p. 651, 1999.

[SPE 09a] SPENCE E.H., "The epistemology and ethics of internet information", in D'ATRI A., SAUA D. (eds), *Information Systems: People, Organizations, Institutions and Technologies, ITAIS: The Italian Association for Information Systems*, Heidelberg, 2009.

[SPE 09b] SPENCE E.H., "A universal model for the normative evaluation of internet information", *Ethics and Information Technology*, vol. 11, p. 4, 2009.

[SPE 10] SPENCE E.H., "Information, knowledge and wisdom: groundwork for the normative evaluation of digital information and its relation to the good life", *Ethics and Information Technology*, vol. 13, pp. 261-275, 2010.

[STO 04] STORCH J.L., RODNEY P., STARZOMSKI R., *Toward a Moral Horizon: Nursing Ethics for Leadership and Practice*, Pearson, Prentice Hall, Toronto, 2004.

[TAB 10] TABUTEAU D., "Editorial", *Les tribunes de la santé*, Presses de Science Politique, no. 29, pp. 3-5, 2010.

[TIS 99] TISSERON S., "Nos objets quotidiens", *Hermès*, vol. 25, pp. 57-66, 1999.

[TOU 04] TOURREILLES J.M., "SIH: 1, 2, 3 … partez!", *ENSP*, Rennes, pp. 15-184, May 2004.

[VAC 97] VACHER B., *La gestion de l'information en entreprise. Enquête sur l'oubli, l'étourderie, la ruse et le bricolage organisés*, ADBS, Paris, 1997.

[VAC 04] VACHER B., "Du bricolage informationnel à la litote organisationnelle. Ou comment considérer le bricolage au niveau stratégique?", *Revue Sciences de la Société*, vol. 63, pp. 133-150, October 2004.

[VAC 09] VACHER B., "Articulation entre communication, information et organisation en SIC", *Les Enjeux de l'information et de la communication*, pp. 1-25, 2009.

[VAC 12] VACHER B., "L'invisible et structurante matérialité de l'information et de la communication organisationnelle: une grille de lecture", *Communication & Organisation*, vol. 30, p. 230, 2012.

[VAN 08] VAN STRIEN W., Opvangen zwakheden maakt beeldtechnieken waardevoller (interview with G.J.C. Lokhorst), Ethiek, Onderzoek en Bestuur, pp. 20-25, March 2008.

[VEN 13] VENOT A., *Informatique médicale, e-santé*, Springer, 2013.

[VÉZ 06] VÉZINA S., Les enjeux éthiques dans les programmes de dépistage: Le cas du Programme québécois de dépistage du cancer du sein, Institut National de Santé Publique Québec, Laval, January 2006.

[VUL10] VULLIET-TAVERNIER S., *De l'anonymat dans le traitement des données de santé*. Médecine & Droit, Elsevier Masson, pp. 22-25, 2010.

[WAR 90] WARREN S., BRANDEIS L., "The right to privacy", *Harvard Law Review*, vol. IV, 1890.

[WAT 93] WATERMAN A.S., "Two conceptions of happiness: Contrasts of personal expressiveness (eudaimonia) and hedonic enjoyment", *Journal of Personality and Social Psychology*, vol. 64, pp. 678-691, 1993.

[WIE 48] WIENER N., *Introduction to Cybernectics*, MIT, 1948.

[WIL 09] WILLCOCKS L., WHITLEY E.A., "Developing the information and knowledge agenda in information systems: insights from philosophy", *Information Society*, vol. 25, pp. 190-197, 2009.

[WOL 95] WOLTON D., "Information et Communication", *Libération*, p. 8, 19 January 1995.

[WRE 07] WRESCH W., "500 million missing web sites: Amortya sen's capability approach and measures of technological deprivation in developing countries", in ROOKSBY E., WECKERT J. (eds), *Information Technology and Social Justice*, Information Science, Hershey, 2007.

[ZHE 07] ZHENG Y., "Exploring the value of the capability approach for E-developing", *Paper Presented at the 9th International Conference on Social Implications of Computers in Developing Countries*, Sao Paulo, Brazil, 2007.

Index

Other titles from

in

Information Systems, Web and Pervasive Computing

2009

BONNET Pierre, DETAVERNIER Jean-Michel, VAUQUIER Dominique
Sustainable IT Architecture: the Progressive Way of Overhauling Information Systems with SOA

PAPY Fabrice
Information Science

RIVARD François, ABOU HARB Georges, MERET Philippe
The Transverse Information System

ROCHE Stéphane, CARON Claude
Organizational Facets of GIS

VENTRE Daniel
Information Warfare

2008

BRUGNOT Gérard
Spatial Management of Risks

FINKE Gerd
Operations Research and Networks

GUERMOND Yves
Modeling Process in Geography

KANEVSKI Michael
Advanced Mapping of Environmental Data

MANOUVRIER Bernard, LAURENT Ménard
Application Integration: EAI, B2B, BPM and SOA

PAPY Fabrice
Digital Libraries

2007

DOBESCH Hartwig, DUMOLARD Pierre, DYRAS Izabela
Spatial Interpolation for Climate Data

SANDERS Lena
Models in Spatial Analysis

2006

CLIQUET Gérard
Geomarketing

CORNIOU Jean-Pierre
Looking Back and Going Forward in IT

DEVILLERS Rodolphe, JEANSOULIN Robert
Fundamentals of Spatial Data Quality

Printed and bound by CPI Group (UK) Ltd, Croydon, CR0 4YY

27/10/2024

14580727-0003